A SEMANTIC STRUCTURE ANALYSIS

OF

T I T U S

by

John Banker

Edited by

John Callow

Summer Institute of Linguistics

7500 W. Camp Wisdom Rd.

Dallas, TX 75236

Library of Congress Catalog Card No. 87-61267
ISBN 0-88312-916-7

Copies may be obtained from
Bookstore
Summer Institute of Linguistics
7500 West Camp Wisdom Road
Dallas, Texas 75236

PREFACE

The earlier work on Titus, "A Literary-Semantic Analysis of Titus" (1980), was the result of the input of many of our SIL colleagues including John Austing, John Beekman, Pam Bendor-Samuel, Richard Blight, John Callow, Stephen Echerd, Daniel Heath, Paul Williams, and Michael Kopesec, who was editor. This was considered a preliminary edition, and was later revised and expanded by Michael Kopesec.

In September 1983 the present author was assigned the task of readying this work for publication. Because of new developments in the theory of the semantic structure of written communication and the present emphasis on more rigorous notes in support of all important exegetical decisions, a further extensive revision was made. This present Semantic Structure Analysis, then, builds on the work of all who have contributed to the project from the beginning until now, and I heartily acknowledge the contribution each one has made. Special acknowledgment is due John Callow who has served as general consultant for my work on Titus and who has provided many valuable insights into the analysis, to say nothing of the training in the theory that he has so ably given. I also would like to acknowledge the help of Harold Greenlee and John Tuggy who have made valuable suggestions.

Thanks is also due June Austing, Elaine Beekman, and Faith Blight for their many hours of faithful work in preparing the manuscript for publication. I also wish to express my thanks to my wife, Betty, who has helped with the editing and proofreading and has taken over many of my responsibilities so that I could give much more time to this project.

The Greek text used in this Semantic Structure Analysis is from the third edition of the United Bible Societies' Greek New Testament.

John Banker

TABLE OF CONTENTS

ABBREVIATIONS

AG	Arndt and Gingrich (See References)
AV	_Authorized_ (or _King James_) _Version_
CONT	content
ICC	_The International Critical Commentary_
METR	metaphor
METY	metonymy
NEB	_The New English Bible_
NIV	_The New International Version of the Bible_
PERS	personification
PROM	prominence
REL	relation
RL	receptor language
RSV	_The Revised Standard Version of the Bible_
SSA	_Semantic Structure Analysis_
SSWC	_Semantic Structure of Written Communication_
SYN	synecdoche
TEV	_Today's English Version of the Bible_
TRNS	translation
TXT	text
UBS	United Bible Societies
amplif.	amplification
circum.	circumstance
contr.	contrast
desc.	description
exc	exclusive
grds.	grounds
ident.	identification
inc	inclusive
neg.	negative
reas.	reason
sg	singular
spec.	specific
valid.	validation

0. GENERAL INTRODUCTION

0.1 The Theory on Which a Semantic Structure Analysis Is Based

This volume is an analytical commentary on Paul's letter to Titus. It is based on a theory of semantic structure set forth in "The Semantic Structure of Written Communication" (Beekman, Callow, and Kopesec 1981). It has been prepared with the needs of the Bible translator particularly in view, though it should be useful to all serious students of God's Word. Like other commentaries, it aims to arrive at the meaning that the original writer intended to communicate to the original recipients. It differs from most other commentaries, however, in that it is consciously based on a theory of the structure of meaning. Consequently, a consistent and comprehensive approach to the analysis of the meaning is applied to the total document, whether that meaning is conveyed by the smallest segments of the written communication, such as words and their component parts; or whether it is conveyed by the largest segments, such as paragraphs and various combinations of paragraphs.

Unlike previous Semantic Structure Analyses, this one does not include a detailed section on the theory and presentation of semantic structure analyses. The person who is building up his own collection of SSA's does not need this section to reappear in every SSA. So, for economy's sake, this section has been left out of the Titus SSA, but the reader may refer to previous SSA's (Colossians, 2 Thessalonians) for this information. A new, updated volume on the theory and presentation of semantic structure analyses will be prepared and published separately. The Titus SSA, however, does include a chart of relations for easy access to this important tool. Also, it would be well to mention the following:

1. Parentheses are used in the display text to enclose implicit material that has been made explicit. Note, however, that in some cases it is difficult to decide what is implicit material and what is actually a component of meaning of the Greek word being translated.
2. An asterisk following a word indicates that the word is not being used in its primary meaning in contemporary English.
3. The literal English gloss following the Greek text at the beginning of each note follows the order of the Greek text, except in those cases where it would confuse the total meaning of the English sentence or clause.

0.2 The Use of a Semantic Structure Analysis

For the translator, who not only must determine the exegesis of a passage but also must determine how to resolve a myriad of translation problems, it sometimes becomes sheer drudgery to wade through the detailed reasoning backing up the exegetical decisions in the SSA or similar commentaries. On the other hand, the detailed reasoning is necessary to determine the best analysis. Any interpretation presented must be backed up with solid reasoning, and there is no way this can be done without adequate, detailed analysis, including reference to the Greek text. To discover whether or not the reasoning is solid, the translator must study the analysis which has been presented.

Does the translator who wants to use the SSA, then, have any other appropriate option than reading every part of the SSA? One approach is to use the display text of the SSA along with other commentaries and versions, and where there is obvious agreement, the translator may move ahead with confidence. Where there is a difference between the display and other texts, or there appear to be a number of alternatives, then the translator may consult the notes in the SSA on the particular verse, or portion of a verse, being studied, in order to see what factors led to the decision represented in the display. The translator should then be better informed so that he can make his own factually-based judgment as to the best interpretation. Also, the notes in the SSA may supply information which the translator needs that is difficult to find elsewhere. If the translator is searching for such information as he works on a particular verse, it would be well for him to consult the SSA notes for that verse to see if his problem is dealt with.

For easier reference, the Titus SSA labels the notes on each verse, or part of a verse, as to whether they deal with the relationships between units (REL), prominence (PROM), variant textual readings (TXT), or general content (CONT). There are also a few notes that seek to help the translator with special problems of translating into languages other than English (labelled TRNS).

Although the method of using the SSA described above is possible, and helpful, nevertheless, in order to obtain the greatest benefit from an SSA, it should be read through in its entirety. Who knows better than the translator the importance of context in understanding each part of a discourse, no matter how small that part may be. So, the more one studies the SSA as a whole, the better he will understand each part. Also, it is impossible for the display text alone to convey all the necessary information the translator needs when translating a passage into another language, so it really is important that the notes be checked, too. Moreover, once in a while, alternate rendering to the rendering in the display text is given in the notes.

0.3 The Display Text Is Not Strictly a Model for Translation

Finally, it should be understood that the SSA display text is not a translation in the common sense. It is a verbalization of the analysis of the meaning of the Greek text, presented in propositional English surface structure form, and with various restrictions. For instance, abstract nouns are avoided as much as possible and the finite form of the verb is normally used. Words are used only in their primary senses. For "live" metaphors, the point of similarity (i.e., the full meaning of the figure intended to be communicated by the original author) is given in the display text. As a result, the display text does not always sound like natural, flowing English, which should mark any good translation. The addition of implicit material may make it seem too overloaded with information and too interpretative for a translation. Its primary purpose is to be a source of information, not a model for word-by-word translation into any real language. However, in some of its patterns, it will more closely approximate patterns of many of the world's languages than normal English or Greek would. For example, if a language naturally uses abstract nouns in more or less the same way English or Greek does, it would be expected that translation using abstract nouns would in many cases (each case needs to be examined for itself) be more natural and effective than following the propositional form of the display text in which abstract nouns are avoided. But, if the language does not normally use abstract nouns, then the propositional form of the display text is built to give the information the translator needs to turn abstract nouns into verbal constructions. At the same time, a natural translation into the language will still not follow the display text word-for-word, but will follow its own patterns.

0.4 CHART OF RELATIONS

Prominence	Relation type	Subtype	Member	Paired member
EQUAL NATURAL PROMINENCE	Chronological (time in focus)		sequential	
			simultaneous	
	Nonchronological (time not in focus)		conjoining	
			alternation	
UNEQUAL NATURAL PROMINENCE	Orientation		orienter	-CONTENT
			circumstance	-HEAD
			introduction	-HEAD
			opening	-BODY
			BODY	-closing
	Chronological		$step_n$	-GOAL
			occasion	-OUTCOME
	Nonchronological	Restatement	HEAD	-equivalent
			GENERIC	$-specific_n$
			generic	-SPECIFIC
			contraction	-amplification
		Clarification	HEAD	-comparison
			HEAD	-illustration
			HEAD	-manner
			contrast	-HEAD
		Logical	RESULT	-reason
			RESULT	-means
			MEANS	-purpose
			condition	-CONSEQUENCE
			concession	-CONTRAEXPECTATION
			HEAD	-grounds
		Associative	HEAD	-comment
			HEAD	-parenthesis
CONCEPT-COMMUNICATION UNIT RELATIONS			CONCEPT	-identification
			CONCEPT	-description

NOTES:

1. Since the Epistle to Titus is nonnarrative, not all the narrative relations are included in this chart.
2. The relations are given in the order in which they are most commonly found in the Greek of the New Testament thus, a RESULT is usually followed by the reason for it, as signalled by **hoti**, **gar**, **dia** + accusative, etc.
3. The naturally prominent member of a paired relation is shown in caps. In one or two cases, there does not seem to be a natural head, e.g., contraction-amplification.
4. It should be noted that marked prominence devices can be used to make the less prominent member of a pair as prominenet as the one which is naturally prominent. And thematic prominence can reverse the natural prominence, so that, for example, a purpose will be of greater prominence than its means.

1. THE INTRODUCTION TO THE SEMANTIC STRUCTURE ANALYSIS OF TITUS

1.1 The Communication Situation

1.1.1 The Identification and Status of the Participants

The participants involved in the letter are clearly stated: the apostle Paul (1:1) is identified as the addressor, and Titus (1:4), an associate of Paul, is identified as the addressee. The Pauline authorship of this letter was a fairly consistently accepted fact up until the modern critical era. Today, there is a wide range of views by Biblical scholars. Many fully accept the traditional view, holding that Paul was responsible for the epistle (as well as the other Pastoral Epistles, 1 and 2 Timothy) in its present shape. On the other end of the scale are those who subscribe to the pseudonymous view, which holds that some second century author used Paul's name to gain apostolic authority for the epistle. In between these polar positions are views that involve varying degrees of editorial intervention by a person other than Paul who either assisted in the writing as an amanuensis, or who posthumously collected and compiled fragments of Paul's writings.

The problems which critics see in Pauline authorship include the fact that there is an obvious difference in vocabulary and style between the Pastoral Epistles and the other epistles of Paul, the assumption that there are theological differences between the Pastoral Epistles and the other Pauline epistles (though this would be very difficult to prove), and the fact that the communication situation as described in the Pastoral Epistles does not fit into the life of Paul as described in Acts and his other epistles.

In the present analysis, the traditional view of Pauline authorship (though not necessarily excluding the use of an amanuensis) is assumed for the following reasons:

1. As far as history and tradition are concerned, this view has far better support.
2. The pseudonymous view, in trying to solve the above problems, renders the discourse itself incoherent in the sense that the discourse condemns the very thing that the pseudonymous writer would be practicing--untruthfulness (cf. references to truth and falsehood in 1:1,2,4,12,14; 2:7; 3:3). Many proponents of the pseudonymous view declare that the author had no intention to deceive but that he was only writing in the apostle's name, writing in the name of an authority being a fairly common practice, even among Christians, at that time. But this is especially hard to believe in the light of personal references to Paul's life such as Titus 3:12-14, and especially 2 Tim. 4:6-8. As Kelly (p. 33) says, "It is one thing to publish under the name of Paul or some other apostle a treatise, whether in the form of a letter or of something else, which the author sincerely believes to express the great man's teaching, or which he even believes to have been disclosed to him by the self-same Spirit which used the great man as his mouthpiece. It is quite another thing to fabricate for it a detailed framework of concrete personal allusions, reminiscences, and messages, not to mention outbursts of intensely personal feeling, which one knows to be pure fiction but which one puts together with the object of creating an air of verisimilitude." Any interpreter who suggests that the author wrote in the second century has to deal with the problem that there are many references to other

well-known first century personages in the Pastoral Epistles--Timothy, Titus, Luke, Mark, etc.--who are portrayed as contemporary with the author.
3. From a purely linguistic perspective, unless the overtly declared communication situation has been too grossly violated, that communication situation is the one that should be assumed in interpreting features of the discourse. In this particular case, since those who argue against the traditional situation have been unable to present convincing evidence for the suggested alternative communication situations, and since the traditional view can be shown to be consistent with the discourse, the traditional situation is the one accepted or assumed.
4. Though certain lexical items and the style of the Pastoral Epistles are distinct from the other epistles of Paul, there are sound linguistic answers potentially applicable to this apparent problem:
   a. A writer may change in vocabulary and style over a period of time, or he may change his vocabulary and style to fit different communication situations.
   b. The differences in vocabulary and style may be due to the vocabulary and style of the amanuensis which Paul used in the Pastoral Epistles. Again, they may be the amanuensis' own personal vocabulary and style (though communicating accurately the thoughts of Paul), or they may be the vocabulary and style that he feels would be most appropriate for those to whom he is writing.

For a good discussion of the problem of authorship and the communication situation in general, see J.N.D. Kelly's introduction to his commentary on the Pastoral Epistles.

The addressee is Titus (1:4), the Gentile Christian (Gal. 2:3) and colleague of the apostle Paul. From Gal. 2:1 it is seen that he was one of Paul's earliest co-workers; he accompanied Paul and Barnabas to the Jersualem council, which was very early in the ministry of Paul. From the references to Titus in 2 Corinthians (2:13; 7:6,13,14; 8:6,16,23; 12:18), it can be seen that Paul had considerable confidence in Titus, since he assigned him to a number of significant and delicate tasks. Then, in the reference to Titus in 2 Tim. 4:10, it can be seen that Titus was consistent and loyal in his commitment and dedication both to the Lord and to Paul.

From Titus 1:5, it can be concluded that Paul had gone to Crete with Titus, and for a period of time worked together with him there in the establishment of the Cretan church. He then departed, leaving Titus to continue the task which they had begun together there. Later on, when Artemas or Tychicus came, presumably to replace Titus, Titus was to join Paul in Nicopolis (3:12).

While the epistle is addressed to Titus only, its purpose is more than solely to instruct Titus what he is to do in Crete. By establishing his own authority in 1:1-3, Paul gives apostolic authority to all Titus is to instruct and urge upon the believers. Verse 2:15, in the middle of the hortatory section of the epistle, again stresses the authority with which Titus is to instruct and exhort, "Teach, urge, and correct with full authority; let no one disregard you." No doubt the epistle was to be read to all the believers and was to serve as a document to which Titus could appeal for authority, as he instructed and exhorted the church. There were many false teachers in Crete and many believers who were ready to follow them (1:10-16). Titus needed all the authoritative backing possible to lead the people in true faith; and to be as effective as possible, this authority needed to be directed through him. The epistle, then, fills the functions of instructing Titus how to deal with the situation in Crete, giving him the authority he needs, and presenting the believers with an authoritative treatise on how they should live. The first and second functions are seen not only in the instructions for organization of the churches (1:5c-9) and for dealing with the false teachers and their followers (1:10-16; 3:8d-11), but also in all that Titus is to instruct the believers.

Some, however, would understand that Paul directed his injunctions for the Cretan believers through Titus as a way of toning them down so that they would not come across too strongly. Not that the Cretan believers didn't need strong persuasion, but that culturally it would have been the wrong way to handle it. The objection to this analysis is that it is uncharacteristic of Paul not to speak directly to those he is instructing, and that it would be difficult to prove that the Cretans, unlike the other peoples whom Paul instructed directly, would culturally need to be instructed through another person. In most of his other epistles Paul exhorts the believers directly, and when needed, he does not mince words (cf. 1 Cor. 4:21; 2 Cor. 10-13; Gal. 1:6-10). Some of the statements that Paul makes in the epistle to Titus itself do not sound like toned-down language. Note especially the reference to the Cretans' character in the quote from one of their own prophets, "Cretans are always liars, evil brutes, lazy gluttons" (NIV). And then he adds his own comment, "This testimony is true."

1.1.2 The Status of the Cretan Church

At the time of the writing of this letter, the Cretan church could be characterized as young and experiencing a good deal of growing pains. **Kata polin** `in each city' (1:5) indicates that the church had spread to many areas on the island. The reference to **holous oikous** `whole households' (1:11) confirms that the growth of the church on Crete had advanced to the point where entire families, not merely scattered individuals, were active believers. However, the fact that Paul seems to equate **presbuteros** `elder' (1:5) with **episkopos** `bishop' (1:7), the fact that these leaders are only now being appointed, and the fact that there is no mention of other officers in the church, such as deacons, deaconesses, etc., indicate that the church was at that time probably still fairly unorganized.

The church also was apparently not morally strong. This is very likely the reason why the qualifications for Christian leaders (1:6-9) involved matters of general morality. Paul again deals with these matters of morality in the instructions for the Cretan believers in general in 2:1-10. Another clue to the moral weakness of the church is Paul's acceptance of the truth of the judgment of the Cretan prophet that "Cretans are always liars, evil brutes, lazy gluttons" (1:12).

1.1.3 The Occasion and Purpose of the Letter

As has been intimated above, the purpose of the letter is to give Titus authoritative instructions on how to deal with the present situation in the Cretan church. It would seem that the most immediate problem is how to deal with false teaching. There are many false teachers in Crete (1:10) who are leading believers astray (1:11). When Paul states the purpose of Titus' ministry in Crete in 1:5, he is probably referring to correcting this situation when he uses the phrase **hina ta leiponta epidiorthōsē** `in order that you might correct those matters that need to be corrected' (see the notes for support for this translation). Paul instructs Titus how to deal with false teaching in 1:10-16 and 3:8d-11. But dealing with the false teaching is only one aspect of solving the problem. The church must be firmly established by the teaching of sound doctrine (2:1-15; 3:1-8c). The second purpose of Titus' ministry in Crete as stated in 1:5 is to "appoint elders in each town."

1:9 shows that the elders, along with Titus, are to be involved in dealing with the false teachers' teaching and the teaching of sound doctrine, "He [i.e., each one appointed to be an elder] must hold firmly to the trustworthy message as it has been taught, so that he can encourage others in sound doctrine and refute those who oppose it." (However, the major responsibility is on Titus himself, as shown by the fact that the imperatives dealing with correcting the false teachers and their followers and the teaching of sound doctrine are second person singular.)

The importance of teaching sound doctrine in order to remedy the situation in Crete and to establish the believers in the faith in general is shown by the fact that considerably more attention is given it than to dealing with false teaching. It is important in understanding the epistle to distinguish between correct behavior and correct belief. Those sections that deal with sound doctrine (2:1-14; 3:1-8c) have prescribed correct behavior as the content of the exhortation paragraphs, and correct belief as the content of the grounds paragraphs supporting the exhortations. The opening of the epistle itself introduces this relationship in the statement of the purpose of Paul's apostleship as furthering "the faith of God's elect and the knowledge of the truth that leads to godliness" (1:1 NIV, underlining mine).

As far as the occasion for actually sending the letter is concerned, it may have been sent by means of Zenas and Apollos. From 3:13 we know that they visited Crete. It is not explicitly mentioned whether they had come from Paul or not. Kelly's position (p. 258) is that "they are almost certainly the bearers of the letter." If this is true, it would seem that Paul used the occasion of their visit to Crete to give a further authoritative boost by means of this letter to Titus' ministry there among people who were not always willing to listen to the truth. In fact, Paul may have specifically requested that they stop by Crete.

1.2 The Overview

1.2.1 The constituent organization of Titus

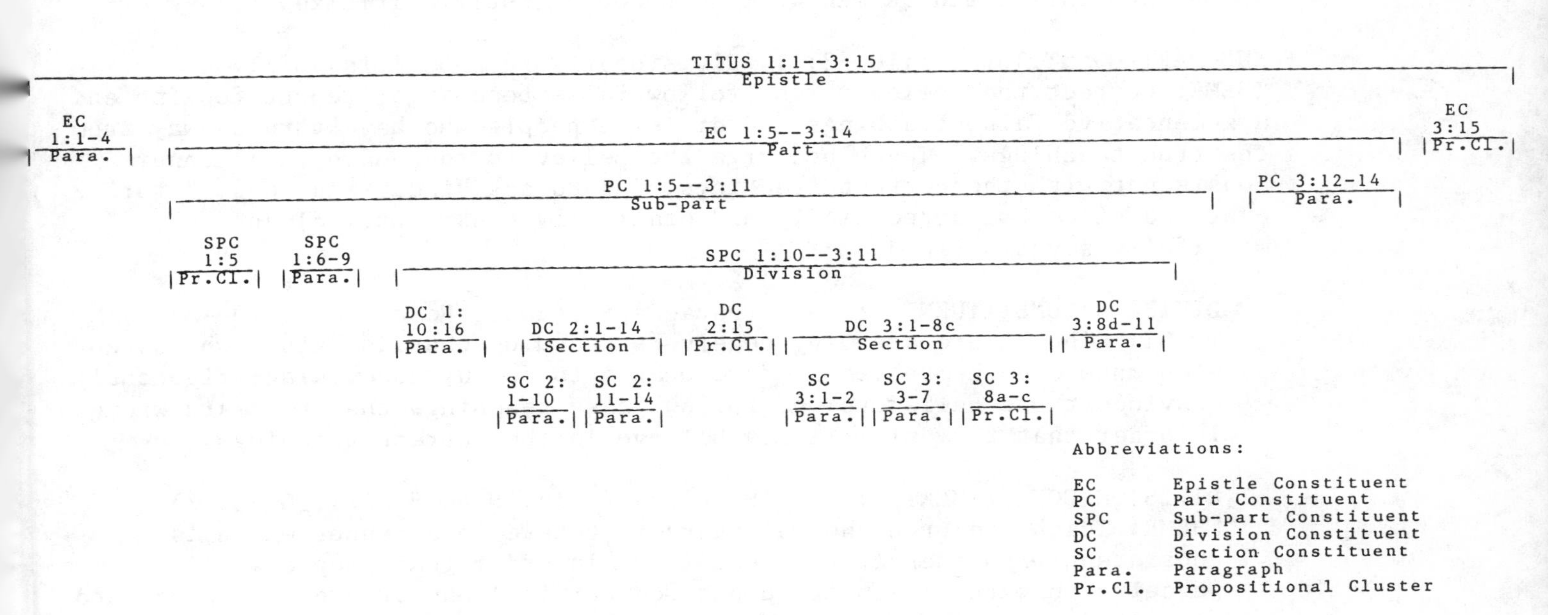

1.2.2 The Thematic Outline of Titus

TITUS 1:1--3:15 (Epistle)
THEME: I left you behind in Crete for these purposes: You are to correct those believers who follow false teachings, and urge all the believers to behave in a manner consistent with the correct teachings; and you are to appoint elders whom no one can justly criticize.

EPISTLE CONSTITUENT 1:1-4 (Paragraph) (Role: opening of the Epistle)
THEME: I, Paul, have been appointed by God as his servant and as an apostle of Jesus Christ in order that I might lead God's people to know, believe, and practice the true teachings. I write this letter to you, Titus. I pray that God will continue to bless you.

EPISTLE CONSTITUENT 1:5--3:14 (Part) (Role: Body of the Epistle)
THEME: I left you behind in Crete for these purposes: You are to correct those believers who follow false teachings, and urge all the believers to behave in a manner consistent with the correct teachings; and you are to appoint elders whom no one can justly criticize.

PART CONSTITUENT 1:5--3:11 (Sub-part) (Role: $Head_1$ of the Body)
THEME: I left you behind in Crete for these purposes: You are to correct those believers who follow false teachings, and urge all the believers to behave in a manner consistent with the correct teachings; and you are to appoint elders whom no one can justly criticize.

SUB-PART CONSTITUENT 1:5 (Propositional Cluster) (Role: Head of 1:5--3:11)
THEME: I left you behind in Crete for these purposes: You are to correct the matters that need to be corrected, and appoint elders in each town.

SUB-PART CONSTITUENT 1:6-9 (Paragraph) (Role: $specific_1$ of 1:5)
THEME: Appoint as elders men whom no one can justly criticize.

SUB-PART CONSTITUENT 1:10--3:11 (Division) (Role: $specific_2$ of 1:5)
THEME: Correct the believers who follow false teachings; reject foolish and argumentative false teachings and divisive people who have turned away from the true teachings. Teach and urge the believers to behave in a manner consistent with the correct teachings, and to act kindly and do good for everyone since God acted kindly and graciously toward us(inc) and mercifully saved us(inc).

DIVISION CONSTITUENT 1:10-16 (Paragraph) (Role: Head A of 1:10--3:11)
THEME: Since there are many deceivers teaching what is false, who do not even know God themselves and are unable to do any good thing, rigorously convince those believers who follow false teachings that they are wrong in order that they will firmly believe in the correct teachings.

DIVISION CONSTITUENT 2:1-14 (Section) (Role: Head B of 1:10--3:11)
THEME: Teach and urge the believers to behave in a manner which is consistent with the correct teachings, in order that people will perceive that the teachings about God our(inc) Savior are very good, and since God very graciously sent Jesus Christ to earth in order that God might save all people and since God graciously trains us(inc) to behave in a godly manner.

SECTION CONSTITUENT 2:1-10 (Paragraph) (Role: Head of 2:1-14)
THEME: Teach and urge the believers to behave in a manner which is consistent with the correct teachings in order that people will perceive that the teachings about God our(inc) Savior are very good.

SECTION CONSTITUENT 2:11-14 (Paragraph) (Role: grounds for 2:1-10)
THEME: God very graciously sent Jesus Christ to earth in order that God might save all people and God graciously trains us(inc) to behave in a godly manner.

DIVISION CONSTITUENT 2:15 (Propositional Cluster) (Role: manner of 1:10--3:11)
THEME: With full authority teach these things (1:10--2:14), urge the believers to do them, and correct those believers who do not follow them.

DIVISION CONSTITUENT 3:1-8c (Section) (Role: Head B′ of 1:10--3:11)
THEME: Remind the believers to act appropriately toward authorities, to act kindly toward everyone, and to do what is good for all people, since God acted kindly toward us(inc) and mercifully saved us(inc), even though formerly we(inc) were behaving sinfully.

SECTION CONSTITUENT 3:1-2 (Paragraph) (Role: Head of 3:1-8c)
THEME: Remind the believers to act appropriately toward authorities and kindly toward everyone.

SECTION CONSTITUENT 3:3-7 (Paragraph) (Role: Grounds for 3:1-2)
THEME: God acted kindly toward us(inc) and mercifully saved us(inc), even though formerly we(inc) were behaving sinfully.

SECTION CONSTITUENT 3:8a-c (Propositional Cluster) (Role: Restatement of 3:1-7)
THEME: I want you to confidently teach this trustworthy message (3:3-7) to the believers in order that they will be constantly concerned with doing what is good for others.

DIVISION CONSTITUENT 3:8d-11 (Paragraph) (Role: Head A′ of 1:10--3:11)
THEME: Have nothing to do with foolish disputes about genealogies and about the Jewish law; and do not allow divisive people who have turned away from the true teachings to influence the believers.

PART CONSTITUENT 3:12-14 (Paragraph) (Role: $head_2$ of the Body)
THEME: Make every effort to come to me at Nicopolis. Help Zenas and Apollos on their journey. All the believers should likewise learn to devote themselves to doing good deeds for people who especially need help.

EPISTLE CONSTITUENT 3:15 (Propositional Cluster) (Role: closing of the Epistle)
THEME: Everyone who is with me greets you and the other true believers there. I pray that our(inc) Lord Jesus Christ will continue to act graciously toward all of you.

2. THE PRESENTATION AND DISCUSSION OF THE SEMANTIC UNITS OF TITUS

TITUS 1:1--3:15 (Epistle)

THEME: I left you behind in Crete for these purposes: You are to correct those believers who follow false teachings, and urge all the believers to behave in a manner consistent with the correct teachings; and you are to appoint elders whom no one can justly criticize.

DISPLAY

RELATIONAL STRUCTURE	CONTENT
opening	(1:1-4) I, Paul, have been appointed by God as his servant and as an apostle of Jesus Christ in order that I might lead God's people to know, believe, and practice the true teachings. I write this letter to you, Titus. I pray that God will continue to bless you.
BODY	(1:5--3:14) I left you behind in Crete for these purposes: You are to correct those believers who follow false teachings, and urge all the believers to behave in a manner consistent with the correct teachings; and you are to appoint elders whom no one can justly criticize.
closing	(3:15) Everyone who is with me greets you and the other true believers there. I pray that our(inc) Lord Jesus Christ will continue to act graciously toward all of you.

COHERENCE OF THE EPISTLE

This epistle follows the pattern for Greek letters--the opening, the body, and the closing--so it is structurally (i.e., organizationally) coherent.

As with its boundaries, it is not necessary to verify the epistle's coherence for the purpose of proving that it is separate from some other unit. But it is important to demonstrate that it is a coherent unit in itself. The more coherent it can be shown to be, the more evidence there is for its integrity, for the fact that it is authored by one person (though perhaps with the help of an amanuensis) and not a collection of bits and pieces of whatever number or size.

Its coherence is shown on the epistle level by the occurrence in the opening of concepts that relate to important themes in the body. (**Paulos**... **apostolos**... **kata**...) **epignōsin alētheias tēs kat' eusebeian** (1:1), which could well be translated "(Paul...an apostle...for...) the knowledge of the truth that leads to godliness" (as NIV), previews one of the main thematic relationships of the body of the epistle--that sound doctrine motivates and produces godly living. This is the basic relationship between paragraphs 2:11-14 and 2:1-10, and between paragraphs 3:3-7 and 3:1-2, two very important units of the body.

Further evidence of coherence between the opening and the body (and possibly even the closing) are the following references (or possible references in some cases) to correct doctrine whether signified from the believing perspective by **pistis** 'faith', from the teaching perspective by **hugiainousa didaskalia** 'sound teaching/doctrine' or by **alētheia** 'truth':

pistin eklektōn theou `faith of God's elect' 1:1 (opening)
koinēn pistin `common faith' 1:4 (opening)
hugiainōsin en tē pistei `they may be sound in the faith' 1:13 (body)
hugiainontas tē pistei `being sound in the faith' 2:2 (body)
tous philountas hēmas en pistei `those loving us in faith' 3:15 (closing)

(Each of these is analyzed in this SSA as referring to correct faith in the sense of correct doctrine though it could well be argued that the first and last references might have different meanings.)

parakalein en tē didaskalia tē hugiainousē `to exhort in sound teaching/doctrine' 1:9 (body)
ha prepei tē hugiainousē didaskalia `those things which are consistent with sound teaching/doctrine' 2:1 (body)
epignōsin alētheias `knowledge of the truth' 1:1 (opening)
entolais anthrōpōn apostrephomenōn tēn alētheian `commandments of men who turn away from the truth' 1:14 (body)

The concept of salvation as represented by forms of **sōtēr** `Savior', **sōzō** `save', and **sōtērios** `saving, bringing salvation' occurs in the opening and body:

tou sōtēros hēmōn theou `of our Savior, God' 1:3 (opening); 2:10; 3:4 (body)
Christou Iēsou tou sōtēros hēmōn `of Christ Jesus our Savior' 1:4 (opening)
Iēsou Christou tou sōtēros hēmōn `of Jesus Christ our Savior' 3:6 (body)
tou megalou theou kai sōtēros hēmōn Iēsou Christou `of our great God and Savior, Jesus Christ' 2:13 (body)
esōsen hēmas `he (God) saved us' 3:5 (body)
hē charis tou theou sōtērios `the saving grace of God' 2:11 (body)

Sōtēr `Savior' occurs more often in Titus than in any other New Testament book. Of the eleven occurrences of **theos** `God' in Titus, four are with **sōtēr**; of the four occurrences of **Iēsous Christos**, three are with **sōtēr**. **Esōsen** `he saved (us)' occurs as the main verb in perhaps the most important grounds paragraph in the epistle. These facts suggest the importance of salvation in the theme of the epistle as a whole.

The chiastic structures of the main part of the body and the interweaving of the body's themes which is accomplished by this type of structure are the best evidence for the coherence of the epistle, especially for its body. These factors will be taken up later in the appropriate places.

PROMINENCE AND THEME

The body is certainly the most naturally prominent of the three major constituent parts of the epistle. Therefore, the epistle-level theme statement is that of the body, unless the theme of the opening or closing is marked highly prominent in some way. Though the opening of Titus does contain information relevant to the theme of the body, that information does not appear to be marked as being prominent enough to form part of the epistle-level theme statement.

EPISTLE CONSTITUENT 1:1-4 (Paragraph) (Role: opening of the Epistle)

THEME: I, Paul, have been appointed by God as his servant and as an apostle of Jesus Christ in order that I might lead God's people to know, believe, and practice the true teachings. I write this letter to you, Titus. I pray that God will continue to bless you.

DISPLAY

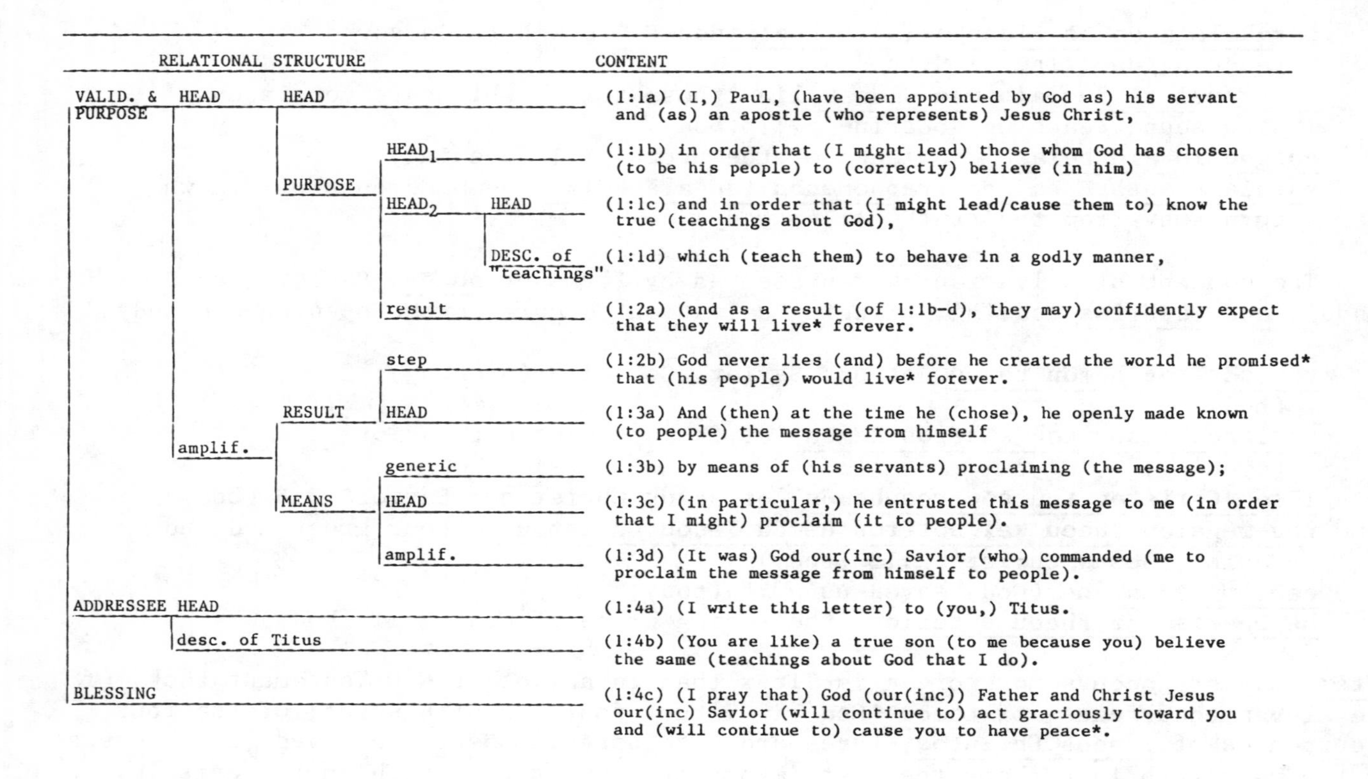

RELATIONAL STRUCTURE	CONTENT
VALID. & PURPOSE — HEAD — HEAD	(1:1a) (I,) Paul, (have been appointed by God as) his servant and (as) an apostle (who represents) Jesus Christ,
PURPOSE — HEAD₁	(1:1b) in order that (I might lead) those whom God has chosen (to be his people) to (correctly) believe (in him)
HEAD₂ — HEAD	(1:1c) and in order that (I might lead/cause them to) know the true (teachings about God),
DESC. of "teachings"	(1:1d) which (teach them) to behave in a godly manner,
result	(1:2a) (and as a result (of 1:1b-d), they may) confidently expect that they will live* forever.
amplif. — RESULT — step	(1:2b) God never lies (and) before he created the world he promised* that (his people) would live* forever.
HEAD	(1:3a) And (then) at the time he (chose), he openly made known (to people) the message from himself
MEANS — generic	(1:3b) by means of (his servants) proclaiming (the message);
HEAD	(1:3c) (in particular,) he entrusted this message to me (in order that I might) proclaim (it to people).
amplif.	(1:3d) (It was) God our(inc) Savior (who) commanded (me to proclaim the message from himself to people).
ADDRESSEE — HEAD	(1:4a) (I write this letter) to (you,) Titus.
desc. of Titus	(1:4b) (You are like) a true son (to me because you) believe the same (teachings about God that I do).
BLESSING	(1:4c) (I pray that) God (our(inc)) Father and Christ Jesus our(inc) Savior (will continue to) act graciously toward you and (will continue to) cause you to have peace*.

THE OPENING OF THE EPISTLE

Standard Greek letters of Paul's day had a formalized opening consisting of the sender's name, the addressee's name, and a brief salutation, normally just "Greetings" (chairein, cf. Acts 23:26). In situations where needed, the identification of the sender or addressee would be expanded. Paul often used this opportunity at the beginning of the letter to make sure that the readers of the letter understood that he spoke with the authority of an apostle. This is certainly the case here in Titus. Although Titus did not have to be reminded of Paul's authority, it is likely that this epistle would be read before the Cretan congregations (notice the plural you in the farewell at the end of the letter), and there were many people in Crete at the time who needed to be persuasively reminded of Paul's authority.

But in Titus, Paul goes even further. He states the function of his apostleship particularly in relation to the message he feels the Cretan believers need at the present moment. Thus this statement acts as a preview of the theme of the epistle as a whole.

Since the normal, unexpanded opening of a Greek letter was not more than one or two abbreviated sentences, it seems inappropriate to represent its structure by means of a schema diagram. However, the opening of Titus and some other New Testament writings are appropriate for schema labelling. The following schema outline applies to some of these:

+ Addressor
± Introductory remarks
+ Addressee
+ Blessing

In epistles where the remarks descriptive of the addressor are brief, they would probably be considered as belonging to the addressor constituent. However, in Romans and Titus the introductory remarks have a more unique function and may be considered as an embedded introduction or preview of the epistle. In Titus the introductory remarks deal with the validation of Paul's authority as an apostle and the purpose of that apostleship especially in reference to the Cretan believers. Therefore this schema-level constituent might be called "validation and purpose" since it deals with both of these matters and one cannot be separated from the other because of the interweaving of both of them.

BOUNDARIES AND COHERENCE

The initial boundary of this unit coincides with the beginning of the epistle discourse, its final boundary is marked by the end of the formalized greeting or blessing which characteristically ends the opening of letters. There is no difficulty in discerning the initial and final boundaries of the opening since they are similar to all of Paul's epistles and are more or less like the structure of the Greek letter of the day.

PROMINENCE AND THEME

The naturally prominent constituents of a standard formalized opening are the addressor, addressee, and the greeting or blessing. But, as mentioned above, in the opening of Titus Paul also deals with the very important and relevant factor of establishing his authority and at the same time gives the purpose of his authority and commission, especially in reference to the Cretan believers. Thus there is a preview of the theme of the epistle right in the opening--the Cretan believers are to be taught God's truth and correct belief which results in godly lives, **apostolos...kata pistin eklektōn theou kai epignōsin alētheias tēs kat' eusebeian** 'an apostle...in reference to the faith of God's elect and knowledge of the truth that has reference to/leads to godliness'. The long expansion of the opening and the relevance of the expansion to the theme of the epistle as a whole argue for its prominence, so a representation of this part of the opening is included in the theme statement of the opening. As noted above, this schema-level constituent is labelled "validation and purpose" in the display diagram.

Regarding the representation of the validation and purpose constituent (1:1-3) in the theme statement, Paul's statements about his being a servant of God and an apostle of Jesus Christ in 1:1a have natural prominence as the means for the purpose propositions in 1:1b-2a. Since 1:2b-3d is an amplification of the Head constituent 1:1a-2a, the only information from this amplification added to the theme statement is the information already added by necessity to 1:1a ("appointed by God") to provide a verb in a means clause. (See the notes for 1:1a.)

As mentioned above, the purpose of the apostleship, as expressed in 1:1b-2a, is marked as prominent by its evident preview of the theme of the epistle as a whole. In the theme statement an attempt is made at shortening these longer purpose propositions to make as brief a statement as possible, "know, believe, and practice the true teachings." Although it might be argued that **pistin** 'faith' refers to initial trust in Christ here, the fact that the whole epistle deals with soundness in faith (cf. 1:13; 2:2) and doctrine (cf. 1:9; 2:1) has led us to interpret **pistin** here as having more to do with sound or correct faith.

And, although **tēs kat' eusebeian** 'which accords with godliness' as a descriptive phrase does not have natural prominence, it seems that the great stress given in the epistle to the practice of godliness marks it as prominent and a very important part of the theme, thus the inclusion of "practice" in the theme statement.

The blessing has been rendered generically in the theme statement as follows: "God" stands for the Godhead (here "God our Father and Christ Jesus our Savior") and "bless" for both "act graciously toward" and "cause you to have peace."

NOTES ON 1:1-4

1:1a. **(I,) Paul, (have been appointed by God as) his servant and (as) an apostle (who represents) Jesus Christ,** (**Paulos doulos theou, apostolos de Iēsou Christou** 'Paul servant of-God, and apostle of-Jesus Christ')

CONT The context suggests that the service aspect of **doulos** 'slave/servant' is in focus rather than the total subservience aspect since Paul is talking about his task here in the opening of the epistle rather than the nature of his relationship with God.

CONT The word **apostolos** 'apostle' here designates a special class of people with primary authority in the church. Paul was an authorized representative of Jesus Christ on the highest level and should be recognized as such not only by Titus but especially by the believers who were being influenced to listen to the teachings of the false prophets. Since the apostles were a special class of Christian leaders, **apostolos** has been rendered in the display text as a noun, rather than a verbal construction, in order to represent clearly the concept of "apostle" in scripture.

The terms **apostolos** 'apostle' and **Iēsou Christou** 'Jesus Christ' are linked by the genitive construction. The semantic relationship is probably that of representation--Paul was representing Jesus Christ. In secular literature, **apostolos** sometimes meant "ambassador, delegate, messenger," and so the concept of representation is clearly part of the meaning of apostle. On the other hand, the sense of "an apostle commissioned by Jesus Christ" is also possible. We have chosen "represent" for our rendering--"an apostle (who represents) Jesus Christ."

REL The relation between **doulos theou** 'servant of God' and **apostolos Iēsou Christou** 'apostle of Jesus Christ' is marked by the connective particle **de**. Harold

Greenlee (personal communication) remarks about **de** in this construction, "I believe **de** is used because the function of **apostolos** is different than the function of **doulos**, hence there is some contrast. If he had said `apostle of God and apostle of Jesus Christ,' he would have used **kai**."

CONT/REL 1:1a, **Paulos doulos theou, apostolos de Iēsou Christou** `Paul servant of God, and apostle of Jesus Christ' has no verbal form and might be interpreted semantically as a stative construction. The following prepositional phrases represent event propositions with some type of dependence on 1:1a. The relationship between 1:1a and 1b-c is probably means-purpose. The problem is that constructions that are completely stative do not adequately function as means in means-purpose constructions and in some languages cannot be used at all in these constructions. Therefore, some type of event word is needed to indicate adequately the means-purpose relationship between 1:1a and 1:b-c. But what should this word be?

Actually **doulos** `servant' and **apostolos** `apostle' are in a sense event words though they denote people. **Paulos...apostolos Iēsou Christou** `Paul...apostle of Jesus Christ' could be understood here in the sense of (1) "(I,) Paul, have been sent/appointed by Jesus Christ to represent him," or (2) "(I,) Paul, represent Jesus Christ." The context of verse three, **en kērugmati ho episteuthēn egō kat' epitagēn tou sōtēros hēmōn theou** `through the preaching which I have been entrusted with by the command of our Savior God', and the apparent function of 1:1-3 of demonstrating the validity of Paul's work, would strongly suggest that the first option above is the correct one. In five other epistles Paul establishes his authority by beginning the epistle referring to himself as an apostle of Jesus Christ "by the will of God" (**dia thelēmatos theou** 1 Cor. 1:1; 2 Cor. 1:1; Eph. 1:1; Col. 1:1; 2 Tim. 1:1). Gal. 1:1 and 1 Tim. 1:1 are similar, and Rom. 1:1 basically has the same thoughts. In Titus the explicit reference to God's appointment (that is, other than **doulos theou** and **apostolos Iēsou Christou**) is not made until verse three as indicated above.

The full meaning of **doulos theou** `servant of God' here is more difficult to ascertain. This is because it is not recognized as a title to the same extent as **apostolos** `apostle', though Moses and Old Testament prophets were called "servants of God." The question is whether **doulos theou** `servant of God' here focuses on the fact that Paul serves God in a certain task or the fact that he is a servant of God appointed by him for a certain task. The stress on Paul's God-given authority in 1:1-3 which parallels most of his other epistles, and the meaning of **apostolos Iēsou Christou** `apostle of Jesus Christ' as suggested above, indicate that "(I,) Paul, (have been appointed by God as) his servant" is probably closer to Paul's intended meaning than "(I,) Paul, serve God."

1:1b. in order that (I might lead) those whom God has chosen (to be his people) to (correctly) believe (in him) (kata pistin eklektōn theou `according/pertaining-to faith of-(the)-elect of-God')

REL There is a difference among commentators as to the meaning of **kata** here. The normative meaning of **kata**, which is usually translated as "according to," is a very common one in the New Testament and seems to be thought of by many as the basic meaning of **kata** with the accusative when it is not in reference to place or time. But it should be realized that **kata** has a normative meaning only in those constructions where one of the two (or more) concepts it relates is a standard of some type. The problem in 1:1b is determining whether **pistin eklektōn theou kai epignōsin alētheias tēs kat' eusebeian** `faith of God's elect and knowledge of truth pertaining to godliness' is intended by Paul to be a standard or not. This should be kept in mind in considering the following interpretations of the meaning of kata in 1:1b:

1. "According to." A minority of commentators take the view that the message of Paul's apostleship is "according to the faith of God's elect and the knowledge of the truth" in the sense that Paul's message is the same as that shared by God's elect people. Now, no commentator is going to say Paul meant that whatever the faith/doctrine of God's people was at a certain time, that was the faith he preached. So Scott says, "Paul's work as an apostle is in keeping with the new revelation to which the elect have responded....Paul's teaching agrees with that new knowledge which has come to Christians through the gospel." But Paul is not talking here about how well he measures up to the faith and knowledge of the truth. He is saying that he has been commissioned by God as his servant and by Christ as his representative with the implication that he preaches the faith revealed by God. This is certainly borne out in 1:3 where he says that the preaching of that revelation has been entrusted to him by the commandment of God. 1:3 and scripture in general teach that revelation follows the pattern as described by the following diagram:

   Revelation--->Paul--->God's elect

   But the above interpretation advocated by a minority of commentators seems to indicate the following:

   Revelation Revelation
↓ ↓
God's elect<--->Paul

   or possibly even:

   Revelation--->God's elect--->Paul

   As Ellicott says, "the faith or knowledge of individuals cannot, without much explaining away, ever be the rule or norma of the apostle's office." It is difficult to see why Paul would want to emphasize that what he preached wasthe same as what God's elect believed when he could and did stress constantly that his revelation was directly from God.
2. "In relation to, with respect to" (Arndt and Gingrich II.6). This, too, is a common meaning of kata with many references in the New Testament. In fact, it could be argued that it is in a sense a more basic meaning than the normative one since it is more neutral in meaning. It is easier to see the progression from "in respect to" to "according to" when a standard is involved, than the progression from a basic meaning of "according to," which signifies that a standard is to be expected, to those other meanings of kata, such as "in respect to" where no standard is involved. For example in John 18:31, kata ton nomon humōn krinate auton `judge him kata your law'. It could be said that kata basically means "in respect/relation to (your law)" but because of the normative standard of the law it takes on a finer meaning here of "according to (your law)." Kelly translates apostolos de Iēsou Christou kata pistin eklektōn theou as "an apostle of Jesus Christ concerned with the faith of God's elect." There is no doubt that this fits the context and is certainly consistent with Paul's apostleship as revealed in other Scripture (Acts 9:15; 26:16-18; Rom. 1:5).
3. "Of goal, purpose `for the purpose of, for, to'" (Arndt and Gingrich II.4). Others refer to this use of kata as "destination." The abstract sense is related to the locative sense "of direction `toward, to, up to'" (Arndt and Gingrich II 1.b). Like 2 above, this sense fits the context and is consistent with other Scripture that deals with Paul's apostleship.

2 and 3 support the relationship shown in the display. The display text is consistent with the meaning advocated by a majority of commentators.

CONT In the Greek text 1:1b-2a is a very compact structure with no verbs at all, thus the need to supply implied verbs in several places in the propositionalized text. For the action that Paul must take to accomplish his task on the behalf of God's elect we have supplied the word "lead" here in the display text, but "teach" or other verbs with a similarly appropriate meaning might be used. Even "bring" or "cause" would be appropriate.

CONT As has been mentioned above in Prominence and Theme for 1:1-4, there is strong indication from the context of the epistle as a whole that **pistin** 'faith' here has to do with the soundness or correctness of the elect's faith, rather than only initial trust in Christ. Some of the more prominent statements of the epistle have to do with the soundness of faith or doctrine (1:9,13; 2:2). Therefore "correctly" has been supplied in the display text, "to (correctly) believe (in him)."

1:1c-d. **and in order that (I might lead/cause them to) know the true (teachings about God), (1d) which (teach them) to behave in a godly manner,** (**kai epignōsin alētheias tēs kat' eusebeian** 'and knowledge of-truth which pertains-to godliness')

CONT In the Pastoral Epistles **eusebeia** in some contexts quite clearly translates in English as "religion" (1 Tim. 6:5; probably 1 Tim. 3:16), in other contexts clearly as "godliness, piety" (1 Tim. 2:2; 6:11), but in still other contexts, as here, it is more difficult to ascertain whether its sense is closer to "religion" or to "godliness." This is the only occurrence of **eusebeia** in Titus but in Titus 2:12 the related adverb **eusebōs** definitely refers to godly, holy living as shown by its clear contrast to **asebeian** 'godlessness, impiety' in the same sentence and the similarity in its behavioral sense with its immediate constituents **sōphronōs** 'with self-control' and **dikaiōs** 'righteously'. Since the whole epistle deals so much with godly living, it is very probable that that is the meaning of **eusebeia** here in the introduction of the theme. One of the main themes of the book is that the great truths of the gospel are incentives for godly living. (See 2:1-14 and 3:1-8c.)

REL Here again in 1d, as in 1b, there is no contextual or lexical reason why **kata** should not mean "pertaining to, is concerned with," i.e., showing that there is a definite relation between the truth (of the gospel) and godliness but not indicating that one of these concepts is the normative one for the other. Paul's task is to make sure that God's people understand the true teachings from God, teachings that are concerned with godliness. This is the very theme of the epistle. This has been propositionalized as "the true (teachings about God), which (teach them) to behave in a godly manner." An alternate rendering would be "the true (teachings about God), (teachings) which pertain to how (God wants people) to behave."

REL Again with the theme of the whole epistle in mind, it would seem probable that **tēs kat' eusebeian** 'which pertains to godliness' describes God's truth as inherently being concerned with godliness. Thus "which pertains to godliness" is in a descriptive relationship with "the knowledge of the truth." Another possible sense here would be a delimiting or identificational one in which "the true teachings that pertain to godliness" especially denotes those specific teachings that pertain to godliness and only those. So "which pertains to godliness" would have an identificational relation with "the truth." The description relation is adopted in the display since such passages as 3:3-8c teach that the great truths of the gospel are incentives for godly living, thus implying that the gospel as a whole is concerned with godliness.

1:2a. **(and as a result (of 1:1b-d), they may) confidently expect that they will live* forever.** (**ep′ elpidi zōēs aiōniou**, `in hope of-life eternal′)

REL The preposition **epi** with the dative has as its most common logical meaning `on the basis of′ and this often propositionalizes as a reason or grounds relationship, though it does not always do so when in the combination **ep′ elpidi** as will be discussed later. **Ep′ elpidi zōēs aiōniou** `in hope of life eternal′ or `on the basis of the hope of life eternal′ could be grammatically connected directly to **Paulos doulos theou, apostolos de Iēsou Christou** with the relationship "(I,) Paul, (am) a servant of God and an apostle (who represents) Jesus Christ because I confidently expect to live forever."

But this basically seems out of step with what Paul is saying in verse one. He is discussing the sphere of his assignment as an apostle, not any personal reasons for his commitment to the apostleship. And the whole context, especially 1:1a and 1:3, is written to stress the fact that his apostleship is definitely from God and not something he has chosen of himself to do. As far as Paul′s credentials are concerned, no one in Crete is going to be particularly impressed by the fact that Paul′s motivation in serving as an apostle is because he hopes to live forever.

Since **pistin** `faith′ and **epignōsin** `knowledge′ are closely coordinated, it may seem best to connect the **epi** phrase with the whole **kata pistin...eusebeian** construction. The rendering for 1:2a would be:

reason

(1:2a) (The people of God believe correctly in him and they come to know the true teachings about him, which teach them to behave in a godly manner,) because they hope to live forever.

The problem with this interpretation is that in it the focus has changed from Paul′s sphere or purpose of ministry to motivations for true faith and knowledge and godliness, and this change in focus cannot otherwise be substantiated. It does not fit in with the recognizable themes of 1:1-3--the authority and sphere of Paul′s apostleship. It would have little more than a comment relationship in this context. We would instead expect that the **epi** phrase would have to do with the sphere/purpose of Paul′s apostleship. Actually, if the motivation is not to be given heavy stress, this reason role is very close to, and can be more succinctly expressed by, either a purpose or result role (which would also be true if **epi** was taken to relate only to **eusebeian** `godliness′).

Therefore **ep′ elpidi** here is probably not to be understood with the most common logical meaning of **epi** `on the basis of′ but either as having a purpose or result role.

Regarding purpose, Kelly says, "Paul′s point is not, as some suppose (translating **epi** by `in′), that as an apostle he is sustained by the `hope of eternal life′; this narrows the thought unduly, as well as missing the parallelism with the preceding clause. Rather he is suggesting that it is his function to promote that `hope′. For **epi** with the dative meaning `with a view to′, `for the sake of′, cf. Eph. ii.10; 1 Thess. iv.7; 2 Tim. ii.14." Kelly relates the **epi** phrase to **apostolos Iēsou Christou.**

Regarding result, of the seven other occurrences of **ep′** (or its alternate **eph′**) **elpidi** in the New Testament (Acts 2:26; 26:6; Rom. 4:18; 5:2; 8:20-21; 1 Cor. 9:10c,d), in only two of them, Acts 26:6 and Rom. 5:2, does **epi** clearly have the meaning "on the basis of." In a third, Rom. 4:18, it may have that meaning.

Following is a detailed study of five of those occurrences of **ep′ elpidi**:

For 1 Cor. 9:10c-d, **opheilei ep′ elpidi ho arotriōn arotrian, kai ho aloōn ep′ elpidi tou metechein** ‵he that plows should plow in hope, and he that threshes in hope of sharing (in the harvest)′, the propositionalization would appear to be:

condition	If a person is plowing,
HEAD	he ought to be able to confidently expect that he will receive a part of what will be harvested; etc.

and probably not:

*If a person is plowing, he ought to be able to plow because/since he confidently expects to receive a part of what will be harvested.

Acts 2:26b-27a, **eti de kai hē sarx mou kataskēnōsei ep′ elpidi hoti ouk egkataleipseis tēn psuchēn mou eis hadēn** ‵moreover my flesh/body will live in hope, because you will not abandon my soul to Hades′, appears to be best propositionalized as:

HEAD	I confidently expect that my body will continue to live/exist,
reason	because you will not abandon my soul to Hades.

certainly not:

*My body will continue to exist because I confidently expect that it will exist because you will not abandon my soul to Hades.

Rom. 8:20-21a **tē gar mataiotēti hē ktisis hupetagē ouch hekousa alla dia ton hupotaxanta, eph′ helpidi hoti kai autē hē ktisis eleutherōthēsetai apo tēs douleias tēs phthoras....** ‵for the creation was subjected to frustration, not by its own choice but by the will of the one who subjected it, in hope that the creation itself will be liberated from its bondage to decay....′ (NIV). It is difficult to see how "because" or "on the basis of" is appropriate here. It cannot be translated "the creation was subjected to frustration because it hoped to be liberated" or "the creation was subjected to frustration not by its own choice, but by the will of the one who subjected it, because he hoped that it would be liberated." It would possibly be propositionalized as follows:

contrast	HEAD		Those things which God created were subjected (by God) to being frustrated
		contr.	not because those things themselves wanted to be frustrated
	reas.	HEAD	but because the one who subjected them willed to subject them.
HEAD			(But those things which God has created) may confidently expect that they will no longer be subjected to being destroyed/decayed.

Rom. 4:18a-b hos par′ elpida ep′ elpidi episteusen eis to genesthai auton patera pollōn ethnōn ʻwho against hope in hope believed and so became father of many nations′. Propositionalization number 1 below is probably nearer the intended meaning than number 2:

1.

concession	Although he (Abraham) and his wife were very old and there was no basis for him to confidently expect that they would have a child,
HEAD	yet he confidently expected and believed that he would have a child
result	and as a result, he became the father of many nations.

2.

concession		Although he (Abraham) and his wife were very old and there was no basis for him to confidently expect that they would have a child,
HEAD	HEAD	yet he believed that he would have a child
	reason	because he confidently expected that he would have a child
result		and as a result, he became the father of many nations.

Note TEV for this verse, "Abraham believed and hoped, even when there was no reason for hoping, and so became ʻthe father of many nations.′"

How do these findings apply to ep′ elpidi zōēs aiōniou ʻin hope of eternal life′ in Titus 1:2a? These references show that within the construction ep′ elpidi in the New Testament, epi does not always, nor even in the majority of cases, clearly mean "on the basis of," propositionalizing as a reason/grounds relation.

It seems that in some cases there is a narrow difference between ep′ elpidi meaning "(I do such-and-such) because/since I hope" and ep′ elpidi meaning "(I do such-and-such) hopefully/confidently expecting that"--in other words, the difference between hope being the basis of an action and hope being a state of mind attendant with the action. The latter may sometimes express itself in a manner construction, but as we have seen in these four examples from the New Testament, conjoined or other relationships are also possible. Thus, in the TEV translation of Rom. 4:18, "Abraham believed and hoped," ep′ elpidi is not taken to mean "on the basis of hope" but as an attendant state of mind expressed as a clause parallel to "Abraham believed." In Rom. 8:20-21, eph′ helpidi presumably refers to the hopefulness there was in a situation that might have seemed hopeless. TEV translates, "[20]For creation was condemned to lose its purpose, not of its own will, but because God willed it to be so. Yet there was the hope [21]that creation itself would one day be set free from its slavery to decay...."

In Titus 1:2a, the meaning of ep′ elpidi as "on the basis of hope" may also be questioned. Perhaps it is more difficult to make a decision here, but the context at least suggests that instead of a reason/grounds proposition, the appropriate proposition may be one which indicates the resultant state of mind and assurance of God′s people who follow the teaching regarding correct belief and knowledge of the truth that leads to godliness. This would be a result proposition--"(and as a result (of 1:1b-d), they may) confidently expect that they will live forever." (See display.)

There is not much difference in meaning between rendering the epi phrase as result or as purpose. 1:2a propositionalized in a purpose role would be, "in order that they may confidently expect that they will live forever."

CONT Because the present-day meaning of hope in English tends to have a component or connotation of uncertainty while the Greek word as used here in the Scripture did not, "confidently expect" has been used instead of "hope."

CONT "Live" is marked with an asterisk in the sequence "live forever" since "live" here does not refer to the physical life of our earthly bodies, which is the primary meaning of "live" in English.

1:2b. **God never lies (and) before he created the world he promised* that (his people) would live* forever.** (**hēn epēggeilato ho apseudēs theos pro chronōn aiōniōn**, ‵which promised the unlying God before times eternal′)

REL The question might be asked as to whether **hēn** ‵which′ specifically refers back to **elpidi** ‵hope′ or to **zōēs aiōniou** ‵eternal life′. Though **elpidi** ‵hope′ is the grammatical head of this genitive construction, semantically eternal life is more prominent since it is something real to be experienced, while hope has more to do with man′s conceptual relation toward the reality of eternal life. The relationship is comparable to the orienter-content relation where the content is more prominent than the orienter unless the orienter is marked as prominent. The fact that eternal life is more prominent than hope can be shown by the fact that if we translate "God promised eternal life to his people," we probably will communicate fully the content of God′s promise; whereas, if we translate "God promised hope to his people," we have not communicated what the content or goal of that hope is. Because of this, it cannot be clearly claimed on the semantic level that **elpidi** must be the specific antecedent of **hēn** on the grounds that **elpidi** is the head of the genitive construction. For this reason, and also because elsewhere we do not find God promising "hope," but we do find "life" promised in the other Pastoral Epistles (1 Tim. 4:8 and 2 Tim. 1:1) and also in 1 John 2:25, "eternal life" has been identified as the antecedent of **hēn** ‵which′. This is also the view held by the majority of commentators and results in a simpler construction. At the same time, there is probably not any appreciable difference in meaning between God promising eternal life and God promising the hope of eternal life.

CONT A second question in 1:2b is concerned with the intended meaning of the words **pro chronōn aiōniōn** literally "before times eternal." Some commentators and translators prefer to translate it here as "ages ago, long ages ago" and refer it to promises in the Old Testament. One of the reasons given for this interpretation is that God's promising something to his people before his people existed is either impossible or not as probable as God's promising to his people when they were actually in existence. However we take the interpretation that **pro chronōn aiōniōn** is referring to eternal times because:

1. The concept of God acting on man's behalf before man existed is scriptural as shown by Eph. 1:4, "For he chose us in him before the creation of the world (**pro katabolēs kosmou**) to be holy and blameless in his sight" (NIV).
2. Reference to pre-creation eternity is undoubtedly the primary meaning of **pro chronōn aiōniōn**. Note that Arndt and Gingrich translate it as "before time began." None of the references which are given by Arndt and Gingrich with the combination **pro...aiōnōn/aiōniōn** definitely refer to time after creation and all have the possibility of referring to eternal times before creation: **pro chronōn aiōniōn** 'before times eternal, before the ages, before time began' 2 Tim. 1:9, Titus 1:2; **pro tōn aiōnōn** 'before the ages' 1 Cor. 2:7; **pro pantos tou aiōnos** 'before all the ages' Jude 25a (cf. Ps. 54:20 in the Septuagint [55:19] **theos ho huparchōn pro tōn aiōnōn** 'God who exists before the ages').
3. A significant point in Titus 1:2-3 is that God's promise was revealed at his appointed time (**kairois idiois**) by the proclamation entrusted to Paul and others. There is a definite contrast between **pro chronōn aiōniōn** and **kairois idiois** which is marked by **de**. Since 1:2-3 talks about the revelation of the message (**ton logon**) through proclamation/preaching (**en kērugmati**) rather than the manifestation of the promise, it seems that Paul is saying that the specific promise referred to in 1:2, which was made **pro chronōn aiōniōn**, was not revealed to any human being until God's appointed time, that is, until the preaching of the gospel of Christ. Cf. 2 Tim. 1:9-10 and 1 Cor. 2:6-10 where events done **pro chronōn aiōniōn/pro tōn aiōnōn** are not revealed until the coming of Christ.

Regarding the problem of to whom the promise was announced/made if it was made before man was created,

1. In the Greek text of Titus 1:2 there is no formal reference as to whom the promise was made, thus implying that in Greek no such formal explicit reference is required with **epēggeilato** 'he promised'. Therefore, this is not a linguistic problem as far as Greek is concerned, though it may be as far as translation into other languages is concerned.
2. The exegetical problem is certainly not insurmountable, though it is difficult to know the correct answer. The promise could have been announced/made within the Godhead or possibly Paul is using **epēggeilato** 'he promised' in a sense in which the announcement to those who receive the promise is not necessarily made at the time of the original statement of the promise.

In the English rendering in the display text, no one is indicated as the recipient of the promise in the orienter proposition (though this is indicated in the content proposition) since the statement "before he created the world God promised to people" could be taken as impossible. Certainly in English itself the recipients do not have to be made explicit in the orienter proposition. If, however, it is felt that English "promise" necessarily indicates a statement that must be made in the presence of the recipients of the promise, then perhaps "vow" in the sense of "to declare with assurance and solemnity" (Funk and Wagnalls) would be a better term for the display text. Thus the asterisk after "promised" in the display text indicates that "promised" is possibly not being used in its most common English sense, since the recipients of the promise were not living when the promise was first made.

The majority of commentators and translators follow the interpretation that refers to eternal times.

The clearest way to express "before eternal times" is probably "before God created the world."

1:3a. **And (then) at the time he (chose), he openly made known (to people) the message from himself (ephanerōsen de kairois idiois ton logon autou** `and/but he-revealed in-times his-own the word of-him')

REL The conjunction de could also be translated "but." The relation between 1:2b and 1:3a is progression (step-goal relationship) although the time references are in contrast.

CONT **Kairois idiois** could mean "at its own time," i.e., "at the proper time, at the right moment," or it could mean "at his (God's) own time." Since the whole context stresses God's action, certainly "at God's own time" is the basic meaning here although a rendering of "at the proper time" would probably also indicate the same idea in this context. In the display text "at the time he (chose)" is used to render "at his own time" in a more propositionalized form. "Determined" or "appointed" would be alternate choices to "choose."

TRNS "To people" is supplied to make explicit the beneficiaries of God's revelation of his message. "People" is used since in English it can be an all-inclusive, nondifferentiating word. However, in some languages the inclusive first person plural pronoun is more appropriate.

CONT/REL Beginning with 1:2a the topic has been eternal life. The relative clause beginning with **hēn** `which' (1:2b) describes eternal life as being promised by God from eternity. The **de**, the contrastive time reference "at his own time," and the contrast between "promised" and "revealed" are all natural indicators that the topic is still being talked about, and so we would expect a second relative clause beginning at 1:3a with "eternal life" as its antecedent too. Instead we find that, at least on the lexical level, a new topic is introduced, **ton logon autou** `his word/message'. Hendriksen is probably right when he says, "From eternity God promised life everlasting, but `in due season'...he revealed it. Strictly speaking, however, it was not life everlasting itself in its glorious heavenly phase that was revealed to earth-dwellers (how could it be?), but the word of God with respect to it. Hence, the change from `life everlasting' in verse 2 to `his word' in verse 3." It may be, too, that Paul now desires to focus on the message as a whole. But it would be ignoring the context to say that what Paul is now talking about no longer has any reference to eternal life. Certainly he has in mind eternal life as an important part of the revealed gospel message which has been entrusted to him. These considerations also show that it is much more probable that **logon autou** means "the word/message from himself" rather than "the word/message about himself."

1:3b-c. **by means of (his servants) proclaiming (the message); (3c) (in particular,) he entrusted this message to me (in order that I might) proclaim (it to people).** (en kērugmati ho episteuthēn egō 'by proclamation which I have-been-entrusted-with')

REL This means proposition is considered as marked prominent by the fact that it states Paul's authority in proclaiming the gospel as an amplification of Paul's statement of his authority in 1a ("servant of God and apostle of Jesus Christ"). Authority is the major theme in this sandwich-type structure.

REL/PROM The order of 1:3b-c with **en kērugmati** 'by proclamation' before the relative **ho** 'which' would tend to indicate that God's chosen means for revealing his message was that of public proclamation--no persons specified. Since Paul was not the only person entrusted with proclaiming the gospel message, **en kērugmati** is best understood generically. However, since Paul is specifically in focus here, as shown by the fact that he says "by the proclamation which I myself (free nominative pronoun **egō** 'I, I myself') have been entrusted with," this specific statement is more prominent than the preceding generic one. This corresponds with the general observation that in a generic-specific relationship where there is only one specific, the specific is often more prominent than the generic.

CONT Grammatically, the relative **ho** 'which', being neuter, refers back to **kērugmati** 'proclamation, preaching' which is also neuter rather than to **ton logon** 'word, message' which is masculine. Semantically, however, it is difficult to divide the message from the proclamation of it. In fact, the word **kērugma** may refer to the proclaiming of the message or to the message itself. Here both are in mind since the revelation cannot be made manifest in the full sense unless it is proclaimed to the people. This is shown in the display text of 1:3b by the use of both "message" and "proclaim."

CONT In 1:3b and c, Paul is stressing the fact that God himself entrusted the proclamation of his revealed message to Paul with the implication that, when he speaks, he speaks with authority from God. This needs to be established at the very beginning of the epistle so that the whole epistle will be seen as authoritative.

1:3d. **(It was) God our(inc) Savior (who) commanded (me to proclaim the message from himself to people).** (kat' epitagēn tou sōtēros hēmōn theou, 'according-to command of-the Savior of-us, God')

CONT/PROM A more literal rendering of 1:3d might be "(it was) God our(inc) Savior (who) commanded (me to be entrusted with proclaiming his message to people)" but this is much more involved and difficult to translate into other languages. Also the agent of both the entrusting and the commanding is God. The purpose of 1:3d is to emphasize Paul's God-given authority to proclaim the revealed message. "It was" has been supplied before "God" to represent the prominence given in the Greek to the fact that God himself entrusted Paul with the proclamation of the revelation. That there is prominence here is clearly indicated by the fact that the whole **kata** phrase could have been left out and God would probably have been understood as the agent of the entrusting, but this needed to be emphasized with full force.

1:4a-b. **(I write this letter) to (you,) Titus. (4b) (You are like) a true son (to me because you) believe the same (teachings about God that I do).** (**Titō gnēsiō teknō kata koinēn pistin**: 'to-Titus true child in-respect-to a-common faith')

CONT Although it may be true that Titus was converted by Paul and this is signified by **teknō** 'child', what may be more in focus is that Titus is as a true son to Paul because he holds firmly to the same faith. **Kata koinēn pistin**, as Huther says, "gives the point of view from which Titus can be considered the genuine son of the apostle." For this reason "(because you) believe the same (teachings about God that I do)" is used in the display. This concept of true faith is pivotal to the epistle.

1:4c. **(I pray that) God (our(inc)) Father and Christ Jesus our(inc) Savior (will continue to) act graciously toward you and (will continue to) cause you to have peace*. (charis kai eirēnē apo theou patros kai Christou Iēsou tou sōtēros hēmōn.** 'grace and peace from God Father and Christ Jesus the Savior of-us')

CONT/TRNS There is no verb at all in the Greek text of 1:4c, nor does Paul use a verb in any of his "blessings." "May" is suggested by the optative form **plēthuntheiē** 'may (it) be multiplied' in the blessings of 1 Pet. 1:2 and 2 Pet. 1:2. In 3 John 1:2 **euchomai** 'I pray' is used in a blessing of a slightly different type. In 2 John 1:3 the future form of the verb "to be," **estai**, is used in a blessing of the type used in Titus, and NIV translates, "Grace, mercy and peace from God the Father and from Jesus Christ, the Father's Son, will be with us in truth and love." "I pray that" is used here in the display text since "may" is an obscure device in English. The determining factor in a translation into another language as to which of the above ("may," "I pray," "will") is to be used will probably be the form which is most appropriate in the Receptor Language. Or a language may have other forms that are appropriate here.

CONT/TRNS **Charis** 'grace' represents an event and, therefore, should be propositionalized as a verb. Since there is no one English verb to represent "grace," it has been suggested in other SSA's that "act graciously" or "be gracious" be used in the SSA display text with the same general denotation as in contexts other than blessings where God's unmerited favor is being discussed, since, "for Paul, 'grace' is the word that characterizes all God's favorable attitudes and actions towards sinful men" (Callow 1982:24).

In many languages, however, there will necessarily be a clear distinction between the verb used in a blessing to describe God acting graciously (in the Christian sense) and the verb used to describe God's action in graciously saving us, for instance (cf. 2:11).

CONT For the meaning of **eirēnē** 'peace' we quote from the discussion of this word as found in the opening of Colossians in the Colossians SSA (Callow 1983a:28), "It is generally agreed among the commentators that peace is the state enjoyed by the recipients of God's grace, and it is also generally considered that it is similar in meaning to the Hebrew word shalom, which is often translated by **eirēnē** in the Septuagint. The Hebrew word, however, means more than internal peacefulness or outward freedom from war, strife, etc. It corresponds more nearly to the English word 'well-being', a state of blessedness or prosperity of body and soul. How far the ideas associated with the Hebrew word carried over into the Greek word **eirēnē** is very hard to say, especially when it is being used in a letter in the place where a conventional salutation would be used. There is a further minor semantic complication in that, whereas 'grace' clearly comes from the Godhead, 'peace' is man's experience, so that the original preposition meaning 'from' strictly has the meaning of 'cause to come to pass'."

EPISTLE CONSTITUENT 1:5--3:14 (Part) (Role: Body of the Epistle)

THEME: I left you behind in Crete for these purposes: You are to correct those believers who follow false teachings, and urge all the believers to behave in a manner consistent with the correct teachings; and you are to appoint elders whom no one can justly criticize.

DISPLAY

RELATIONAL STRUCTURE	CONTENT
$HEAD_1$	(1:5--3:11) I left you behind in Crete for these purposes: You are to correct those believers who follow false teachings, and urge all the believers to behave in a manner consistent with the correct teachings; and you are to appoint elders whom no one can justly criticize.
$head_2$	(3:12-14) Make every effort to come to me at Nicopolis. Help Zenas and Apollos on their journey. All the believers should likewise learn to devote themselves to doing good deeds for people who especially need help.

BOUNDARIES AND COHERENCE

The initial boundary of the body of the epistle is indicated by the ending of the formalized opening of the epistle, specifically the ending of the blessing. The end of the body is indicated by the beginning of the closing of the epistle. 3:15 is set off from the body in that it has the characteristics of the closings of Paul's epistles--final greetings and a benediction. 3:12-14 are not considered as part of the closing since 3:12 and 13 deal with specific instructions for Titus while 3:14 returns to the theme of the body.

Regarding the coherence of the body, it is distinct from the opening and closing in that it is basically hortatory and carries the main message of the epistle. As is discussed elsewhere, the constituent 1:5--3:11 has many factors demonstrating its coherence. Although the instructions found in the final constituent of the body, 3:12-14 (especially in 3:12-13), are of a different type, still they are instructions. (**Aspasai** `greet' in the closing could hardly be called an instruction.) And then there is the tie between 1:5--3:11 and 3:12-14 that has to do with doing good for others. The theme or motif of doing good works is found throughout 1:5--3:11 and will be discussed later.

STRUCTURE

On the higher levels, the structural organization of the body of the epistle to Titus is basically chiastic. Topics are introduced together in pairs and the second topic introduced is discussed first, after which the author returns to discuss the first topic introduced.

On the highest level, the topic of correcting the situation in the church in Crete (**ta leiponta epidiorthōsē** `the matters remaining/lacking you should correct') is introduced first (1:5b), followed by the introduction of the topic of appointing elders (**katastēsēs kata polin presbuterous** `you should appoint for each town elders' (1:5c; for the reasons for considering these as two separate topics see the discussion under Boundaries and Coherence for 1:5). Then in 1:6-9 the appointing of elders is elaborated upon. When that topic is finished, Paul proceeds to the first topic introduced, the correcting of the situation in the Cretan church, which he discusses in 1:10--3:11. (It seems best to consider **epidiorthōsē** `correct' as introducing not only the correcting of those who are following false doctrine, but also the positive side of teaching sound doctrine.)

On the next level down (1:10--3:11), the topics are introduced in 1:9b and c, but this time in the "tail" of a tail-head link since 1:9b-c is actually a part of the paragraph on the appointing of elders. This introduction is also obscured somewhat by the fact that the explicit agents in this introduction are the elders, while the explicit agent in the following discussion of these topics is Titus. However, there is such a strong semantic relationship between these introductions and the actual discussion of the topics that there can be little question that 1:9b and c are meant as introductions to these topics (as well as functioning within the paragraph on appointing elders itself). The topic of urging the believers to follow sound doctrine (**hina dunatos ē kai parakalein en tē didaskalia tē hugiainousē** 'that he may be able both to exhort in sound teaching/doctrine' 1:9b) is introduced first, while the topic of correcting/refuting those who oppose sound doctrine (**kai tous antilegontas elegchein** 'and refute those who oppose (sound doctrine)' 1:9c) is introduced second. Then in 1:10 Paul immediately starts to deal with those who oppose sound doctrine and continues with this topic through 1:16. (Notice that the most prominent verb of 1:10-16, **elegche** 'convince/correct', is the same verb which occurs in the introduction in 1:9c, **elegchein**.) In 2:1 he returns to the topic he introduced first, teaching and urging the believers to follow sound doctrine, and continues on with this topic, most obviously until 2:14, but, as will be discussed later, actually through 3:8c. (Note the similarity between **en tē didaskalia tē hugiainousē** 'in sound doctrine' in 1:9b and **ha prepei tē hugiainousē didaskalia** 'what is consistent with sound doctrine' in 2:1 which is the generic Head of 2:1-10. The main verb of the introduction, **parakalein** 'urge, exhort', is the same as one of the two most prominent verbs of the discussion of the topic, **parakalei** 2:6.)

So far, the chiastic arrangement discussed has had, as its constituent parts, the introduction of topics and the discussion of those topics. However, the discussion of the topics in 1:10--3:11 is also organized chiastically. As mentioned above, the first topic discussed in 1:10--3:11 is that of dealing with those who follow false teaching (1:10-16), and this is followed by a discussion of the topic of teaching the believers to live according to sound doctrine (2:1-14). 2:15 does not deal so much with the content of the teaching as with the manner of teaching-- **meta pasēs epitagēs** 'with all authority'; **mēdeis sou periphroneitō** 'let no one disregard you'. So, in this sense, 2:15 stands apart from the first two topics, though otherwise definitely connected with them, since they are the things that are to be taught "with full authority." In 3:1-8c Paul returns to the discussion of teaching the believers to live lives which are consistent with sound doctrine, while in 3:8d-11 he returns to the first topic of 1:10--3:11, how to deal with false teaching. Thus, there is a chiastic arrangement.

Following are descriptions of the higher level chiastic arrangements discussed above. Lower case letters indicate introductions to topics while higher case letters indicate the discussion of those topics.

a	1:5b	Correct the situation
b	1:5c	Appoint elders
B	1:6-9	Appoint elders
A	1:10--3:11	Correct the situation

- -

x 1:9b Urge believers to follow sound doctrine
y 1:9c Convince those who oppose sound doctrine that they are wrong
Y 1:10-16 Convince those who follow false teaching that they are wrong
X 2:1-10 Teach and urge believers to follow sound doctrine
Z 2:15 Teach, urge and convince with full authority
X′ 3:1-8c Urge believers to follow sound doctrine
Y′ 3:8d-11 Reject false teaching and false teachers

The preceding can be summed up by the following formulae:

a = x + y = Y + X + Z + X′ + Y′
b = B

There remains but one part of the body outside this chiastic arrangement--3:12-14. The earlier analysis of Titus (Kopesec 1980a) treats this as secondary matters, and certainly the first two topics of 3:12-14, the instructions for Titus to come to Nicopolis (3:12) and to help Zenas and Apollos on their way (3:13), being personal, time-specific matters which are separate from the main themes of the epistle, could well be called "secondary matters." However, 3:14 appears to return to the primary matters again since it states that the believers should learn to devote themselves to good works, an idea that is closely related to the theme of the epistle as a whole. At the same time, 3:14 has a formal connection with 3:13--**de kai** `and also′--and a semantic connection too, since 3:13 deals with meeting the needs of two specific persons, Zenas and Apollos, while 3:14 deals with meeting the needs of people in general. It may be that 3:13 with its specific need to be met gives Paul one further opportunity to stress the importance of good works in general. 3:12-14 does appear to be an entity, though a rather loosely-connected one. But it does not seem quite appropriate to label it as "secondary matters" when verse 14 definitely is closely connected with the major themes of the epistle. So 3:12-14 is labelled as "$head_2$ of the Body."

PROMINENCE AND THEME

Since 1:5--3:11 deals with matters that concern the work in Crete as a whole, while 3:12-14 deals more with personal, time-specific matters, 1:5--3:11 is considered as the major Head of the body, while 3:12-14 is labelled as "$head_2$." Therefore, only the theme of the major Head is included in the theme statement for the body of the epistle.

PART CONSTITUENT 1:5--3:11 (Sub-part) (Role: $Head_1$ of the Body)

THEME: I left you behind in Crete for these purposes: You are to correct those believers who follow false teachings, and urge all the believers to behave in a manner consistent with the correct teachings; and you are to appoint elders whom no one can justly criticize.

DISPLAY

RELATIONAL STRUCTURE	CONTENT
HEAD	(1:5) I left you behind in Crete for these purposes: You are to correct the matters that need to be corrected, and appoint elders in each town.
$spec._1$	(1:6-9) Appoint as elders men whom no one can justly criticize.
$spec._2$	(1:10--3:11) Correct the believers who follow false teachings; reject foolish and argumentative false teachings and divisive people who have turned away from the true teachings. Teach and urge the believers to behave in a manner consistent with the correct teachings, and to act kindly and do good for everyone since God acted kindly and graciously toward us(inc) and mercifully saved us(inc).

BOUNDARIES AND COHERENCE

The initial boundary has been discussed under Boundaries and Coherence for the body (1:5--3:14).

The final boundary of this constituent is determined to be between 3:11 and 3:12 for the following reasons:

1. The main themes of correcting those following false teaching and urging the believers to follow sound doctrine end at 3:11 (except for the brief return to the theme or motif of "good works" in 3:14).
2. In 3:12, for the first time in the epistle, people other than Paul and Titus are mentioned by name.
3. The actions asked of Titus in 3:12-13 are specific, one-time actions which, when once accomplished, no longer need to be dealt with; the prescribed actions in 1:5--3:11 are actions that are to be carried out repeatedly over a period of time.

This constituent coheres in that it deals with all the instructions and teaching that Paul prescribes to Titus which deal with the church in Crete in general, rather than with personal, time-specific matters. It includes the various specifics of the generic Head in 1:5, "I left you behind in Crete for these purposes: You are to correct the matters that need to be corrected and appoint elders in every town as I have directed you." See more on this under Boundaries and Coherence and Prominence and Theme for 1:5.

PROMINENCE AND THEME

There are two contrasting factors that must be taken into consideration in determining the theme statement for 1:5--3:11:

1. The prominence of 1:5 as generic Head of this sub-part of the epistle argues for the theme of 1:5 as the principal theme of this constituent. Since Paul begins this the main part of his message to Titus with a generic representation of all he is going to say in this constituent, he has, in effect, given us the main theme of this most important part of the letter right in the first verse of this constituent. Do we really need to add to what he has himself stated as the theme of this constituent?
2. One might argue, however, that this theme statement (1:5) excludes explicit reference to the very important part of the theme of this sub-part that deals with teaching sound doctrine, and that, although Paul no doubt implicitly includes this as part of **ta leiponta epidiorthōsē** 'correct the matters that need to be corrected', it is so important that it should be included explicitly in the theme statement for 1:5--3:11. Paul actually writes more to Titus on teaching sound doctrine than on any other topic, and the units dealing with sound doctrine contain various prominence-marking components of substantial weight.

It seems that there are three choices before us: (1) use only the generic 1:5 as the theme statement, (2) use the theme statements of the specifics of 1:5 and leave out the theme statement of the generic, or (3) use a combination of both. Based on the considerations stated in paragraph 2 above, choice number 3 seems best and the theme statement for 1:5--3:11 is based upon it. As an alternate solution, only the generic Head for 1:5--3:11 (as it appears in 1:5) could be used for the theme statement.

Note that in the theme statement presented for 1:5--3:11, the order Paul uses in 1:5 as to correcting the matters that need to be corrected and appointing elders is maintained. The amount of space given to correcting the things that need to be corrected and many other prominence-marking signals indicate that what Paul mentions first in 1:5 is really the most important part of his message, though, of course, the appointing of elders is very important for maintaining these things on the long-term basis.

The basic theme for 2:1-14, which covers much of the same area as 3:1-8c, is used to represent all of 2:1--3:8c. The chiastic structure of 1:10--3:11 supports this. Instead of following word for word Paul's generic statement in 1:5 regarding correcting the matters that need to be corrected, the reference has been made more specific, "correct those who follow false teachings." This is basically the theme statement for 1:10-16 with close parallels to the theme of 3:8d-11.

Further support for the theme statement for 1:5--3:11 as presented above is the introduction to 1:10--3:11 which Paul gives in 1:9b-c, "in order that he may encourage the believers in sound doctrine and refute/correct those who are opposed to sound doctrine."

SUB-PART CONSTITUENT 1:5 (Propositional Cluster) (Role: Head of 1:5--3:11)

THEME: I left you behind in Crete for these purposes: You are to correct the matters that need to be corrected, and appoint elders in each town in the manner I directed you.

DISPLAY

RELATIONAL STRUCTURE	CONTENT
means	(1:5a) I left you behind in (the land of) Crete for these purposes:
$HEAD_1$ (hortatory purpose)	(1:5b) You (are to) correct the matters that need to be corrected,
$HEAD_2$ (hortatory purpose)	(1:5c) and you (are to) appoint elders (in the church) in each town in the manner I directed you.

BOUNDARIES AND COHERENCE

See the preceding for the initial boundary.

1:5-6 present problems in analysis because of apparent skewing between the form and the semantic structure, and so it is difficult to determine the final boundary of this constituent. Grammatically, it appears that the **hina** construction does not stop at the end of verse five but continues on until the end of verse six, since verse six begins with a conditional clause **ei tis estin anegklētos...** 'if anyone is blameless...' and there is no nonsubordinate finite verb or main clause in verse six, the conditional clause depending on the subjunctive verb in the **hina** clause, **katastēsēs** 'you might appoint'. In verse seven, however, there is a nonsubordinate finite verb, **dei** 'it is necessary', and thus the rest of the paragraph on the appointing of elders is no longer a part of the **hina** clause which begins in verse five.

Also basic to the analysis of the final boundary and role of this constituent is the correct understanding of the meaning of **ta leiponta epidiorthōsē** (1:5b). **Epidiorthoō**, which occurs only here in the New Testament, and its cognates **diorthoō, diorthōma, diorthōsis** all have the senses of "setting right, correcting, reforming."

In its primary sense it does not basically mean "to complete." Arndt and Gingrich give as the meaning of **epidiorthoō** here "'set right' or 'correct in addition' (to what has already been corrected) **ta leiponta** 'what remains' Tit. 1:5.... Simply 'correct' is also possible." **Ta leiponta** could also mean "what is lacking, the defects" (Arndt and Gingrich). Therefore, a possible rendering for 1:5b would be "in order that you might correct the matters that need to be corrected" or, "in order that you might set right those matters that need to be set right."

Since this is a generic statement of Paul's reason for leaving Titus in Crete (**Toutou charin apelipon se en Krētē**) and the idea of "correcting" or "setting right" is close to the idea represented by **elegche**, the main verb of the Head proposition of 1:10-16, i.e., "convince that they are wrong" or "correct, reprove," it is evident that 1:10-16 could be a specific of 1:5b "correct the matters that need to be corrected."

Following are possible analyses for 1:5ff.:

1. 1:5b-c has a purpose role only.
   a. 1:5 deals wholly with the appointing of elders. **Ta leiponta epidiorthōsē** 'you might set right the matters that need to be set right' is a generic statement for the specific **katastēsēs kata polin presbuterous** 'you might appoint elders in each town', **kai** being taken in the less common yet possible sense of "namely, that is" (Arndt and Gingrich I.3, though this reference is not given in Arndt Gingrich). Hendriksen translates, "For this reason I left you behind in Crete, that you might straighten out the things that remain to be done, namely, that you might appoint elders in each city...."
   b. Same as a. above except that the appointing of elders is only one of the things to be set right, the others would be dealing with the false teaching and teaching behavior conforming to sound doctrine. Thus **ta leiponta epidiorthōsē** 'you might set right/correct the matters that need to be set right/corrected' is a generic for the main specific topics discussed in the epistle. 1:5a-b acts as an introduction to the main specific themes of the epistle (1:5c--3:11), but not as a generic Head since most of the specific themes are hortatory.
   c. **Ta leiponta epidiorthōsē** 'you might set right/correct the matters that need to be set right/corrected' refers to something other than **katastēsēs...presbuterous** 'you might appoint elders'. This analysis takes **kai** in its most common sense of "and." And the fact that a similar chiastic structure operates on the next level down makes it a plausible solution (see Structure of the body of the epistle, 1:5--3:14). **Ta leiponta epidiorthōsē** refers to the other main topics discussed in the epistle but not to the appointing of elders. These topics are correcting those people who follow false teaching and teaching the believers to behave in accordance with sound doctrine. 1:5a-b acts as an introduction to the main specific themes of the epistle except for the appointing of elders.
   d. 1:5 as a whole acts as an introduction for 1:6--3:11. It is not to be divided on this level.
2. 1:5b-c has both a purpose and hortatory role, but the hortatory role is more significant.
   a. 1:5b, **ta leiponta epidiorthōsē** 'you might set right/correct the matters that need to be set right/corrected', acts as a generic exhortation for 1:5c **katastēsēs...presbuterous** 'you might appoint elders'. Since 1:5c is the only specific under the generic, 1:5c would be considered more naturally prominent than 1:5b.

b. 1:5b acts as a generic exhortation for 1:5c and the other specific Head exhortations of 1:5--3:11.
c. 1:5b acts as a generic exhortation for the specific Head exhortations in 1:10--3:11 but not for 1:5c.
d. 1:5 as a whole acts as generic Head for 1:5--3:11. It is not divided on this level. The units of 1:6--3:11 are specifics of 1:5 as a whole rather than being specifics of 1:5b or c.

As for the role 1:5b-c is playing, purpose or hortatory, Paul's purpose in reiterating the instructions he had previously given are certainly hortatory and not just an explanation of what he had ordered (**dietaxamēn**) Titus before he left Crete. His statements here about appointing elders are as hortatory as they were when Paul first gave them earlier. Therefore, it seems better to understand 1:5b-c as "hortatory purpose" rather than purpose alone.

Regarding the generic-specific relationships, it would seem that analyses 1a and 2a do not handle the total context as well as the other solutions. **Ta leiponta epidiorthōsē** 'you might set right/correct the matters that need to be set right/corrected' is at least as close in meaning to **elegche** 'convince, correct, reprove' as it is to a presumed deficient organizational situation calling for the appointing of elders. And it seems as if Paul's reason for leaving Titus in Crete would not be just to appoint elders, when his main focus in the epistle is on dealing with false teaching and teaching the believers to behave in a way consistent with sound doctrine.

It is more difficult to determine, however, whether 1:5c is to be included as one of the specifics of 1:5b (analysis 2b), is something completely separate from 1:5b (analysis 2c), or is to be included with 1:5a-b to function together as a generic head for 1:6--3:11 (analysis 2d).

In favor of analyzing 1:5c as the first specific of 1:5b are the following:

1. If it is assumed that the appointing of elders is one thing needed to remedy the situation in Crete, which would be suggested by 1:9b-c (**hina dunatos ē kai parakalein en tē didaskalia tē hugiainousē kai tous antilegontas elegchein** 'in order that he (the elder) may be able to encourage others in/by sound doctrine/teaching and refute/convince those who oppose (sound doctrine)', then **katastēsēs...presbuterous** 'you might appoint elders' would come within the range of meaning of **ta leiponta epidiorthōsē** 'you might set right/correct the matters that need to be set right/corrected'.
2. With this analysis there is no need to set up a second Head for 1:6-9 as in the third analysis below, where the Head for 1:6-9 is actually an implicit restatement of part of 1:5c.

In favor of analyzing 1:5b as a generic Head for 1:10--3:11 with 1:5c as something wholly separate from 1:5b, i.e., not a specific of it, are the following:

1. **Ta leiponta epidiorthōsē** 'you might set right/correct the matters that need to be set right/corrected' equates very well with the idea of correcting those who follow false doctrine. Note especially the first specific Head that would come under this generic, 1:13b-c, "convince them (the Cretan believers who follow false teaching) that they are wrong in order that they (firmly) believe the correct teachings." The setting right/remedying (**epidiorthōsē**) of the situation consists both in the repudiating of their present beliefs (as **elegche** 'correct,

convince that they are wrong' would indicate) and the teaching of correct behavior and doctrine which are dealt with in 2:1--3:8.
2. This analysis retains the meaning of kai as "and," its primary and by far its most commonly used meaning.
3. Though this analysis represents a structure which appears unbalanced as far as our present-day thought patterns are concerned, it is parallel to other chiastic structures in the epistle, especially to that on the next level down where 1:9b and c form an introduction to 1:10--3:11 (see Structure of the body of the epistle, 1:5--3:14). Thus, it has the possibility of being a completely appropriate analysis as far as structure is concerned.

In favor of analyzing 1:5 as a whole as a generic Head for all of 1:5--3:11 are the following:

1. As with the analysis immediately above, epidiorthōsē and kai are taken in their primary meanings.
2. 1:5a, which certainly relates to 1:5c, is not separated from 1:5c in the way it is in the analysis immediately above.
3. The diagramming difficulties of the analysis immediately above, in which the specifics for 1:5b are separated from the generic Head by the specific of 1:5c, are overcome. Of course, this relates basically to diagramming rather than difficulties in structure per se. Since there is an underlying chiastic structure here in 1:5--3:11 and on other levels also, such a structure cannot be said to be inappropriate.

It can be seen from the above that each of these three analyses has good support. If we follow the rule that a word should be taken in its primary sense unless the context clearly shows that a secondary sense is intended, then the primary meaning of kai as "and" would suggest that either the second or third solution is perhaps the correct one. It is interesting to note that, although many commentators take kai as meaning "namely" and mention the appointing of elders either as if it were the only thing intended by Paul in setting things right, or as one of the things to be set right (though very few refer to the other topics of the epistle as coming under setting things right), standard translations tend to translate kai as "and" (AV, RSV, NIV, TEV, though NEB has "and in particular"). It would seem that commentators have not taken possible chiastic structure into account in their analysis here.

The third solution has been chosen for the display, since it keeps the good points of solutions 1 and 2, while it does not have some of their questionable points. It is true, however, that this solution must set up an implicit proposition as Head of 1:6-9.

Grammatically, 1:5-9 is not in hortatory form. It does not contain one imperative. But semantically, it seems to function as a hortatory unit or units. As a reiteration of the earlier instructions/commands, it is also hortatory. And since 1:5b is some type of generic representation of the main part of the body of the epistle, which is unquestionably hortatory, it too must be hortatory to a certain extent. Obviously, Paul is not repeating these instructions to Titus merely as a recounting of the work in Crete. They are meant as a set of authoritative instructions to which Titus can refer and, probably more significantly, to which Titus can refer the Cretan believers, in order to properly establish the church in Crete.

There is no doubt that the conditional construction beginning at verse 6, ei tis estin anegklētos... `if anyone is blameless...', added to the means-purpose construction, makes for a somewhat over-extended construction. Some modern translations start a new sentence at 1:6: "An elder must be blameless...." (NIV). "They are to be men of irreproachable character...."(20th Century). Others handle the problem by making hōs egō soi dietaxamēn `as I instructed you' a hortatory statement: "In doing so, observe the tests I prescribed...." (NEB). "Remember my instructions: an elder must be without fault...." (TEV).

Two things will be noticed in these translations: (1) A fresh start either at the beginning of verse 6 or with the beginning of the last clause of verse 5 and (2) hortatory-type statements: "must be," "are to be," "Remember," "Observe." The rendering in the display text for 1:6a "(Appoint as elders men like this:)" seems to be based upon the full semantic structure.

It could be maintained that this implicit proposition does not need to be of a hortatory type since 1:6-9 is basically identificational in function. However, since the generic katastēsēs `appoint' has been interpreted as hortatory, it seems best to use a hortatory proposition here also.

PROMINENCE AND THEME

Although it is much more common for a means proposition to be more prominent than the purpose proposition, here the purpose propositions are considered to be more prominent than the means for the following reasons:

1. Toutou charin `for this purpose' in 1:5a marks the purpose as prominent.
2. "I left you behind in Crete" by itself has no significant tie-in with the theme of the epistle, whereas "correct the matters that need to be corrected" and "appoint elders" does.

However, the means is retained in the theme statement to give proper orientation for the purpose.

NOTES ON 1:5

1:5a-b. **I left you behind in (the land of) Crete for these purposes: (5b) You (are to) correct the matters that need to be corrected, (Toutou charin apelipon se en Krētē, hina ta leiponta epidiorthōsē** `for-purpose this I-left you(sg), in Crete, in-order-that the (things) lacking you(sg)-might-set-right')

REL/TRNS This clause is introduced by hina `in order that' which signals that 1:5b is the purpose of 1:5a. It has been presented in the display as a command for the reasons discussed under Boundaries and Coherence for 1:5 above. As far as translation into other languages is concerned, it would not necessarily need to be translated in hortatory form as long as its reference to prescribed instructions is communicated otherwise.

CONT/TRNS As discussed earlier under Boundaries and Coherence for 1:5, the verb epidiorthōsē has the idea of "setting things right, correcting," and the force of the epi- may signify "in addition" though not necessarily. The substantive ta leiponta means "the things lacking" or "the defects." Any translation for this generic Head should be consistent with the specifics of combating false teaching and exhorting the believers to correct doctrine and practice (that is, if the generic-specific analysis proposed in this SSA is followed).

1:5c. **and you (are to) appoint elders (in the church) in each town in the manner I directed you. (kai katastēsēs kata polin presbuterous, hōs egō soi dietaxamēn,** 'and appoint according-to city elders, as I you(sg) commanded')

CONT The preposition **kata** has a distributive function here. Elders were to be appointed "town by town." "In the church" makes explicit the clearly implied idea that the appointments were in the church and not in the civil government.

CONT **Presbuterous**, literally "elders," is used here as a designation of officials to be appointed in the local Christian congregation. Note that the basic meaning here is not that of age but of position.

CONT Arndt and Gingrich list **hōs** here "as a comparative particle, indicating the manner in which something proceeds 'as, like'...corresponding to **houtōs** = 'so, in such a way.'" It is also possible that it has a narrower sense, "appoint elders which is what I commanded you (when I departed from you)." However, since it seems more probable that Paul would have told Titus not only to appoint elders but how to do so, the first choice seems the better and it is used in the display.

SUB-PART CONSTITUENT 1:6-9 (Paragraph) (Role: $specific_1$ of 1:5)

THEME: Appoint as elders men whom no one can justly criticize.

DISPLAY

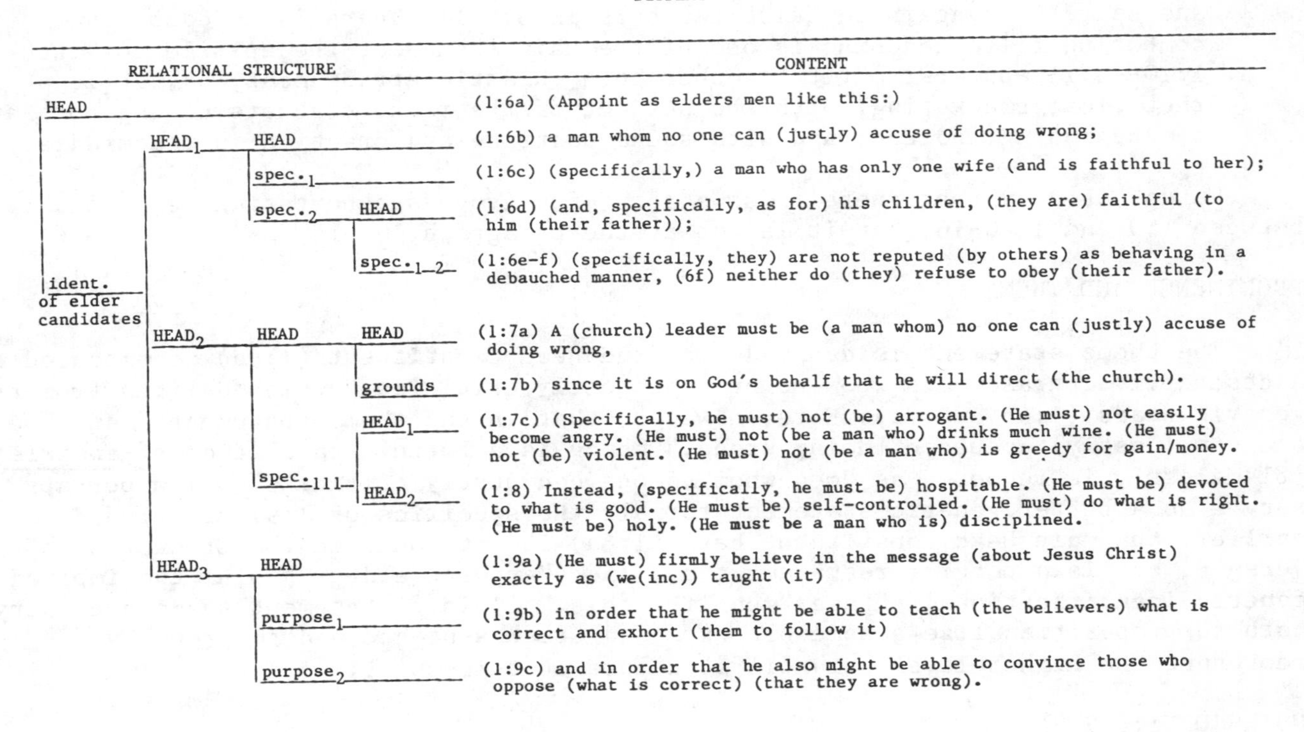

BOUNDARIES AND COHERENCE

The initial boundary has been discussed under 1:5. The end of 1:9 has been chosen as the final boundary of this unit for the following reasons:

1. All of 1:6-9 deals with the appointing of elders, but elders or their appointment are not mentioned again in the whole epistle.
2. The only argument for this unit being larger than 1:9 is that 1:10-16 (or some part of it) is grounds for the appointing of elders. Although there is a gar 'because, since, for' at the beginning of 1:10, which often indicates a grounds relation, and there is no doubt that Paul had in mind that good elders were needed to combat the false teaching (tous antilegontas elegchein 'refute those who oppose (correct doctrine)' 1:9c), the unit on false teachers (1:10-16) functions better as a complete unit in itself because:
   a. It has its own exhortation, 1:13 elegche autous apotomōs 'correct them rigorously' (imperative mood in the Greek).
   b. 1:10-16 is coherent as a whole. Even though Paul starts talking about the false teachers (1:10-11, possibly 12) and then mentions those being deceived by them (1:13b-14b, possibly 12), he quickly returns to the false teachers (1:14c-16). So there is rhetorical bracketing ("sandwich" structure) which indicates the unity of 1:10-16. And in 1:13 the imperative is second person singular, not second or third person plural which we would expect if Paul were still talking about the elders. The following hardly seems appropriate: "You(sg) must appoint elders because you(sg) must rebuke those being deceived by the false teachers."
   c. 1:10-16 is more developed than 1:9, a point that does not carry a lot of weight in itself, but that shows how concerned Paul was with false teaching; and he returns again to false teachers in 3:9-11. There is no doubt that combating false teaching is one of the main themes of the epistle to Titus.
   d. 1:10--3:11 appears to fit together in a chiastic arrangement, or, at least in rhetorical bracketing, with the subject of the false teachers coming both at the beginning and end, and with sound doctrine and practice in the middle.

We do not deny that there is some sort of a grounds-exhortation relationship between 1:9 and 1:10-16, but it is not at the paragraph level.

PROMINENCE AND THEME

The theme statement is derived from the Head constituent (1:6a) accompanied by a descriptive phrase "men whom no one can justly criticize," which derives from the generic Heads (1:6b and 7a). Note, however, that in the theme statement "men whom no one can (justly) accuse of doing wrong," which is a better translation of anegklētos 'blameless', is rendered as "men whom no one can justly criticize" which perhaps serves as a better generic statement for all the specifics of 1:9. As alluded to earlier, the main Head constituent here (1:6a) is not found in the Greek text of verse 6, but is a partial restatement of 1:5c ("appoint elders") plus the implied generic identificational phrase "men like this." This restatement seems necessary both to propositionalize a somewhat extended Greek sentence and to properly represent the higher-level semantic structure at this point.

NOTES ON 1:6-9

1:6a-b. **(Appoint as elders men like this:) (6b) a man whom no one can (justly) accuse of doing wrong;** (ei tis estin anegklētos, 'if anyone is blameless')

REL 1:6-9 identifies those who are potential candidates for appointment as elders. 1:6 is in a generic relation with the other propositions in 1:6 since it occurs first in the list and is more generic than the others. It is also shown to be generic by the fact that 1:7a basically repeats the same information that a church leader should be one whom no one can justly accuse of doing wrong, thus returning to the most significant or generic information in the preceding unit. 1:7a acts as a generic Head for the rest of the qualifications in 1:7c-8.

CONT Basically **anegklētos** designates a person who is without accusation or reproach. Here it would mean, as Nicholson says, "one who is without reproach in his personal life, his family life, and his public life." A translation such as "without fault" (TEV) is from the point of view of the man's character itself rather than that of the (justified) reaction of others to that character. There are many indications in the epistle that Paul is very concerned about the view outsiders had of the church and thus the gospel itself (see esp. 2:5,8,10), so it would seem better to follow the more literal meaning "without accusation, irreproachable." In the display text, "justly" is added to show that what is being talked about here is a man's character that is not justly liable to accusation. Beside here and 1:7a, **anegklētos** 'blameless' is found elsewhere in the New Testament in 1 Cor. 1:8; Col. 1:22; 1 Tim. 3:10.

1:6c. **(specifically,) a man who has only one wife (and is faithful to her); (mias gunaikos anēr**, 'of-one wife husband')

CONT **Mias gunaikos anēr**, literally "man/husband of one woman/wife," has been interpreted by commentators--

1. with the focus on faithfulness to one's wife;
2. with the focus on not having more than one wife at a time;
3. with the focus on not remarrying whether
   a. the first wife has been divorced
   b. or, the first wife has died;
4. as excluding a man who has never married.

Since it appears that this proposition is in some type of specific relation to "blameless" of 1:6a, **mias gunaikos anēr** is to be interpreted in reference to what is or is not sin rather than in reference to a criterion of special dedication, etc. This agrees with the context of the epistle as a whole where much is made of the importance of the believers' conducting themselves in such a way that unbelievers have no grounds to defame the gospel (see esp. 2:5,8,10). Thus, it is difficult to see how **mias gunaikos anēr** would exclude any man who had remarried after his wife had died or a man who had never married. Certainly the New Testament teaches that death breaks the marriage relationship and leaves the survivor of the marriage free to remarry. Paul's own life and his discourse in 1 Corinthians chapter 7 show that an unmarried man would be acceptable as an elder.

Since this is the only statement Paul makes about the prospective elder's relationship with his wife, we would expect it to be a generic statement rather than a specific one, i.e., Paul is probably more concerned here with the blameless marital relationship of the prospective elder in general rather than some specific facet of that relationship. Therefore, we would expect that **mias gunaikos anēr**, first of all, indicates to the reader that the prospective elder is to be one that has been completely faithful in his marital relationship. It must be remembered that the word **anēr** means both "man" and "husband," and that **gunē** means both "woman" and "wife," and so **mias gunaikos anēr** has the possibility of meaning to the original reader something more generic than the English "husband of one wife." Furthermore, in 1 Tim. 5:9 Paul states that a widow who is to be put on the list of widows must be **henos andros gunē** 'woman/wife of one man/husband', and certainly having more than one husband at a time is not being referred to there. Based on all these considerations, it appears that **mias gunaikos anēr** focuses more on the faithfulness of the marital relationship in general rather than only polygamy.

The next question to ask is whether polygamy is intended to be excluded here, or whether **mias gunaikos anēr** is so idiomatic that it would not necessarily exclude polygamy to the Greek, as it very obviously does in a literal English translation. If the latter is, in fact, true, then it would not be necessary to propositionalize as "a man who has only one wife and is faithful to her," but only as "a man who is faithful to his wife," i.e., a generic statement about his sexual morality having no explicit reference to polygamy. Since it is difficult to answer the above question, for the display text the following rendering is used: "(Specifically,) a man who has only one wife (and is faithful to her)." However, there is a possibility that "a man who is faithful to his wife" is a more idiomatic rendering of **mias gunaikos anēr**.

1:6d. **(and, specifically, as for) his children, (they are) faithful (to him (their father)); (tekna echōn pista,** 'having believing/faithful children')

CONT Pistos has the senses of "faithful, trustworthy" or "believing." Although the majority of commentators interpret **pista** as meaning "believing (in Christ)," Lock has a good point when he says, "perhaps 'believing,' 'Christian'....More probably, as suiting the following qualifications better, 'trustworthy,' 'loyal.'"

The following would tend to support the interpretation that pista here means "faithful (to their father/parents)":

1. There appears to be a pattern in Titus of a positive generic followed by two or more negative specifics (1:7; 1:13c-14; 2:3a-b). There is a clear positive generic-negative specific relationship between pista in its sense of "faithful" (i.e., "faithful to their parents") and **mē...anupotakta** 'not disobedient, not unruly' where the object of their obedience is their parents. **Mē en katēgoria asōtias** 'not having the reputation of being debauched' is a further extension of this. They are faithful to their parents in that they are obedient to them and do not live a wild, debauched life.
2. In considering the explicit role relationships wholly contained within the phrase **tekna echōn pista** 'having faithful/believing children', the explicit participants are **tekna** 'children' and the elder-candidate father (the nominative masculine singular ending on the participle **echōn** refers back to **anēr** 'man, husband'). Therefore, the relationship signalled by the word **pista** 'faithful/believing' is most likely to be one between those explicit participants, i.e., the children and their father, unless there is some other overriding factor that would signal a different relationship.
3. In the parallel passage in 1 Timothy chapter 3, the qualifications for the overseer (**episkopos**) do not mention that the children should be believers (**pistos** or any other term that could be interpreted as meaning believers does not occur), but they do deal with the parent-child relationship, "He must manage his own family well and see that his children obey him with proper respect. (If anyone does not know how to manage his own family, how can he take care of God's church?)" (1 Tim. 3:4-5 NIV; cf. 1 Tim. 3:12.)

Since **pistos** occurs in the New Testament, and specifically in the Pastorals, with both the meaning of "faithful" and "believing" according to the context, and since there seems to be nothing in the context that would indicate that it means "believing" here instead of "faithful," seemingly the only support for the interpretation that it means "believing (in Christ)" here would have to be that the primary meaning of **pistos** at the time of the writing of Titus was "believing" or, at least, that the primary meaning of **pistos** when modifying nouns signifying people was "believing." This would be very hard to prove though it seems to be implied in the interpretation of a majority of commentators in reference to this verse.

A third interpretation would be that they were "trustworthy children" in a more general sense, that is, in their dealings with their parents or anyone else; but the three points in favor of a parent-child relationship outlined above would suggest that that relationship was more in focus.

Based on all these considerations, we have rendered **tekna echōn pista** as "(as for) his children, they are faithful (to him)." However, it is possible that the meaning "believing" was intended by Paul and the display text rendering for this would be "(as for) his children, they believe (in Jesus Christ)."

References in the Pastoral Epistles where **pistos** appears to have the meaning of "believing" or "believers" are: 1 Tim. 4:3,10,12; 5:16; 6:2a,b. References where it means "faithful" or "trustworthy" are: 1 Tim. 1:12,15; 3:1,11; 4:9; 2 Tim. 2:2,11; Titus 1:9; 3:8.

1:6e-f. **(specifically, they) are not reputed (by others) as behaving in a debauched manner, (6f) neither do (they) refuse to obey (their father).** (**mē en katēgoria asōtias ē anupotakta**. 'not in accusation of-debauchery or unruly')

CONT There are two other occurrences of **katēgoria** 'accusation' in the New Testament. **Katēgoria** in John 18:29 refers to a formal accusation, and in 1 Tim. 5:19 it refers to either a formal or non-formal accusation. The meaning here in Titus would seem quite general, ranging from formal accusation to reputation--anything that would put the children of the elder candidate, and thus the elder candidate himself, in a bad light. As with **anegklētos** 'blameless' above, Paul, in this paragraph (and also in 2:1-10, see esp. 2:5,8,10), is concerned with outsiders' view of the church, and therefore he mentions not only the sin or negative quality itself but also other people's views of the person involved. In this verse "not having the reputation of" seems to be a good translation for **mē en katēgoria**, and this has been propositionalized as "they are not reputed (by others)."

CONT The basic meaning of **asōtia** is "indulging the flesh in an excessive manner." In its other occurrences in the New Testament, Eph. 5:18 and 1 Pet. 4:4, the contexts are those of sensual pleasures. The same is true with the cognate adverb **asōtōs**, as found in Luke 15:13. Thus, the meaning focuses more on the abandonment of oneself to excessive sensual pleasures rather than a more generic abandonment of oneself to a life completely without principle of any kind. Some translators render **asōtias** here as "wild," but notice that that is a figurative use of the word and also "wild" is more generic than **asōtia**. "Debauched" is probably the best English equivalent as understood in the sense listed first under "debauchery" in *Funk and Wagnalls Standard College Dictionary*, "Gross indulgence of one's sensual appetites."

CONT The neuter plural form of the adjective **anupotakta** `insubordinate' shows that it refers back to **tekna** `children' and not to **katēgoria** `accusation' (fem. sg.). Thus, it is not strictly a part of the accusation but is a further qualification of the children, "not disobedient."

1:7a. **A (church) leader must be (a man whom) no one can (justly) accuse of doing wrong,** (**dei gar ton episkopon anegklēton einai** `for it-is-necessary (that) the overseer blameless be')

REL This verse begins with **gar** which often signals a reason or grounds relationship. However, it is not at all clear that **gar** represents that relationship here. There seem to be two possible interpretations:

1. **Gar** here represents a reason or grounds relationship, "Appoint as elders men who are blameless...since an elder/overseer must be blameless since he will be a steward of God."
2. **Gar** here indicates continuation or connection (Arndt and Gingrich 4): "Appoint as elders men who are blameless....An elder/overseer must be blameless since he will be a steward of God."

It is more probable that the second interpretation is correct. What seems to be happening is that Paul is restating in 1:7a the generic qualification for elders, i.e., that they be blameless, giving a reason/grounds why they should be blameless (1:7b), and then giving a long list of specific qualifications (1:7c-9) in addition to the ones that he has already given (1:6c-f). On the higher level, it does not make sense for a unit which is basically composed of specifics of "blameless" (1:7-9) to give grounds support to the statement "Appoint as elders men who are blameless." It is much more probable that **gar** introduces an amplification unit or second Head regarding qualifications for elders. In interpretation number 1 above, the first grounds constituent, "since an elder/overseer must be blameless" is too repetitious of the Head statement and, thus, does not really add grounds support to it. It may well be that the rather complex description of the **tekna** (`children') made it necessary, grammatically, to start another unit. Since there is no suggestion that 1:6b-f is more prominent than 1:7-8, or vice-versa, they are treated as separate Heads of equal status.

REL/TRNS Even though there is no imperative in the Greek text, it might be maintained that 1:7a "It is necessary (**dei**) that an overseer be blameless" is hortatory. In a sense this is so, but what seems to be more in focus is the identification of the right persons as candidates for elders. Note also that in many languages hortatory forms cannot be used with stative verbs or ideas; one cannot say, "He must be a man who is blameless." In these languages, then, other constructions will have to be used.

CONT There is a lexical change here from **presbuterous** `elders' (1:5) to **episkopon** `overseer' (1:7). Most commentaries identify both terms as referring to the same person, the first relating to his position and/or qualifications of experience and the second, to the work he is expected to perform. A few commentaries regard the overseer as an executive officer chosen from the group of elders. The analysis presented in the display follows the majority view, because in the other passage where elders and overseers are mentioned, Acts 20:17-28, those referred to as elders are said to have been made "overseers" (**episkopos**) of the "flock" by the Holy Spirit, signifying the work they are to perform. Also, the whole organization of the paragraph points to one position and not two.

Episkopos 'overseer' also occurs in Phil. 1:1; 1 Pet. 2:25; and 1 Tim. 3:2. SSA of Titus 1:7b-9

1:7b. **since it is on God's behalf that he will direct (the church).** (hōs theou oikonomon, 'as God's steward')

REL Hōs theou oikonomon, literally "as God's steward," is interpreted as being a grounds constituent, since grounds fits the context best. The alternate possibility, "An overseer must be blameless while he is directing (the church) on God's behalf" (Head-circumstance), would not be as pointed nor as forceful.

PROM In the genitive construction theou oikonomon 'steward of God', theou 'of God' occurs before the head noun, indicating marked prominence on "of God."

1:7c. **(Specifically, he must) not (be) arrogant. (He must) not easily become angry. (He must) not (be a man who) drinks much wine. (He must) not (be) violent. (He must) not (be a man who) is greedy for gain/money.** (mē authadē, mē orgilon, mē paroinon, mē plēktēn, mē aischrokerdē, 'not arrogant, not quick-tempered, not given-to-much-wine, not violent, not fond-of-shameful-gain')

REL Here again in the $Head_2$ unit, anegklētos 'blameless' seems to act as a generic characteristic of the candidate for elder while the succeeding characteristics are more specific qualities. The first five characteristics are negative ones that must not be found in the elder candidate.

CONT Authadēs means "arrogance" especially in the sense of being domineering, overbearing, and self-willed (it occurs elsewhere in the New Testament only in 2 Pet. 2:10).

CONT Paroinos may be translated as "drinks much wine, drunkard, addicted to wine" (see also 1 Tim. 3:3). Oinos 'wine' normally refers to fermented juice of the grape (Arndt and Gingrich). Some commentators take paroinos in an extended sense which is also found in Greek literature. Lock says, "Perhaps quite literally--'not given to much wine';...but this is not necessarily implied: perhaps only 'blustering,' 'abusive,' like a man who has been drinking." However, it seems best to take it in its literal sense because:

1. The literal sense would probably be its primary meaning (note that Arndt and Gingrich do not give its extended meaning).
2. In 1 Tim. 3:8 where Paul describes the characteristics that a deacon should have and in Titus 2:3 where he describes the characteristics older Christian women should have, he says that they should "not be addicted to much wine" (oinō pollō), a statement that must be taken in its literal sense. Therefore, we should not be surprised at all but, on the contrary, expect to see this characteristic listed in the qualifications for elders.

CONT Aischrokerdē 'fond of shameful gain' could be understood (1) in the sense of a man's habit or tendency to obtain riches through dishonest means, or (2) "in the setting of gain before one as an object in entering the ministry" (White). Arndt and Gingrich give as the meaning of aischros 'ugly, shameful, base'. In its use in the New Testament other than with kerdos 'gain' it seems to have the sense of "shameful, disgraceful" (1 Cor. 11:6; 14:35; Eph. 5:12). Since the occurrence of aischrokerdēs here in Titus 1:7 is in a list of qualifications, it would seem that a translation of the more generic sense of the word would more likely cover Paul's intended meaning. In other words, if it is translated as "not seeking dishonest gain," it might tend to exclude those who are not actually dishonest in the sense of embezzling, etc., but who only would serve for purposes of the money or advantage involved. Thus, a translation such as "not greedy for gain" might be more appropriate. This would propositionalize as "(He must) not (be a man who) is greedy for gain/money" (cf. aischrou kerdous in 1:11 which has the same general meaning; aischrokerdēs also occurs in 1 Tim. 3:8, the adverb aischrokerdōs in 1 Pet. 5:2).

1:8. **Instead, (specifically, he must be) hospitable. (He must be) devoted to what is good. (He must be) self-controlled. (He must) do what is right. (He must be) holy. (He must be a man who is) disciplined.** (alla philoxenon, philagathon, sōphrona, dikaion, hosion, egkratē, `but hospitable, a-lover-of-good, self-controlled, upright, holy, disciplined')

CONT Regarding philoxenos `hospitable', an elder must be the kind of man who is ready to welcome travelers (as in 3:13), but there seems to be no reason why this should be limited to travelers alone; other strangers or even friends, especially within the body of believers, who are in need, should be received into the elder's home for needed lodging and food. Since ho xenos can mean "the host," that is, one who offers hospitality, in some contexts and "the stranger" in others, it seems very probable that philoxenos is also no longer to be understood in the narrower literal sense "lover of strangers" only but as the more generic "hospitable." (Note, too, that xenia means "hospitality" and xenizō `receive as a guest'.) Philoxenos is found elsewhere in the New Testament only in 1 Pet. 4:9 and 1 Tim. 3:2.

CONT The question might be asked whether philagathos (found only here in the New Testament) means "loving good" in the sense "loving to do good to/for others" or "loving those things (not material things) that are good" (cf. Phil. 4:8), which would be more generic. Agathos may describe what is morally good (see, e.g., Rom. 2:7,10) or what is specifically beneficial to others (Gal. 6:10). It would seem that a translation as generic as possible is needed here.

CONT "(He must) be self-controlled," or "(he must be able to) control himself" (sōphrona) is the virtue opposite to the negative traits of passion described in the previous verse. Here the mind by God's grace is in control and not the passions. Sōphrōn is found also in 2:2,5, and its cognates in 2:6 (sōphronein `be self-controlled') and 2:12 (sōphronōs `in a self-controlled manner').

CONT Although some commentators see dikaios here as having special reference to one's relationship with one's fellow man, it seems better to keep it generic as in Arndt and Gingrich, "`upright, just, righteous,'...conforming to the laws of God and man, and living in accordance with them."

CONT Hosios has the idea of "devout, pious, pleasing to God, holy" (Arndt and Gingrich), "faithful in all one's duties to God" (Barnes). Its orientation is toward God. Most of its other references in the New Testament describe God the Father or Christ, except for 1 Tim. 2:8 and Acts 13:34.

CONT It is difficult to make a distinction in English translation between sōphrōn and egkratēs. Both might be translated "self-controlled" or "disciplined." Egkratēs is found only here in the New Testament but the cognate noun, egkrateia, is found in Gal. 5:23; Acts 24:25; 2 Pet. 1:6, and the cognate verb egkrateuomai in 1 Cor. 7:9; 9:25.

1:9a. **(He must) firmly believe in the message (about Jesus Christ) exactly as (we(inc)) taught (it)** (**antechomenon tou kata tēn didachēn pistou logou**, 'holding-to the according-to the teaching faithful word')

REL The construction in verse nine is participial having changed from the infinitival construction of 1:7-8. This change potentially, though not necessarily, signals a switch from the specific-generic relationship with **anegklēton** 'blameless' to a new relationship. When it is considered that the substance of verse nine focuses more on the orthodoxy of the prospective elder's doctrine and his ability to teach others correctly rather than the fact that he be blameless in the eyes of others (probably both within and outside the church), it may well be that verse nine deals with a final requirement for elder candidates that does not quite fit under the generic **anegklēton** 'blameless' of 1:7a. Therefore, 1:9 is treated as a third Head in the display rather than as another specific under Head 1:7a.

CONT **Antechomenon** 'hold to, be devoted to' seems to have as its basic meaning here a firm belief in and conviction of the truth of the apostolic message, a conviction that will not be swayed by any opposition. Antechō is found elsewhere in the New Testament in Matt. 6:24; Luke 16:13; and 1 Thess. 5:14.

CONT There is a question as to whether **pistou** 'faithful, trustworthy' refers to the apostolic message as inherently trustworthy or whether it refers to the faithfulness of what they believe in its being exactly the same as what was taught them by Paul (note ICC "paraphrased" text, "holding firmly a preaching that is loyal to our doctrine" and Ellicott's statement, "the faithful word is so on account of its accordance with apostolic teaching"). This interpreration is quite well expressed in The Twentieth Century New Testament, "who holds doctrine that can be relied on as being in accordance with the accepted Teaching." The word/message which the candidates for elder hold to is trustworthy as measured by the norm of the teaching. This interpretation fits the context well since Paul is trying to ensure soundness and purity in doctrine in the whole epistle. In translations such as NIV, "the trustworthy message as it has been taught," it is difficult to know what interpretation is being taken, but it sounds like the message in itself is trustworthy and "trustworthy" does not specifically refer to the fact that trustworthiness here consists of the message being the same as the teaching. The rendering in the display text follows the interpretation which sees trustworthiness of the message as based here upon its conformity with the teaching they had received from Paul and Titus, because this fits the context better and no arguments against this position that are based upon grammatical considerations are given in available commentaries.

CONT Most commentators refer **tēn didachēn** 'the teaching' to the teaching of Paul, that is, the apostolic message which he taught the Cretans. Since Titus was presumably involved in the teaching, this has been propositionalized as "exactly as we(inc) taught (it)." This could be considered a first person dual inclusive for languages which make the distinction between dual and plural. An alternate would be to consider that Paul was only referring to his own teaching in the light of his remarks in 1:1-3 about his being entrusted with the proclamation of the message of God. This would be propositionalized as "exactly as I taught (it)."

1:9b. **in order that he might be able to teach (the believers) what is correct and exhort (them to follow it)** (**hina dunatos ē kai parakalein en tē didaskalia tē hugiainousē** 'in-order-that able he-may-be both to-exhort in/by the teaching which is-sound')

REL A purpose relation is signalled by **hina** `in order that'. The conjunction **kai** is the first element of a **kai...kai** `both...and' set. It has been represented in the display text of 1:9c as "and...also."

CONT In the face of the false doctrine being taught by the false teachers (1:10-16) the believers must be taught correct doctrine and strongly exhorted to follow it. **Parakalein** `exhort' describes the way the teaching is to be put across while **en tē didaskalia tē hugiainousē** `by/in sound teaching' describes the subject matter and at least alludes to the fact that it is taught. In the propositionalized form each of these factors needs to be represented. Thus the rendering in the display text, "in order that he might be able to teach (the believers) what is correct and exhort (them to follow it)." Some commentators prefer to translate "encourage by means of sound teaching" but it is difficult to see any other object of the encouragement or exhortation than the following of sound doctrine. Anything else would not fit the context as well as "encouragement/exhortation to follow sound doctrine."

CONT "The believers" is supplied to show who is to be taught and exhorted. A more generic word such as "people" could also be used.

CONT **Hugiainousē** literally "sound, healthy" is not a live metaphor since in contemporary usage it also had the meaning of "reasonable, true, correct." Thus, it had similar senses to the following dictionary entries given for the English adjective "sound": "Founded in truth; valid. Correct in views or processes of thought" (Funk and Wagnalls). This Greek word has been rendered as "correct" in the display text. **Hugiainō** in its figurative sense is also found in 1:13; 2:1,2; 1 Tim. 1:10; 6:3; 2 Tim. 1:13; 4:3.

1:9c. **and in order that he also might be able to convince those who oppose (what is correct) (that they are wrong).** (**kai tous antilegontas elegchein.** `and those contradicting to-convince')

PROM There is marked prominence on **tous antilegontas** `those contradicting' indicated by its occurrence before the infinitive **elegchein** `to convince'.

CONT By being firmly devoted to and convinced of sound doctrine, the elders will better be able to convince those who contradict or oppose sound doctrine that they are wrong. See further discussion of **elegchō** in 1:13b.

CONT An alternate rendering for "what is correct" in both 1:9b and 1:9c These alternates are not based on different interpretations but on different ways of propositionalizing the Greek word **didaskalia** `teaching, doctrine'.

SUB-PART CONSTITUENT 1:10--3:11 (Division) (Role: specific$_2$ of 1:5)

THEME: Correct the believers who follow false teachings; reject foolish and argumentative false teachings and divisive people who have turned away from the true teachings. Teach and urge the believers to behave in a manner consistent with the correct teachings, and to act kindly and do good for everyone since God acted kindly and graciously toward us(inc) and mercifully saved us(inc).

DISPLAY

RELATIONAL STRUCTURE	CONTENT
HEAD A	(1:10-16) Since there are many deceivers teaching what is false, who do not even know God themselves and are unable to do any good thing, rigorously convince those believers who follow false teachings that they are wrong in order that they will firmly believe in the correct teachings.
HEAD B	(2:1-14) Teach and urge the believers to behave in a manner which is consistent with the correct teachings, in order that people will perceive that the teachings about God our(inc) Savior are very good, and since God very graciously sent Jesus Christ to earth in order that God might save all people and since God graciously trains us(inc) to behave in a godly manner.
manner	(2:15) With full authority teach these things, urge the believers to do them, and correct those believers who do not follow them.
HEAD B′	(3:1-8c) Remind the believers to act appropriately toward authorities, to act kindly toward everyone, and to do what is good for all people, since God acted kindly toward us(inc) and mercifully saved us(inc), even though formerly we(inc) were behaving sinfully.
HEAD A′	(3:8d-11) Have nothing to do with foolish disputes about genealogies and about the Jewish law; and do not allow divisive people who have turned away from the true teachings to influence the believers.

BOUNDARIES AND COHERENCE

As has been discussed earlier under Structure for the body of the epistle in unit 1:5--3:14, 1:10--3:11 is organized chiastically. Following is additional evidence for this chiastic organization:

1. The topics/themes of 1:10-16 and 2:1-14 are shown to be closely related by the following:
   a. In the manner constituent 2:15, the repetition of lalei `speak, teach′, parakalei `urge′ and elegche `correct′, which are the only three imperative verbs of 1:10--2:14, indicates the close referential coherence of at least 1:10--2:14. Note that parakalein `urge′ and elegchein `correct′ are found in the introduction to 1:10--2:14 in 1:9b-c, as well as in the main propositions of 1:10--2:14 (parakalei `urge′ and lalei `speak, teach′ substitute for one another as can be seen from the fact that parakalei acts as a substitute for lalei in 2:6). Thus, both the introduction and summarizing manner constituent contain the main imperative verbs of 1:10--2:14, showing the coherence of this unit.
   b. De at the beginning of 2:1 indicates some type of relationship between 1:10-16 and 2:1ff. De here seems to have two functions. It indicates a contrast on the lower levels between the teaching and character of the false teachers and the correct teaching that Titus must give to the believers which issues in godly behavior. It thus also indicates a change in topic from that which relates to false teaching to that which relates to sound teaching, i.e., contrastive topics. However, the paragraph level themes are not in contrast, since they deal with how Titus is to attack the general problem of doing away with false teaching and encouraging the believers to follow sound teaching. They are two steps that he must take and so are not contrastive.
2. The type of chiastic organization in 1:10--3:11 is one in which two contrastive topics are discussed, each in a definite unit of its own, and then there is a noticeable break before the second topic is amplified. Finally, the first topic is taken up again and amplified. So, instead of the more common organization of the amplification of topics A A′ B B′, the order is A B B′ A′. While we are dealing here with the amplification of topics, the paragraph/section-level themes tend to be equally prominent so they are all treated as separate, though closely related, Heads. The topics/themes of 1:10--2:14 are shown to be amplified chiastically in 3:1-11 by the following:

a. 3:1-8c as an amplification or further treatment of the same general topic as in 2:1-14.
   1) Both of these sections consist of a hortatory constituent presenting various specific instructions as to how believers should live godly lives, each followed by a grounds constituent giving motivation for such behavior.
   2) These two grounds constituents are also related semantically by three occurrences of what might be called an "appearance" motif or "epiphany" formula which forms an important part of these grounds constituents. Two of them occur in the first grounds constituent at 2:11 and 2:13, and the third in the second grounds constituent at 3:4. These occurrences of the "epiphany" formula present various attributes of God our Savior (grace and glory in 2:11 and 2:13 respectively, and kindness and love in 3:4) as important grounds for holy living. (See notes on these constituents, especially the notes on 2:11.) These occurrences of the "epiphany" formula tie the two grounds constituents together along with the hortatory paragraphs they support.
   3) Grace and salvation are very important concepts in both of the two grounds constituents.

b. 3:8d-11 as an amplification or further treatment of the same general topic as in 1:10-16.
   1) In 1:10-16, the believers are to be instructed not to hold to Jewish myths (**Ioudaikois muthois**) and commandments of men who reject the truth (**entolais anthrōpōn apostrephomenōn tēn alētheian** 1:14). In 3:9, Titus is told to have nothing to do with disputes about genealogies (**zētēseis kai genealogias**) and arguments and quarrels about the (Jewish) law (**ereis kai machas nomikas**). In 1 Tim. 1:4 where Paul is also talking about people who teach false doctrine, he mentions that these people have been devoting themselves to "myths and endless genealogies" (**muthois kai genealogiais aperantois**). This passage in 1 Timothy which relates myths with genealogies tends to show that Paul is talking about the same general subject when he mentions myths in 1:10-16 and the genealogies in 3:8d-11. In both of these constituents he is instructing Titus and the believers to have nothing to do with these various facets of false teaching.
   2) In 1:10-16, Paul describes the false teachers and tells Titus how to deal with those who follow false teaching. He describes the false teachers as "men who reject the truth" (**anthrōpōn apostrephomenōn tēn alētheian** 1:14). In 3:10-11, Paul tells Titus how he should deal with a **hairetikos anthrōpos** 'a divisive person', or perhaps 'a heretical person'. Paul says, if this person refuses to change these practices, "he has been perverted" (**exestraptai**). So Paul appears to be talking here again in 3:10-11 about people who reject the truth and teach false doctrine.

3. There is another **de** at the beginning of the second discussion of the topic of false teaching. So we find that each time there is a switch to the contrastive topic there is a **de**:

A	1:10-16	False doctrine
B	2:1-14	**De** sound doctrine
B′	3:1-8	Sound doctrine
A′	3:9-11	**De** false doctrine

(For various reasons discussed later, we have decided to begin the second unit on false doctrine at 3:8d rather than at the beginning of 3:9. 3:8d functions as a summarizing statement for 3:3-7 so is still concerned with sound doctrine; the switch to false doctrine comes with the **mōras de** 'foolish however' at the beginning of 3:9. However, this summarizing statement of 3:8d seems to function better as part of the unit which follows it, rather than the unit which precedes it.) These occurrences of de signal the contrastive nature of the material in 1:10--3:11, both in 1:10--2:14 and 3:1-11, thus also indicating the chiastic structure.

PROMINENCE AND THEME

As the discussion in the Boundaries and Coherence section above shows, the chiastic structure of 1:10--3:11 indicates that each of the themes of the four main constituents are closely related. The two outer constituents of the chiasmus are more closely related to each other than to the inner ones, and vice versa. This means two things for the theme statement of 1:10--3:11: The outer themes may be handled together and, if appropriate, their themes may be synthesized. The same holds for the inner themes.

In the theme statement for 1:10--3:11, we have chosen to handle the themes of the two outer constituents together to indicate the close tie between these two constituents. The grounds for 1:10-16 which is included in the lower-level theme is not included in this higher-level theme since it is not marked as being prominent enough to be considered for inclusion at this higher level. Also the theme statement for 3:8d-11 is somewhat shortened, "foolish disputes about genealogies and about the Jewish law" being shortened to "foolish and argumentative false teachings." "Reject" is used as a generic to translate both **periistaso** and **paraitou**. See discussion on the meanings of these words under the notes for 3:9 and 10.

As for the theme for the inner constituents of the chiasmus, the theme statement for 2:I-14 is reduced to the theme of the Head (hortatory) paragraph of 2:1-10. The theme statement for 3:1-8c is slightly shortened by leaving off the specific reference to "authorities" and dropping of "even though formerly we were behaving sinfully," both of which are not as focal on the higher level. The grounds part of this theme statement is retained because it is marked as highly prominent. (See the discussion under Prominence and Theme for 3:1-8c.) "Graciously" is added to the theme of this grounds constituent to represent the grounds constituent of 2:11-14 where God's grace is the topic of the grounds. The general concept of grace is also the central component of 3:3-7 though the word for grace occurs only once there (**chariti** 3:7).

Finally, a reference to "doing good" is included in the theme statement for 1:10--3:11, since that is an apparent motif or theme of the epistle, as seen by its occurrence six times (1:16; 2:7,14; 3:1,8,14), four of these at strategic points in the epistle, though only one in a hortatory construction (3:8). These will be discussed in detail in the notes. It could be argued that "do good works" is a generic for any of the positive commands that deal with Christian llbehavior in the epistle and so, since it is covered by the specific commands, it is not necessary to include it in the theme statement. However, its occurrence at these strategic points in the form of a motif, and its sense of good done on the behalf of others in many of its contexts in the epistle, argue for its inclusion.

DIVISION CONSTITUENT 1:10-16 (Paragraph) (Role: Head A of 1:10--3:11)

THEME: Since there are many deceivers teaching what is false, who do not even know God themselves and are unable to do any good thing, rigorously convince those believers who follow false teachings that they are wrong in order that they will firmly believe in the correct teachings.

DISPLAY

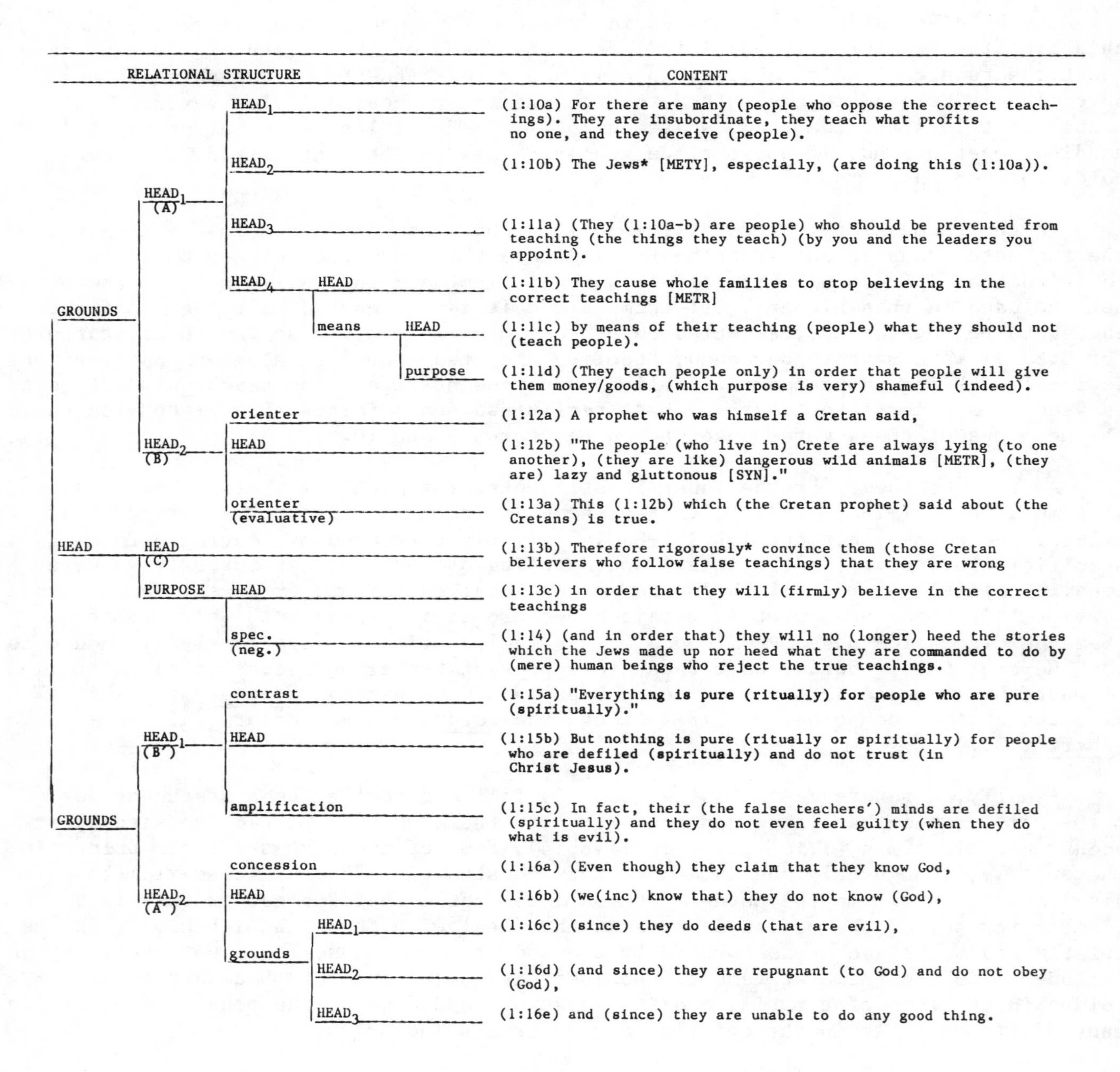

RELATIONAL STRUCTURE	CONTENT
GROUNDS — HEAD 1 (A) — HEAD 1	(1:10a) For there are many (people who oppose the correct teachings). They are insubordinate, they teach what profits no one, and they deceive (people).
HEAD 2	(1:10b) The Jews* [METY], especially, (are doing this (1:10a)).
HEAD 3	(1:11a) (They (1:10a-b) are people) who should be prevented from teaching (the things they teach) (by you and the leaders you appoint).
HEAD 4 — HEAD	(1:11b) They cause whole families to stop believing in the correct teachings [METR]
means — HEAD	(1:11c) by means of their teaching (people) what they should not (teach people).
purpose	(1:11d) (They teach people only) in order that people will give them money/goods, (which purpose is very) shameful (indeed).
HEAD 2 (B) — orienter	(1:12a) A prophet who was himself a Cretan said,
HEAD	(1:12b) "The people (who live in) Crete are always lying (to one another), (they are like) dangerous wild animals [METR], (they are) lazy and gluttonous [SYN]."
orienter (evaluative)	(1:13a) This (1:12b) which (the Cretan prophet) said about (the Cretans) is true.
HEAD — HEAD (C)	(1:13b) Therefore rigorously* convince them (those Cretan believers who follow false teachings) that they are wrong
PURPOSE — HEAD	(1:13c) in order that they will (firmly) believe in the correct teachings
spec. (neg.)	(1:14) (and in order that) they will no (longer) heed the stories which the Jews made up nor heed what they are commanded to do by (mere) human beings who reject the true teachings.
GROUNDS — HEAD 1 (B') — contrast	(1:15a) "Everything is pure (ritually) for people who are pure (spiritually)."
HEAD	(1:15b) But nothing is pure (ritually or spiritually) for people who are defiled (spiritually) and do not trust (in Christ Jesus).
amplification	(1:15c) In fact, their (the false teachers') minds are defiled (spiritually) and they do not even feel guilty (when they do what is evil).
HEAD 2 (A') — concession	(1:16a) (Even though) they claim that they know God,
HEAD	(1:16b) (we(inc) know that) they do not know (God),
grounds — HEAD 1	(1:16c) (since) they do deeds (that are evil),
HEAD 2	(1:16d) (and since) they are repugnant (to God) and do not obey (God),
HEAD 3	(1:16e) and (since) they are unable to do any good thing.

BOUNDARIES AND COHERENCE

For the initial boundary, see the discussion under Boundaries and Coherence for 1:6-9.

There are very strong referential and structural coherence factors within 1:10-16 showing that it is definitely a single coherent unit:

1. The principal class of people referred to in this unit are the tous antilegontas 'those who speak against/oppose (sound doctrine)' who are introduced in 1:9c in a tail-head link. All of 1:10-16 deals with these people. These are the people most commonly referred to as "false teachers" by commentators on Titus and the Pastoral Epistles in general, and it may be well to keep that designation in our discussion of these people, too. The tous antilegontas introduced in 1:9c and described in the first Greek sentence of 1:10-16 (1:10-11) are the same people as the anthrōpōn apostrephomenōn tēn alētheian 'men who turn away from the truth' (1:14) who are further discussed in 1:15-16. They oppose and reject the truth.
2. Furthermore, their traits are all negative ones:

   anupotaktoi 'insubordinate' 1:10

   mataiologoi 'foolish talkers' 1:10

   phrenapatai 'deceivers' 1:10

   holous oikous anatrepousin 'ruining whole houses' 1:11

   didaskontes ha mē dei 'teaching what they should not' 1:11

   didaskontes...aischrou kerdous charin 'teaching...for the sake of shameful gain' 1:11

   memiammenois 'defiled' 1:15

   apistois 'unbelieving' 1:15

   memiantai autōn kai ho nous kai hē suneidēsis 'both their minds and consciences are defiled' 1:15

   tois ergois arnountai 'they deny (God) by their actions' 1:16

   bdeluktoi 'detestable' 1:16

   apeitheis 'disobedient' 1:16

   pros pan ergon agathon adokimoi 'unfit for anything good' 1:16

   To this can be added the description of Cretans in general by one of their own prophets, Krētes aei pseustai, kaka thēria, gasteres argai 'Cretans are always liars, evil beasts, lazy gluttons' (1:12), which Paul seems to use to describe both the ones who are opposed to sound doctrine and those who are being deceived by them.
3. The referential coherence described in 1 and 2 above is built into a coherent chiastic structure:

   A Description of those who oppose sound doctrine 1:10-11
   B Quote (from Cretan prophet) 1:12-13a
   C Exhortation 1:13b-14
   B' Quote/Saying (of Jesus or Christian teaching) and statements based upon it 1:15
   A' Description of those who oppose sound doctrine 1:16

   Note that the quotes are also concerned with the description of the false prophets.

As for the final boundary, 2:1-10 is shown to be separate from 1:10-16 by the marked change in referential coherence and genre:

	1:10-16	2:1-10
Principal personal references	Titus, those who oppose sound doctrine	Titus, various groups within church
Characteristics of participants	negative	positive (to be sought)
Genre	more space given to description than to exhortation	hortatory through whole unit

PROMINENCE AND THEME

The only imperative in the Greek text of this paragraph is **elegche** 'correct, convince' occurring in 1:13b. The propositionalized form of the Greek clause in which it occurs has been rendered in the display text as "Therefore rigorously convince them (those Cretan believers who follow false teachings) that they are wrong." This is obviously the main part of the theme of this paragraph since imperatives are naturally more prominent than other forms, and this proposition comes at the very middle of the chiastic structure supported by grounds both before and after its occurrence.

However, there is a second Greek construction that could also be considered as hortatory, **hous dei epistomizein** 'whom it is necessary to silence' (1:11a). This present analysis considers **hous dei epistomizein** as a part of the description of those who oppose sound doctrine rather than a full-fledged exhortation, since in the Greek structure it is a relative clause in a long list of descriptions of these false teachers. No one is explicitly mentioned as the agent to perform the "silencing" as one would expect in hortatory material. This is because the false teachers are in focus; they are the ones being described by various adjectives, nouns, and relative clauses (note the relative clause immediately following in 1:11b which some commentators analyze as grounds). The whole symmetrical chiastic structure also points to only one exhortation, that of 1:13b; everything else centers around this. In a sense, **hous dei epistomizein** 'whom it is necessary to silence' is a generic expression of all of Paul's descriptions of the false teachers--"these are the kind of people whom it is necessary to silence." There is the possibility that Paul's intent is to silence them only through positive means, the positive means stated in the exhortation of 1:13b-c, "convince them that they are wrong in order that they will be sound in the faith," an exhortation that is probably aimed more at the listeners than the hard-core false teachers themselves. If these believers can be convinced of how wrong the false teachers are, the false teachers will find no profit in their contact with them and the problem will be solved.

It has also been decided to include the purpose constituent 1:13c in the theme statement, since it gives much more significance to the theme than the Head proposition alone. Since 1:14 is a negative restatement of 1:13c, 1:13c is used alone to represent the whole purpose constituent. This succinctly rounds out a representation of the full content of the exhortation.

In the Boundaries and Coherence section above, it has been shown that Paul gives a fully-developed description of the false teachers both before and after the exhortation in 1:13b. The highly emotive words that Paul uses in his description mirror his alarm at the present situation in Crete. He must do his best to see that the believers reject this false teaching and become truly sound in correct doctrine. And so, he does not mince words nor does he limit his description to a brief passing comment. He must show Titus and the believers in general how dangerous these people really are. And it is this fully-developed description that is the grounds for his exhortation to Titus to convince the believers that they are wrong in following the dangerous doctrines of the false teachers, and that they should instead follow sound doctrine. Because of the obvious prominence of this description, it is represented in the theme.

Since the individual descriptions are all basically equally prominent, it is difficult to determine which one(s) of them should represent the description as a whole. In the pre-exhortation description, deception stands out as seen in **phrenapatai** 'deceivers' (1:10) and **pseustai** 'liars' (1:12). "They deny God" stands out as the most prominent clause in the Greek structure of 1:16. However, **pros pan ergon agathon adokimoi** 'they are unfit for any good work' (1:16e), which occurs as the final description in the paragraph, is also included in the theme because the motif or theme of good works also occurs at the end of two other sections and at the very end of the body of the letter, which shows how prominent it is. This is discussed more fully in the notes for 1:16e.

NOTES ON 1:10-16

1:10a. **For there are many (people who oppose the correct teachings). They are insubordinate, they teach what profits no one, and they deceive (people). (Eisin gar polloi [kai] anupotaktoi, mataiologoi kai phrenapatai**, 'For there-are many insubordinate(people), vain-talkers and deceivers')

REL As has been mentioned in the Boundaries and Coherence for 1:6-9, **gar** in 1:10a is analyzed as indicating a relationship other than grounds-exhortation on the paragraph level. The basic problem in considering **gar** as indicating a grounds relationship on the paragraph level is that the resulting relationship between the Heads of each paragraph is illogical, as shown by the following:

HEAD	(1:6-9) [You(sg)] Appoint as elders men whom no one can justly criticize
*grounds	(1:10-16) since [you(sg) must] rigorously convince those Cretan believers who follow false teachings that they are wrong.

Note that in the Greek text the Head of 1:6-9 does not represent an imperative while the Head of 1:10-16 does.

The earlier analysis of Titus (Kopesec 1980a) took **gar** here as showing a grounds relationship for appointing elders, and tried to handle the problem above by dividing up 1:10-16 before the Head (1:13b). But this solution breaks up a unit which we have shown to be very coherent.

Other evidence for the fact that 1:10-16 is to be considered to have some type of conjoined relationship with 1:6-9 is the fact that we should expect the appointing of elders to be something that would need to be done in Crete anyway, whether there were false teachers or not. Even in 1 Timothy where false teachers are also mentioned, the appointing of elders does not have a direct connection with dealing with the false teachers.

Also, if we take **ta leiponta epidiorthōsē** 'correct the matters that need to be corrected' as a generic introduction dealing with the false teachers, it may be significant for our analysis that the relationship indicated between this and the appointing of elders is a conjoined one, as shown by kai 'and', and not one of means-purpose such as "I left you in Crete to appoint elders in order that they might straighten up the problems there."

What appears to be happening, then, is that the problem of the false teachers is a serious one and Paul is taking various steps to deal with it. The first step mentioned coincides with another matter that needs to be taken care of, the appointing of qualified elders. Part of their work will be to encourage the believers in sound doctrine and to refute those who oppose sound doctrine, i.e., the false teachers. The second step is for Titus himself to conduct a major campaign to convince people that the false teachers are deceivers who do not even know God and so must not be followed. The third step is for Titus to teach sound doctrine to the whole church.

Since 1:6-9 definitely functions as a unit and 1:10-16 does also, and since it has been shown that gar cannot function here as indicating a grounds relationship on the paragraph level, gar must be taken as having some other function in this context. Sometimes at the boundary between higher-level units, there is a lower-level relationship between propositions, which crosses that boundary. Here we find a lower-level causal relationship of some type between 1:9c and 1:10a. Since it is a lower-level relationship, we would expect it to be less significant than the higher-level relationship between the larger units. This type of lower-level causal relationship at a higher-level boundary is usually translated by "for" in English. Note that, in English at least, the second part of this relationship is not subordinate to the first. Versions such as TEV and NIV have no problem in starting a new paragraph, even though they use "for" at the beginning of that paragraph. (Note that NEB starts a new paragraph and uses no conjunction here at all.) It appears, then, that "for" has two functions at the beginning of verse 10: it communicates the lower-level causal relationship, and also introduces a new higher-level unit. Gar presumably does the same thing in Greek. It would seem that a semantic structure analysis in propositionalized form should not overlook the function of gar in such a position, therefore, "for" is used in the display text.

Instead of "for," the statement "I say this because" could also be used, but it would have to be understood as a connective between 1:9c and 1:10ff., and not as a Head proposition with 1:10ff. subordinate to it.

TXT Some manuscripts omit the first kai 'and, also' in this verse. The text of the third edition of the UBS Greek New Testament has this kai in brackets and classifies this textual problem as one where "there is a considerable degree of doubt whether the text or the apparatus contains the superior reading." It is common in Greek for kai to occur between an adjective of quantity and one of quality. In addition to the predication that "there are many," a description of their character is also given. Ellicott, in supporting the inclusion of kai, remarks, "its omission being so obviously referable to an ignorance of the idiomatic **polus kai**." Whichever reading is chosen, there is no basic change in the meaning.

CONT The addition of the implied "people who oppose the correct teachings" in the display text is to clarify who is being discussed in this paragraph.

CONT/TRNS The adjective **anupotaktoi** `insubordinate, unruly' describes a course of action indicating that the persons act as if they are subject to no one. The display text preserves the adjectival form in "insubordinate." However, if a verb must be used, "they do not obey (anyone)," or even, "they refuse to obey (anyone)" would be proper translations.

CONT The meaning of **mataiologoi** here perhaps is best understood from the use of **mataios** in 3:9, where the teaching of the false teachers is described as **anōpheleis kai mataioi** `unprofitable and worthless', in contrast to the "profitable" (**ōphelima**) doctrines of the gospel. Lock renders **mataiologoi** as "teachers of worthless doctrine" in his paraphrase. "Worthless" seems to be the prime meaning of **mataios** in the New Testament as a whole.

Another analysis would be that **mataiologoi** focuses in more on the style of teaching and the person of the teacher, rather than focusing on the worthlessness of the subject matter. Thus, Guthrie says, "they are emptyheaded in their teaching, doing much talking but saying nothing." The first analysis above has been chosen since it appears to be more specific to the fuller context. However, the second analysis is also possible, and **mataiologoi** could be rendered as "they talk foolishly" or "they are foolish talkers."

CONT Though a few commentators and versions understand **phrenapatai** to mean "those who deceive themselves," the majority do not, but see the word as being formed from **phrena apatan**, with the literal meaning here of "deceivers of the mind/ mind-deceivers," and a freer rendering of "deceivers," i.e., "they deceive others."

1:10b. The Jews* [METY], especially, (are doing this (1:10a)). (**malista hoi ek tēs peritomēs**, `especially those of the circumcision')

CONT **Hoi ek tēs peritomēs** has been variously translated or understood as "Jews," "Jewish Christians," "those who advocate/preach circumcision." The Greek construction itself does not give clues as to whether the meaning in this context is "Jews/Jewish believers in Christ," or whether Paul is focusing on the fact that these teachers are advocating circumcision for all believers. Of the other five occurrences of **ek peritomēs** in the New Testament in substantive constructions, Colossians 4:11 definitely means "Jews/Jewish Christians" and has no connection with advocating circumcision whatsoever, nor does it appear to have any direct reference to circumcision. It only means "Jew." Rom. 4:12 has reference to the fact that the people are circumcised, but has no reference to advocating circumcision whatsoever. The reference in Acts 10:45 probably should also be included with either Col. 4:11 or Rom. 4:12. Acts 11:2, at first, looks like it may mean "those who advocate circumcision for Gentile Christians," but, in verse 18 of the same chapter, these very people agree with Peter that the Gentiles do not need to be circumcised to be saved (cf. Acts 15:1 with 15:24). Only in Gal. 2:12 does **tous ek peritomēs** appear to definitely mean "those who advocate circumcision for Gentile believers."

Thus in most contexts **hoi ek peritomēs** only means "those who are circumcised," i.e., "the Jews." (Note that, in all five of these occurrences, the people referred to are Jews who have believed in Christ.) In the display text for Titus 1:10b, then, "Jews" is used to translate **hoi ek tēs peritomēs**. This seems to be a better translation than "Those who are circumcised, especially, (are doing this)," since the fact of being circumcised would not be in focus here. On the other hand, based on the one reference in Gal. 2:12, there is a possibility that **hoi ek tēs peritomēs** here in Titus 1:10 refers to people who are preaching circumcision, though one wonders why Paul would use an ambiguous substantive phrase to do so.

"Jews" is asterisked in the display text since, although the word itself has both the sense of race and religion, only that of race is being referred to here. Another way to handle this would be to use "those of Jewish ancestry" in the display text.

CONT **Malista** 'especially' indicates that this movement of opposition to sound doctrine was basically led by Jewish people.

1:11a. **(They (1:10a-b) are people) who should be prevented from teaching (the things they teach) (by you and the leaders you appoint).** (**hous dei epistomizein**, 'whom it-is-necessary to-stop-the-mouths-of')

REL See under Prominence and Theme as to the reasons for considering this constituent descriptive rather than hortatory.

CONT/TRNS No agent is given for silencing the false teachers. Titus is the most obvious agent, since he is the agent of the only imperative of this paragraph (1:13b). However, since it is mentioned in 1:9 that the leaders who are to be appointed are also to refute the false teachers, they are also included as agents in the display text. If we view this constituent as descriptive rather than hortatory, then it is the false teachers who are in focus and not the agents, as is also shown by the fact that the agents are not even mentioned in the Greek. Thus, in languages where no agent is required here on a grammatical basis, none should be included.

1:11b. **They cause whole families to stop believing in the correct teachings** [METR] (**hoitines holous oikous anatrepousin** 'who whole households overturn')

REL Following the Greek structure of a relative clause, this constituent has been analyzed as a further description of the false teachers. For those who analyze 1:11a as an exhortation, 1:11b is more naturally considered as grounds for 1:11a, "(since) they cause whole families to stop believing in the correct teaching."

CONT It is difficult to ascertain the exact meaning of **anatrepousin** 'overturn, upset', since it is used in a figurative sense, though the figure is probably a dead one, having been used in Greek for a long time already (see Arndt and Gingrich). Although some commentators mention the sense of upsetting peace and harmony, perhaps more common is the view that the sense here is to upset the believers' faith. The latter is more probable, since the action of the false teachers which Paul seems to focus on most in 1:10-14 is their deception of believers so that they will turn from sound doctrine and truth. We would expect, from the highly emotive overtones of this paragraph and from the intent structure of the book as a whole, that Paul is trying to deal with a very serious problem indeed, and therefore, "subverting" is more likely to be the sense here rather than merely "disturbing."

PROM There is marked prominence on "whole households," as shown by forefronting.

1:11c-d. **by means of their teaching (people) what they should not (teach people). (11d) (They teach people only) in order that people will give them**

money/goods, (which purpose is very) shameful (indeed). (**didaskontes ha mē dei aischrou kerdous charin**. 'teaching what (they)ought not for-the-sake-of shameful gain')

REL/CONT 1:11d indicates the purpose or motive of the false teachers; they teach for the sake of shameful gain. It is generally agreed that the purpose of their teaching was to profit materially from the teaching, with no concern at all for the spiritual welfare of the people they taught. Their only desire is to make money and this, of course, is shameful. Though some authorities translate "dishonest gain" here, it seems as if a translation that adheres more closely to the literal meaning of "shameful" and that more specifically describes the action of the false teachers would be better. This translation has been attempted in the display text.

TRNS It must be made clear in translation that the shameful act of the false teachers was not the taking of money for their teaching, but teaching only with the motive of making money, with no interest in the spiritual welfare of those being taught.

CONT **Kerdous** 'gain' does not necessarily refer only to money, but other representations of material gain could also be included.

1:12a. **A prophet who was himself a Cretan said,** (**eipen tis ex autōn, idios autōn prophētēs**, 'said certain-one of them, of-their own, a-prophet')

REL There is no conjunction at the beginning of 1:12 to relate it to the preceding constituent. The chiastic structure, as described above, would indicate some type of division here. (Note that there is also asyndeton at the beginning of the saying in 1:15.) **Di' hēn aitian** 'for which reason' in 1:13b indicates that 1:12a-13a is grounds for the exhortation that begins in 1:13b. But it can be seen that the quote, and Paul's testimony that the quote is true, are not complete in themselves without the preceding facts and evidence given in 1:10-11 about the false teachers. Certainly 1:10-11 and 1:12a-13a are meant to reinforce one another as strong evidence for the necessity of carrying out the exhortation in 1:13b-14. These considerations strongly suggest that there are two grounds units before the exhortation, that they are closely related to each other, and that the second unit begins at 1:12a. The strong connection between these two grounds units can be seen in the description of the false teachers as **phrenapatai** 'deceivers' in 1:10, the fact that they subvert whole families (1:11), and the description of the Cretans as always being liars (**aei pseustai**) in the quote (1:12).

CONT Paul, here, makes clear that the content of 1:12b is not to be taken as originating with himself. It originated with one of the Cretans' very own prophets. Note the repetition of **autōn** 'their' and the addition of **idios** '(their) own'.

CONT By "prophet" here, Paul, of course, does not mean that he is a prophet of Yahweh, but one of their own (pagan) prophets. If the "prophet" is Epimenides, as the majority of commentators maintain, it is significant that he was considered a prophet by his own countrymen and the Greeks in general. He was "a religious teacher and wonder-worker of the sixth century B.C." (Kelly) and is said to have prophesied the failure of the Persian expedition against Greece ten years before it took place. In describing him as a prophet here, Paul is emphasizing the reliability of the statement.

1:12b. **"The people (who live in) Crete are always lying (to one another), (they are like) dangerous wild animals [METR], (they are) lazy and gluttonous [SYN]."** (Krētes aei pseustai, kaka thēria, gasteres argai. 'Cretans (are) always liars, evil beasts, idle bellies')

CONT Since the Greek for the first phrase in the quote literally means "Cretans always liars," an alternate rendering for the display text would be "The people (who live in) Crete have always been people who (habitually) lie (to one another)" (cf. Arndt and Gingrich, "Cretans have always been liars").

CONT Kaka thēria 'evil beasts' is a metaphor which is expressed in the display text as a simile. The noun thēria is used here as a figure for people who have a "bestial" nature. The forefronted adjective kaka 'evil' puts marked prominence on the evil character of the "wild beasts." They are ferocious, dangerous. The figurative language means that Cretans were by nature difficult and dangerous to have dealings with.

CONT In gasteres argai 'idle bellies', gasteres 'bellies' is used figuratively to mean "gluttons." The adjective argai 'idle' is also applied to the Cretans. They are lazy as well as gluttonous.

CONT This quotation is a hyperbole in the sense that we would not expect every Cretan to fit all these traits. However, the prophet and Paul himself found that these traits were characteristic of all too many Cretans.

1:13a. **This (1:12b) which (the Cretan prophet) said about (the Cretans) is true.** (hē marturia hautē estin alēthēs. 'this testimony is true')

REL This constituent serves as an evaluative orienter for the quotation. Paul agrees with the statement of the prophet based on his own experience with the Cretans. (Note that this relation is called an "evaluative orienter," whether it comes before or after that which it evaluates.)

1:13b. **Therefore rigorously* convince them (those Cretan believers who follow false teachings) that they are wrong** (di' hēn aitian elegche autous apotomōs, 'for which reason refute/correct them rigorously/severely')

REL Di' hēn aitian 'for which reason, therefore' logically refers back, not only to the quote with its orienters, but also to the evidence which backs up Paul's agreement with the quote regarding the present situation, the evidence he has stated in 1:10-11. As mentioned above, this binds all the pre-exhortation grounds (1:10-13a) together.

CONT We now come to perhaps the most difficult problem in the exegesis of this paragraph. When Paul says, "Correct them rigorously," who does he mean by autous 'them'? Is it the deceivers, or those being deceived? There are arguments for both sides, and commentators seem to be evenly divided on this subject.

The main reason for considering autous 'them' to refer to the deceivers is that all the paragraph so far has been talking about the deceivers, and nowhere does the reference clearly switch to those being deceived. The "deceivers" (phrenapatai) of 1:10 are the same people who in 1:11 "subvert whole families" and "teach what they ought not for the sake of shameful gain," and so most likely would be the same people whom Paul, through the words of the Cretan prophet, characterizes as "liars" (pseustai) in 1:12, especially since autōn 'of them' in 1:12a most naturally refers back to the people being discussed in 1:10-11. In the same way, the autous 'them' of 1:13b also most naturally refers back to the Cretan liars of 1:12 and, thus, the deceivers being discussed in 1:10-11.

On the other hand, the exhortation of 1:13b, "rigorously convince them that they are wrong in order that they may be sound in the faith, not heeding Jewish myths and commandments of men who turn away from the truth" does not seem to be made to people who are themselves deceivers, but to those who are being deceived. This can be seen by the fact that, instead of saying something like, "Don't allow them to teach," or, "Silence them," as one would expect if the deceivers were the topic of 1:13b, the people in focus are to be exhorted to be sound in the faith, not giving heed to false teaching. 1:14 reveals clearly that there are two groups of people being discussed in this paragraph: (1) those who are, or who are in danger of, heeding the myths and commandments of men who have rejected the truth; and (2) those who have actually rejected the truth and are deceiving others by their teaching. And a proper analysis of 1:13b-14 seems to show clearly that it is those of the first group who are to be exhorted in 1:13b. It would seem highly probable that those who in 1:10 are deceivers (phrenapatai), who are turning whole families from the truth (holous oikous anatrepousin 'subvert whole households' 1:11b) and are teaching what they ought not (didaskontes ha mē dei 1:11c), are the same people who themselves reject the truth (anthrōpōn apostrephomenōn tēn alētheian 1:14) and propagate Jewish myths and human commandments instead. (Hendriksen, however, would see those "who reject the truth" as Jewish propagandists who stand wholly outside of the Christian faith and are other than the false teachers of 1:10-11.)

The problem, then, is that there seems to be almost equally valid evidence for proving that those to be exhorted in 1:13b are, by one line of evidence (1:10-13a), the false teachers, and by another line of evidence (1:13c-14), the believers who are being deceived or at least liable to be deceived.

It may be, however, that the problem with the above analysis is that it tends to polarize the people concerned, more than Paul does in his own thinking. It may be that he himself starts out in 1:10-11 to focus mainly on the false teachers themselves, but the distinction between the deceivers and the deceived begins to blur in his stating of the quote. The fact that both the deceivers and the deceived are all Cretans may have something to do with this. And in 1:13b, Paul may have in mind all who are still reclaimable. Some of these would have developed into deceivers themselves, but might be returned to sound faith if corrected rigorously enough. Thus, it is well not to render autous 'them' in 1:13b as "false teachers" or as "those being deceived," but by a somewhat more generic expression, such as that used in the display text, "those Cretan believers who follow false teachings."

CONT Although some render elegche as "rebuke," there is a noticeable difference between Greek elegchō and English "rebuke" in their full spectra of meaning, and it appears that their primary meanings are different. For elegchō, Arndt and Gingrich give the following meanings: (1) "bring to light, expose, set forth"; (2) "convict" or "convince" someone of something, "point something out to someone"; (3) "reprove, correct"; and (4) "punish, discipline," which Arndt and Gingrich qualify as a "heightened" sense of the word. Funk and Wagnalls Standard College Dictionary gives the following present-day meanings for "rebuke": "to reprove sharply; reprimand," and for the noun, "a strong and authoritative expression of disapproval." It can be seen that the primary meaning of "rebuke" has more the sense of censure for past or present misdeeds, than the sense of convincing someone that they are wrong, which appears to be the central meaning of elegchō (though, in some contexts, the meaning of elegchō may be closer to the sense of rebuke).

Since elegchein definitely has the sense of "convince that they are wrong, refute" in 1:9c, which introduces this paragraph (no one translates "rebuke" there), and 1:13b deals with this same subject, it is this same central meaning of elegchō that is intended in 1:13b. We can hardly expect that people will become "sound in the faith" by being "rebuked sharply," but, if they are convincingly shown that they are wrong, they may indeed change. It may be that some translators have thought that "rebuke" is the correct translation here because it has the component of "severity," which is a sense of apotomōs, but the other components of "rebuke" are not equal to those of elegchō in this context. Note that Arndt and Gingrich give "rigorously" as a meaning for apotomōs. Based on these considerations, the display text is translated as "rigorously convince them that they are wrong." Here "rigorously" is to be understood in the sense of "uncompromisingly," (i.e., "in no uncertain terms"), rather than the sense "logically accurate" (cf. Funk and Wagnalls).

1:13c. **in order that they will (firmly) believe in the correct teachings (hina hugiainōsin en tē pistei**, 'in-order-that they-may-be-sound in the faith')

CONT **Pistis** 'faith' may refer to the act of believing or to the body of truth which a Christian is to believe. Here, it undoubtedly refers primarily to the goal of faith, i.e., the body of Christian truth, and is closely related to **tē didaskalia tē hugiainousē** 'sound teaching/doctrine' (1:9) and **tē hugiainousē didaskalia** 'sound teaching/doctrine' (2:1), though here looking at it from the believing side rather than the teaching side. The immediate context agrees with this, since **hugiainōsin en tē pistei** 'they may be sound in the faith' is immediately followed by its specific negated opposites, **mē prosechontes Ioudaikois muthois kai entolais anthrōpōn apostrephomenōn tēn alētheian** 'not heeding Jewish myths and commandments of men who reject the truth'. They are to believe in sound doctrine and not false doctrine.

Another way to look at this is from the perspective of the kind of belief. What is meant here is to "believe correctly" rather than "believe firmly" only. A man may appear to have "great faith," but something would be drastically wrong if his faith were not correct faith, i.e., faith in the correct doctrine. The fact that **hugiainō** (which has a literal meaning of "to be sound, healthy" and is usually translated as "to be sound"), at the time of the writing of Titus, was a dead figure meaning "true, correct, reasonable" gives even more weight to the analysis that what is being talked about here is correct belief. (See Dibelius on 1 Tim. 1:10.)

1:14. **(and in order that) they will no (longer) heed the stories which the Jews made up nor heed what they are commanded to do by (mere) human beings who reject the true teachings.** (**mē prosechontes Ioudaikois muthois kai entolais anthrōpōn apostrephomenōn tēn alētheian**. 'not heeding Jewish myths and commandments of-men turning-away-from the truth')

REL As mentioned above under 1:13c, 1:14 states two negated specifics of believing the correct teachings. In this type of generic-specific relationship, the specifics cover only a small part of the total area covered by the generic, though, as here, often a significant part of that area as far as the context is concerned.

CONT The negative **mē** 'not', with the present tense of the participle **prosechontes** 'giving heed to', may signal either, that the believers should stop heeding these false doctrines if they are at present heeding them, or, not to begin to heed them if they haven't yet done so. The context of verse 13 would suggest that the former is more in focus here.

CONT Arndt and Gingrich give as the meaning of **muthos**, `tale, story, legend, myth, fable', which shows that the word had a rather wide range of meaning. Since it is contrasted here with correct doctrine, as it is in 2 Tim. 4:4, **kai apo men tēs alētheias tēn akoēn apostrepsousin, epi de tous muthous ektrapēsontai** `and they will turn their ears away from the truth and turn aside to myths', it is apparent that the **muthoi** do not represent the truth. Therefore, **muthos** here would have the components of (1) story, (2) false, and (3) a basis for doctrine, since it is not the mere telling of stories that is in focus, but the telling of stories that support doctrine. Note that the "false" component would apply certainly to the doctrine and most likely to the story, too.

CONT **Ioudaikois** `Jewish' indicates the origin and nature of the stories.

CONT The genitive construction, **entolais anthrōpōn** `commandments of men', draws attention to the human origin of the commands. **Anthrōpoi** refers to men in general, mankind, human beings. As in Col. 2:8, it is being used derogatively here and so the addition of "mere" in the display text. Here, the commandments are not only described as being those of mere men but also as commandments of men who reject the truth. The present tense of **apostrephomenōn** `turn away from, reject' indicates either that these people at the time of the writing of the epistle were in the process of turning away from the truth ("men who are now turning away from the truth," Lock), or that they continually reject the truth ("they ever `keep turning away' from the truth whenever it is offered to them," Lenski). It seems better to use the second option as the basis for the display text, since it is more generic than the first, and the point that they are even now turning away from the truth would not appear to be in focus.

1:15a. "Everything is pure (ritually) for people who are pure (spiritually)." (**panta kathara tois katharois**: `all(things) (are) pure to-the pure(ones)')

REL There is asyndeton again at the beginning of the second "saying," even as there was at the beginning of the orienter for the first "saying" (1:12) of this chiastic structure. It is generally agreed that "all things are pure for the pure" is a saying. Kelly says, "The sentence has the ring of a proverb. As Jesus used a similar statement in Mark 7:15 to counter his legalistic Jewish opponents, "Nothing outside a man can make him `unclean' by going into him" (NIV), so Paul does here.

The connection between **entolais anthrōpōn** `the commandments of men' (comparable forms of which elsewhere occur in the New Testament to refer to ritual law in Mark 7:7; Col. 2:22) and the statements about purity and defilement dealing with ritual and moral law (1:15) shows that Paul is explaining how the false teachers have turned aside from the truth in that their commandments and lives are not pleasing to God at all. **Entolais anthrōpōn apostrephomenōn tēn alētheian** `commandments of men turning away from the truth' occurring at the end of the purpose constituent 1:13c-14 acts as a "tail" in a tail-head link between 1:13b-14 and 1:15-16. 1:15-16 does not act as an amplification of the purpose unit but as further descriptive grounds for the Head in 1:13b-14. The description of the negative traits of the false teachers serves as a grounds for the exhortation, the main aim of which is to turn the believers away from the false teachers and their teaching. By showing how bad and wrong they are, Paul hopes to spur Titus and the Cretan believers in general to firm action to prevent adherence to the false teachers and their teaching.

CONT What Paul is saying in verse 15 is difficult to understand unless we assume that some of these human commandments had to do with rules of ritual purification regarding food and possibly other things. 1:15a has been interpreted in various ways. Interpretations are based on the potential meanings of panta 'all (things)' and kathara 'pure'. The fact that panta 'all' is neuter indicates that natural objects, such as food and utensils, could very well be in focus, as in Rom. 14:20 where Paul uses panta kathara to mean "all food is pure (ritually)." Following this interpretation, kathara in Titus 1:15a would refer to ritual purity. Tois katharois refers to people as being pure, and undoubtedly to the sense of spiritual or moral purity instead of ritual purity, since ritual law does not maintain that a person will stay ritually pure, even though he comes in contact with things that are ritually impure. Secondly, the context does not warrant such a sense at all. On the other hand, lexically panta is not limited to natural objects only, but could also refer to a man's actions or anything in an abstract sense. Nevertheless, it is more probable that Paul is referring to ritual, rather than moral/spiritual, purity by panta kathara as the following shows:

1. It is difficult to understand how "all things are morally pure to the morally pure" could be true. As Kelly says, "When modern people quote the apothegm, they usually take the word exclusively in the moral sense and deduce that the man who is himself pure need not fear contamination by anything impure. This is a dangerous half-truth, and far from Paul's meaning."
2. In Col. 2:22, Paul calls rules about ritual purity "the commandments and teachings of men," ta entalmata kai didaskalias tōn anthrōpōn, similar to the phrase here in Titus 1:14, entolais anthrōpōn 'the commandments of men'. Jesus also calls at least some of the ritual purity laws entalmata anthrōpōn 'commandments of men' when he quotes from Isaiah in Mark 7:7. Thus, there seems to be some connection between the "commandments of men" in Titus 1:14 and Paul's remarks about purity and corruption in 1:15--remarks that show very good evidence of some connection with ritual purity with their use of katharos 'pure' and miainō 'defile'. (This does not mean that he uses katharos and miainō to refer to ritual purity only, for he also uses katharos to mean moral or spiritual purity, and miainō to refer to moral defilement, but these remarks take off from the starting point of ritual law.)
3. In Mark 7:15, there is a similar exposition to this one in Titus, since it also has to do with ritual law. Jesus says, "Nothing outside a man can make him 'unclean' by going into him. Rather, it is what comes out of a man that makes him 'unclean'" (NIV). Note that, in the second occurrence of "unclean" here in Mark, Jesus is using "unclean" in its moral sense, but that his starting point is the use of "unclean" in its ritual sense, something very similar to what Paul is doing in Titus 1:14-15.

The majority of commentators take panta kathara 'all (things) (are) pure' to refer to ritual purity.

CONT/TRNS A freer rendering of 1:15a would be, "People who are (spiritually) pure (may treat) everything (as ritually) pure."

1:15b. **But nothing is pure (ritually or spiritually) for people who are defiled (spiritually) and do not trust (in Christ Jesus).** (**tois de memiammenois kai apistois ouden katharon**, 'but to-those having-been-defiled and unbelieving nothing (is) pure')

REL There is what, at first, might seem to be a three-way contrast between 1:15a, b, and c. Notice the de adversative between 15a and b and the alla adversative between 15b and c. Actually, the contrast between 15a and b is a true contrast, while that between 15b and c is a double contrast that almost functions as a Head-equivalent relationship, but is probably more appropriately labeled as amplification. This will be analyzed more fully below.

CONT One question here is whether ouden katharon 'nothing (is) pure' refers to ritual or moral purity, or both. The question is not so much whether moral purity could logically be included, but whether or not Paul is focusing on ritual purity in ouden katharon. The chiastic form of 1:15a-b would tend to point toward ritual purity as the sense of katharon in 15b:

A panta kathara 'all (things) (are) pure'
B tois katharois 'to the pure (ones)'
B′ tois de memiammenois kai apistois 'to the defiled and unbelieving'
A′ ouden katharon 'nothing (is) pure'

The inner constituents of the chiasmus refer to people and thus, in this context, definitely to moral purity. Apistois 'unbelieving' supports this. Panta kathara has been analyzed as referring to ritual purity, and, because of the parallel structure within the chiasmus and the fact that both A and A′ are neuter constructions, it seems as if ouden katharon is also referring to ritual purity. However, when Paul amplifies ouden katharon in 1:15c and says even their minds and consciences have been defiled, he is talking about moral purity. It may be, then, that in ouden katharon 'nothing (is) pure', Paul is not making a distinction as to ritual or moral purity, since he seems to be relating it to ritual purity on one side and moral purity on the other.

CONT Memiammenois has the sense of "defiled, contaminated," a word which, in other contexts, has to do with either ritual or moral impurity. Here the sense intended is moral impurity. Nothing is ritually or morally pure to these people, since their very minds and consciences have been contaminated by sin and unbelief. Compare Haggai 2:10-14 where, because of the Jews′ sin, whatever they do and whatever they offer in the temple is unclean.

CONT Another question is whether Paul changes from the general reference in 1:15a to a specific reference to the false teachers, either at the beginning of 1:15b or 1:15c. The chiastic structure of 1:15a-b would tend to indicate that the generic reference of 15a continues in 15b. The general principle is given in chiastic form. The forefronting of autōn 'their' in 15c before the words it modifies, kai ho nous kai hē suneidēsis 'both the mind and the conscience', suggests a return to specific reference to the false teachers. The forefronting of the free form reference to the topic (i.e., the people being discussed) may well indicate change in topic from general reference back to specific reference to the false teachers. It should be noted, however, that even though the reference in 15b is a general one, Paul has the false teachers in mind as the main example of this generic statement.

CONT Kai apistois is a further description of the persons who are defiled. Apistois may refer to the state of not believing, or it may mean "disloyal." In the display text, the first option has been chosen, since "disloyal" is more specific and may signify unfaithfulness where there was once faithfulness. Here something more general is needed. According to Arndt and Gingrich, "faithless" or "unbelieving" is the sense of apistos that is indicated in every other reference of the word in the New Testament, except for Acts 26:8 where it means "incredible."

"In Christ Jesus" has been supplied to show who should have been the object of their faith. The other option would be "in God," but it seems that faith in Christ is more in focus here, since the false teachers, who are mainly Jewish (1:10), are shown in this paragraph to have, as their basic problem, rejection of Christ as the end of the law. They continue to depend on the law, or even worse, on "Jewish myths" and "the commandments of men."

CONT/TRNS A freer rendering of 1:15b would be "But people who are (spiritually) defiled and do not trust (in Christ Jesus) (cause) everything (they do or touch to become) impure (ritually and spiritually)."

1:15c. **In fact, their (the false teachers') minds are defiled (spiritually) and they do not even feel guilty (when they do what is evil).** (alla memiantai autōn kai ho nous kai hē suneidēsis. 'but they-have-been-defiled, both their mind and their conscience')

REL/CONT Alla does not signal a true contrast here but has an ascensive sense, cf. RSV "their very minds and consciences are corrupted" (underlining mine). 1:15c is probably best analyzed relationally as amplification. As Erdman says, "when Paul states that 'their mind and their conscience are defiled,' he does not formally give it as a reason why, to them, external things are impure; rather, he adds this phrase to describe further the false teachers."

"In fact" is used at the beginning of 1:15c to translate this ascensive sense of alla in reference to "their minds," while "even," in "they do not even feel guilty," translates alla in reference to "their consciences."

CONT In the display text, nous 'mind' is rendered as a noun, since the concept of "mind" would seem to be nearly universal. However, the concept of "conscience" as an entity in itself is not universal, so it is rendered as "and they do not even feel guilty (when they do what is evil)."

1:16a-c. **(Even though) they claim that they know God, (16b) (we(inc) know that) they do not know (God), (16c) (since) they do deeds (that are evil),** (theon homologousin eidenai, tois de ergois arnountai, 'God they-profess to-know, but by-the works they-deny')

CONT The false teachers certainly profess that they know God, but their actions are not those of people who are really God's children. It is difficult to know exactly the extent of those actions, though the context gives an idea of some of them: deceiving others (1:10), leading people astray (1:11), teaching for shameful gain (1:11). They have rejected the truth (1:14) and oppose sound doctrine (1:9). They are undermining the basis of true religion; could anything be more harmful and evil?

CONT/REL/TRNS As commonly translated, the expression "by their works they deny (God)" (tois de ergois arnountai), or "by their works they deny (that they know God)," may be clear enough for the English reader to understand, but it is also easy to see that the logical relationships are skewed. First of all, "deny," in its primary meaning, is a speech orienter, and the context indicates that the content of the denial would be "they know God," i.e., "they deny that they know God." But, in the real world, they never say that they do not know God, but the exact opposite--"they profess that they know God." "Deny," then, is used here with its primary meaning on one level, but with an extended sense on another level. On the formal lexical level, its primary meaning is being contrasted with "profess," but on the level of real-world reference, it has the meaning of "show otherwise," i.e., "they show that they do not know God." But this "showing" is not intentional on the part of the false teachers, so the relationship is not one of means-result, for example:

*RESULT	(1:16b) they show that they do not know him
|*means	(1:16c) by what they do.

The relationship, then, may be one of reason-result, for example:

reason	(1:16b) they do what is evil
|RESULT	(1:16c) as a result, they show that they do not know God.

However, especially since "show" is not used here in the sense of intentionally "showing," whereas, in some languages, it may inherently have that sense, it may be better to render 1:16b-c as Head-grounds:

HEAD	(1:16b) (we(inc) know that) they do not know (God)
|grounds	(1:16c) (since) they do deeds (that are evil).

1:16d. (and since) they are repugnant (to God) and do not obey (God), (bdeluktoi ontes kai apeitheis 'abominable being and disobedient')

REL 1:16d-e is in a participial relationship with **arnountai** 'deny', and so, some type of fairly close semantic relationship is intended. In the earlier analysis (Kopesec 1980a), this was analyzed as a generic-specific relationship. Hendriksen sees the participial phrase (1:16d-e) as "the reason why they commit these evil acts." This would suggest a result-reason relationship.

As for the generic-specific relationship, it seems questionable, since the generic constituent would refer to actions, while **bdeluktoi ontes** 'being detestable' refers to a state; or possibly, there is an action here, but the false teachers are the affectants or goal, and not the agents, i.e., "the false teachers are detested by..."

As far as the result-reason relationship is concerned, it seems that one could say, "they are detestable as a result of their evil works" as well as "they do evil works because they are detestable." In other words, the result-reason relationship is not clear. Also, it is difficult to see a result-reason relationship between "they deny God by their (evil) works" and "they are unfit for any good work."

It seems best to take the participial phrase of 1:16d-e as additional evidential grounds for the conclusion of 1:16b "(we(inc) know that) they do not know (God)."

CONT Some see in **bdeluktoi** 'abominable, detestable' an intended ironic relation to the fact that the false teachers considered certain foods, etc., as detestable. Guthrie says, "This word may here be used ironically, in the sense that those who claim to track down detestable things are themselves detestable." It seems that this could well be true on the basis of the use of "detestable" in similar situations as "defiled" (cf. Lev. 18:30), and the contrastive style of the immediate context with profess-deny and pure-defiled, both contrasts in which the false teachers profess that they have the positive characteristics, but actually have the negative characteristics. Although "pure" is not made explicit again here in 1:16d, it is obviously the opposite of **bdeluktoi** `detestable' (cf. Prov. 17:15, **akathartos kai bdeluktos** `impure and detestable').

But is "detestable" here to be applied to people (because of what they do, of course), or is it to be applied only to their actions and not to their persons? In other words, is "they do detestable things" an accurate translation, or is the more literal translation, "they are detestable," the only acceptable translation? It would seem better to translate literally and not apply **bdeluktoi** only to their actions, even as the related concept **memiammenois** `defiled' (15b) was not translated as only relating to deeds. Notice that the primary meaning here is probably not "deserving to be hated" but that of repugnance because of the sin and defilement connected with the item/person described. **Bdeluktos** is, therefore, close to the meaning of "defiled" but has a very important additional component of repugnancy because of the defilement. From the use of **bdeluktos** and its cognates in general, and especially from the immediate context where the relationship being discussed is that between the false teachers and God, it is evident that God is the primary personality who views the false teachers as repugnant. So the rendering in the display text is, "they are repugnant (to God)." God would also be the one that they refuse to obey.

1:16e. **and (since) they are unable to do any good thing.** (**kai pros pan ergon agathon adokimoi**. `and for every good work unfit')

REL/PROM Although the last part of the participial phrase is joined to the second part by **kai** `and', suggesting equal prominence and function, there are reasons for analyzing the relationship here somewhat differently. **Ergon agathon** `good work/action' is the first occurrence of an important motif or theme of the epistle, "good works." The false teachers not only do not promote good works as Christians should, they are totally unfit to produce any good work. It is interesting that the motif or theme of "good works" comes at the very end of this first paragraph about false teachers (A), as it does at the end of the first section on how Christians should live (B--2:14), the end of the second section on how Christians should live (B'--3:8), and at the very end of the body of the letter, even after the personal, secondary matters are mentioned (3:14). ("Good works" are also mentioned two other places mid-paragraph--2:7 and 3:1.) This repeated occurrence of "good works" at the very end of sections very strongly indicates that this is a prominence-marking device. Thus, in the display text, 1:16e is separated from the other two constituents of the participial construction.

CONT **Ergon agathon** `good work' should probably be taken quite generically. "Good work(s)" occurs often in the Pastoral Epistles with the noun **ergon** and the adjective **agathon**, or the adjective **kalon**, and often in the plural. With either adjective, the meaning is basically the same, as shown by their use in 1 Tim. 5:10a and b where **ergois kalois** and **panti ergō agathō** have the same reference--the good deeds of the widow. In some contexts, these words refer to acts of charity, whether it be the giving of gifts and aid to help people in need, as in 1 Timothy 6:18 and Titus 3:14, or helping people in other ways, as in 1 Timothy 5:10a. In other contexts, they refer to the good work of properly teaching, correcting, and training people in righteousness (2 Tim. 3:17, cf. 1 Tim. 3:1). (If "man of God" in 2 Tim. 3:17 is taken to mean the individual Christian rather than the teacher, then there is still some question as to whether **ergon agathon** would mean good works as something beneficial to others, or good actions in general.) In Titus, 3:14 is the only reference that specifically relates to doing good to supply the needs of others. The other references (1:16; 2:7,14; 3:1,8) appear to be more generic, though 3:1 probably refers either to doing good deeds to benefit others, or good work done for those in authority. It seems very possible that the reference in 1:16 refers not only to good works done to help others, but also to good behavior in general. The false teachers are described as detestable, disobedient, and **pros pan ergon agathon adokimoi** 'unfit for any good deed', or as NIV translates it, "unfit for doing anything good." They deny God by their actions (**ergois**), and they are unable to do any good deed/action (**ergon**). Or more freely, they show that they do not know God by the bad things they do; in fact, they aren't even able to do one good thing. This certainly seems to indicate that **ergon agathon** here refers not only to good done on the behalf of others, but also to good behavior in general. **Erga agatha** (or **kala**) 'good works' (or its singular form), then, is not to be understood as a stereotyped form that always refers to good done on the behalf of others, but as a construction that is both potentially more generic and also more versatile, i.e., less stereotyped (as the fact that both **agatha** and **kala** occur with **erga** also might suggest). In Christian usage in English, "good works" is more stereotyped and tends to mean only good done on the behalf of others.

CONT "Unfit, unqualified" (**adokimoi**) is probably best rendered as "unable to do," since that is the basic meaning of "unfit" or "unqualified," and it is more universal in its ability to be directly translated into other languages.

DIVISION CONSTITUENT 2:1-14 (Section) (Role: Head B of 1:10--3:11)

THEME: Teach and urge the believers to behave in a manner which is consistent with the correct teachings, in order that people will perceive that the teachings about God our(inc) Savior are very good, and since God very graciously sent Jesus Christ to earth in order that God might save all people and since God graciously trains us(inc) to behave in a godly manner.

DISPLAY

RELATIONAL STRUCTURE	CONTENT
HEAD	(2:1-10) Teach and urge the believers to behave in a manner which is consistent with the correct teachings in order that people will perceive that the teachings about God our(inc) Savior are very good,
grounds	(2:11-14) and since God very graciously sent Jesus Christ to earth in order that God might save all people and since God graciously trains us(inc) to behave in a godly manner.

BOUNDARIES AND COHERENCE

For the initial boundary, see Boundaries and Coherence for 1:10-16.

2:1-14 coheres as a hortatory unit (2:1-10) supported by a grounds unit (2:11-14). Gar, which commonly marks grounds, occurs at the beginning of 2:11, and the statements in 2:11-14 that are naturally prominent (2:11-12a,14a) are semantically supportive of the exhortations of 2:1-10. This is shown within the paragraph itself by the fact that the hina purpose clauses (2:12b-c, 14b-d), dependent on two of the naturally prominent statements, 2:12a and 2:14a, express the essence of the exhortations--self-controlled, upright, godly behavior (2:12b-c) and sinless, holy people eager for good works (2:14b-d). In other words, there is a logical progression of exhortation-->grounds/means-->purpose, where both the exhortation and the purpose express godly living.

After the grounds unit of 2:11-14 which has no imperatives or explicit hortatory statements, there comes a grammatical sentence followed by a shorter sentence clearly connected to it. These two sentences (2:15) function as a unit. Each of the four verbal forms of this unit (**lalei** `speak, teach'; **parakalei** `exhort, urge'; **elegche** `correct, reprove'; and **periphroneitō** `disregard, despise') are imperatives, indicating a clear change from supportive material to hortatory material. Though 3:1-2 is also hortatory as shown by the imperative **hupomimnēske** `remind' followed by infinitives expressing the content of what the believers are to be reminded to do, there are basic differences between 2:15 and 3:1-2:

1. Tauta `these things' (2:15a) is the only word that expresses the content of the commands of 2:15 and it is generic, while 3:1-2 deals with a number of specific subjects.
2. 2:15 deals more with the manner of the teaching (**meta pasēs epitagēs** `with full authority', **mēdeis sou periphroneitō** `no one should disregard you') while 3:1-2 deals with the content of the teaching. Paul has been telling Titus what to teach and will continue to do so in chapter three, but in 2:15 he is telling Titus how to teach.

Thus it would seem that 2:15 is a unit in itself.

Before attempting to decide to what unit(s) 2:15 most closely relates, it seems best to determine what the relationship would be. As mentioned above, there is no doubt that 2:15 deals with the *manner* of Titus' teaching. It is to be done with full authority and Titus is to let no one disregard that authority which he represents. It might be asked whether 2:15 possibly has a *summary* role or a *prominence orienter* role. The fact that 2:15 introduces new information--the authority with which Titus is to teach--indicates that the function of 2:15 is not summary alone. SSWC defines the *summary* communication role as the generic repetition of specific information already introduced. If this is a prominence orienter, it is not only stressing the content of the teaching, urging, and correcting, but the fact that the content *must* be taught, urged, and corrected, and that with full authority. Since the information dealing with the manner of the teaching is the only new lexical information in 2:15, we have chosen to label 2:15 as a *manner* constituent.

There is no doubt that 2:15 relates to at least 2:1-10 since the combination of **tauta** `these things' with **lalei** `speak, teach' and **parakalei** `exhort, urge' indicates a definite coherence with the same imperatives occurring in 2:1 and 2:6 respectively, imperatives that govern all of 2:1-10. And the fact that this manner unit comes after 2:14 instead of after 2:10 would suggest that 2:15 relates to all of 2:1-14.

But the third imperative of 2:15, **elegche** `correct, reprove', also occurs in 1:13. (These three imperatives occurring the second time in 2:15 are the only imperatives so far in the epistle.) In using **elegche** here, is Paul consciously thinking of what he has told Titus to do in reference to false teaching in 1:10-16? Certainly, he means for Titus to correct with full authority those who are following false teaching, and it would be that type of people especially who would tend to disregard his authority. Thus, there is good evidence that would support analyzing 2:15 as relating to all of 1:10--2:14.

The next question that comes to mind is, if 2:15 relates to the manner of Titus' teaching, since Titus is also to *teach* the remainder of the material in the epistle (basically 3:1-11; note that 1:5-9 deals with *appointing* elders and not teaching), why shouldn't 2:15 relate to that too? The fact that **tauta** `these things' in this type of a construction typically refers to what has come before (this observation is based on the examples given in the Arndt and Gingrich lexicon) and the fact that the double occurrences of **lalei**, **parakalei**, and **elegche** give coherence to the material preceding and including 2:15 suggests that 2:15 relates much more directly to what precedes it than to what follows.

It appears that Paul in 2:15 has reached a certain peak in the epistle. He has dealt with the false teachers (1:10-16) and then with the teaching of practical godly living (2:1-10) based on the gospel of salvation (2:11-14). After dealing with the appointing of elders, these are the very important points he has wanted to stress. In 2:15 he stresses to Titus the importance of actually carrying out the teaching with full authority, not letting anyone or anything stop him. From this point on Paul expands on these same subjects but does not introduce any new topics that are basically different from those he has already dealt with (except for the secondary matters of 3:12-13). Thus, 3:1-2 adds further exhortations to godly living, 3:3-7 adds further grounds for godly living very similar to those of 2:11-14, and 3:9-11 deals again with problems related to false teaching. This does not mean that everything after 2:15 is anticlimactical since there is another discernible peak at the end of 3:1-8. But it does mean that 2:15 comes at a central point in the body of the letter, and at the very center of the chiastic structure of 1:10--3:11.

Two other structures in the epistle show similarities to 2:15 in its relationship within the chiasmus. The first is that of 1:10-16 where the only imperative comes in the middle of the chiastic structure of that unit, i.e., as C in the structure A B C B′ A′. In the chiastic structure of 1:10--3:11, 2:15 with its four imperatives is also C in an A B C B′ A′ structure. Though 2:1-10 is not in chiastic form, Paul does deal in 2:7-8 with the manner of Titus′ teaching. Though this does not come in the exact middle of the paragraph, it does come with content units both before and after.

Based on all these considerations, we see 2:15 as relating most directly to 1:10--2:14, but also to 3:1-11. It is treated as C in a chiastic structure A B C B′ A′.

Another option would be to take 2:15 as relating only to 2:1-14 and to take 3:8 as somewhat parallel to 2:15 since it, too, comes at the end of an exhortation-grounds section, basically standing outside the content of the teaching and having some reference to the manner of the teaching, though more to the purpose of it. This would make two parallel structures thus:

Exhortation	2:1-10	Exhortation	3:1-2
grounds	2:11-14	grounds	3:3-7
prominence orienter(?)	2:15	prominence orienter(?)	3:8

1:10--3:11 would still be in chiastic arrangement but in A B B′ A′ arrangement. 2:15 would be a part of B instead of being C as in the first analysis above.

One problem with this second option is that 2:15 and 3:8 really seem to have different roles. 2:15 has a manner role while 3:8 appears to be a restatement of 3:1-7. Secondly, 2:15 appears to relate back to more than just 2:1-14 as mentioned above.

PROMINENCE AND THEME

Since 2:1-10 is hortatory throughout while 2:11-14 is the grounds for these exhortations, 2:1-10 is more naturally prominent, and its theme should form at least the basic part of the theme statement for 2:1-14. On this level it seems best to include the theme of the grounds paragraph. Certainly, the great statements Paul makes about grace and salvation and the appearances of Christ in 2:11-14 are important grounds for holy living.

The three motivational purpose constituents of 2:1-10 (5b, 8b-c, 10c) also need to be considered as possible inclusions in the theme statement for 2:1-14 since they, like the grounds paragraph, form the motivation for the exhortations of 2:1-10. They each come at the end of their constituents, but the final purpose clause, coming at the most strategic place at the very end of the paragraph, represents the other two well. It is positive rather than negative like the first one, and is more generic than the second. So a slightly shortened form of it, "in order that people will perceive that the teachings about God our(inc) Savior are very good," is included in the theme. While the inclusion of the motivational purpose makes for a long theme statement, it rounds out the basic structure and essential theme of the section.

SECTION CONSTITUENT 2:1-10 (Paragraph) (Role: Head of 2:1-14)

THEME: Teach and urge the believers to behave in a manner which is consistent with the correct teachings in order that people will perceive that the teachings about God our(inc) Savior are very good.

DISPLAY

RELATIONAL STRUCTURE	CONTENT
HEAD	(2:1) But as for you, teach (the believers) what is consistent with the correct teachings.
spec.$_1$ — HEAD$_1$	(2:2a) (Specifically, tell) the older men (that they should) be temperate, (that they should) behave in such a manner that all people will respect them, (that they should) be self-controlled.
spec.$_1$ — HEAD$_2$	(2:2b) (And tell them that they should) firmly believe in the correct teachings, (that they should) sincerely love (others), (and that they should) always be steadfast.
spec.$_2$ — HEAD$_1$ — HEAD	(2:3a) (As for) the older women, similarly, (tell them that they should) behave in a holy, reverent manner;
spec.$_2$ — HEAD$_1$ — spec.$_{1-2}$ (neg.)	(2:3b) (specifically, they should) not slander (others) (and they should) not be addicted to (drinking) much wine.
spec.$_2$ — HEAD$_2$ — HEAD	(2:3c) (Tell them that they should) teach (the younger women) what is good,
spec.$_2$ — HEAD$_2$ — purpose — ORIENTER	(2:4a) in order that they may train the younger women
spec.$_2$ — HEAD$_2$ — purpose — CONTENT — HEAD	(2:4b-5a) to love (their) husbands (and) love (their) children, (5a) to be self-controlled (and) chaste, to be good workers at home (and) submissive to their own husbands.
spec.$_2$ — HEAD$_2$ — purpose — CONTENT — purpose	(2:5b) (The younger women should behave like this (2:4b-5a)) in order that the message about God will not be spoken against (by anyone).
spec.$_3$	(2:6) As for the younger men, similarly, urge them to be self-controlled in all things.
manner — HEAD$_1$	(2:7a) You yourself (must continually) do what is good in order that (others) will see how they should behave.
manner — HEAD$_2$	(2:7b-8a) Teach sincerely (and) seriously, (8a) (and) teach what is correct which no one can (justly) criticize.
manner — purpose	(2:8b-c) (Do this (2:7a-8a)) in order that anyone who opposes (us(inc)) may be put to shame (8c) (because) there will be nothing bad that he can (justly) say about us(inc).
spec.$_4$ — HEAD	(2:9a) as for slaves, (specifically, urge them) to be submissive to their masters in everything.
spec.$_4$ — spec.$_1$ — HEAD	(2:9b) (Specifically, they should) please (them (their masters));
spec.$_4$ — spec.$_1$ — spec. (neg.)	(2:9c) (in particular, they (slaves) should) not refuse (to obey them (their masters)).
spec.$_4$ — spec.$_2$ — spec. (neg.)	(2:10a) (Specifically, they (slaves) should) not pilfer (things that belong to their masters),
spec.$_4$ — spec.$_2$ — HEAD	(2:10b) instead (they (the slaves) should) always be completely honest/reliable (and thus) show (their masters that they (their masters)) can completely trust them.
spec.$_4$ — purpose	(2:10c) (They (slaves) should behave like this (2:9a-10b)) in order that by means of all (they (the slaves) do) (people) will perceive that the teachings about God our(inc) Savior are very good.

BOUNDARIES AND COHERENCE

For the initial boundary, see Boundaries and Coherence for 1:10-16.

1:10-16 ends with a description of the ungodly behavior of the false teachers. They are defiled, they profess to know God but deny him by their actions, they are detestable, disobedient, and unfit for any good work. As de at the beginning of 2:1 suggests, the topic changes now to one that is in contrast to these false teachers, their behavior and their teachings. Instead of the false teachings of these men, Titus is to "teach those things which accord with sound teaching/doctrine" (**Su de lalei ha prepei tē hugiainousē didaskalia**).

Paul has now come to the second general topic he wants to discuss under the subject of doctrine, the teaching of sound doctrine. He has introduced this in a tail-head link in 1:9b with **hina dunatos ē...parakalein en tē didaskalia tē hugiainousē** 'in order that he might be able to encourage in sound doctrine'. But he has first discussed the subject of refuting those who oppose sound doctrine (1:10-16) which had been introduced in 1:9c in the same general tail-head link.

The coherence of this paragraph is clearly shown by the orderly listing of each of five social strata within the church and by the common semantic domain of the words used to describe the behavior expected of Christians in each of these categories. The words with the root **sōphron-** are the most frequent (2:2,4,5,6). They represent the idea of "sensible judgment, self-control."

Grammatical unity is reflected in the use of the imperative mood to encode the speech orienters (**lalei** 'speak/teach' 2:1, **parakalei** 'exhort/encourage' 2:6), followed by the infinitives to encode the content of the orienters (**einai** 'to be' 2:2,4,9; **sōphronein** 'to be self-controlled' 2:6; and **hupotassesthai** 'to be submissive' 2:9). The two imperatives **lalei** 'speak' and **parakalei** 'exhort' grammatically govern the whole paragraph.

Relational coherence is seen by the use of the comparative **hōsautōs** 'likewise' at the beginning of the second and third specifics (2:3,6), thereby connecting the first, second, and third specifics, and thus also connecting the unit governed by **lalei** (2:1-5) to that governed by **parakalei** (2:6-10).

The following factors indicate that there is a boundary between this paragraph and the next one at the end of 2:10:

1. There is a change of subject matter from the Cretan Christians' prescribed character (2:10) to the basis for that character, namely, the saving grace of God (2:11-14).
2. Accompanying this change of subject matter is a change from present to aorist tense. In 2:1-10, twenty out of twenty-two verbal forms are present tense; while in 2:11-14, six out of eight verbal forms are aorist tense.
3. There is a change from hortatory to expository genre. In 2:1-10, the two main verbs, **lalei** 'speak' (2:1) and **parakalei** 'exhort' (2:6), are imperative in mood. The content of what Titus is commanded to "speak" and "exhort" is given in infinitive forms (2:2,6,9) expressing how people to be addressed by Titus are to behave. These, in turn, are elaborated by participial clauses and other subordinate clauses, giving further expectations or intended outcomes of the commanded behavior. However, in 2:11-14, the main verb **epephanē** 'has appeared' (2:11) is indicative and the verb governing the relative clause beginning in 2:14 (**edōken** 'gave') is also indicative. All other verbal forms are directly or indirectly subordinate to these two.
4. Relationally, **gar** 'for' in 2:11 introduces paragraph 2:11-14 as a grounds for the previous paragraph.

STRUCTURE

Although five different classes within the church are to be instructed in 2:2-10, i.e., the older men, the older women, the younger women, the younger men, and the slaves, the surface structure divides 2:2-10 into only four units, including the younger women in the same unit with the older women. Also, the remarks to Titus in 2:7-8 on the manner of his teaching are included in the surface unit that starts at the beginning of 2:6 with the instruction for the younger men. The structural markers for the four surface structure units are:

1. Forefronting of the topics:

presbutas	'old(er) men'	2:2a
presbutidas	'old(er) women'	2:3a
tous neōterous	'younger men'	2:6
doulous	'slaves'	2:9a

2. Each of these units has, as its first verbal form(s), either an imperative and infinitive (parakalei sōphronein 'urge to be self-controlled' 2:6), an infinitive that relates directly back to one of the two imperatives of the paragraph (**einai** 'to be' 2:2, **hupotassesthai** 'be submissive to' 2:9a); or the comparative adverb **hōsautōs** 'likewise' (2:3a,6).

The constituent that deals with the younger women has none of the above characteristics in 1 and 2 but starts as a **hina** purpose clause subordinated to the part about the older women--**hina sōphronizōsin tas neas philandrous einai**...'in order that they may train the younger women to love their husbands...'

A further detail of the structure of these units is that the second and fourth end with motivational purposes (2:5b, 2:10c), while another motivational purpose comes at the end of the surface structure unit that includes the younger men and Titus' manner of teaching (2:8b-c). Each of these purpose clauses deals with how the outside world should view the church.

In the diagram of the relational structure, each of these four groups is labelled "specific," i.e., $specific_1$, $specific_2$, $specific_3$, $specific_4$. It must be realized, however, that these four "specific" units are actually four groupings of specifics of 2:1, "teach what is consistent with the correct teachings," organized around these four classes within the church.

PROMINENCE AND THEME

Since the generic Head of the paragraph (2:1), "Teach (the believers) what is consistent with the correct teachings," clearly includes each constituent that has been analyzed as a specific, i.e., all of the rest of the paragraph except for 2:7-8, 2:1 is the basic theme of the paragraph.

Behavior is very central to the theme of the paragraph as a whole. Since each of the specifics deals with what is to be taught the believers in respect to their behavior, whereas the generic ha 'those (things) which' (are consistent with the correct teachings) does not make this explicit, the factor of behavior is included in the theme.

2:7-8, the constituent dealing with the manner of Titus' teaching rather than being a specific of 2:1, does not appear to be marked prominent, so is not included in the theme. However, the inclusion of one of the specifics of that manner constituent, such as "sincerely" (see 2:7b), in the theme would very succinctly represent this part of the paragraph, "Sincerely teach..." It would also make a good contrast with the insincerity of the false teachers.

There is a question as to whether a representation of the three motivational purpose clauses (2:5b, 2:8b-c, 2:10c), coming at the end of each of three of the main constituents of the paragraph and all dealing with how the outside world views the believers and their doctrine, should be included in the theme. This repetition of the same general motivational purpose marks it as prominent and so it is included in the theme statement.

NOTES ON 2:1-10

2:1. **But as for you, teach (the believers) what is consistent with the correct teachings.** (**Su de lalei ha prepei tē hugiainousē didaskalia.** 'but you(sg) speak that-which is-consistent-with the sound teaching')

REL **De** along with the forefronted free form of the second person singular pronoun, **su** 'you', does not indicate contrast at the section level but a tail-head contrastive link across the boundary between 1:10-16 and 2:1-14. In contrast with the false teachers' doctrine and negative traits, especially as stated in 1:15-16, Titus is to teach the believers what is consistent with sound doctrine.

That de does not signal a section-level contrast is shown by the incongruity of the following: *"You must rigorously convince those who follow false teaching that they are wrong, but, as for you, teach the believers what is consistent with sound doctrine." These two actions which are to be taken by Titus are not in contrast. They are two things which he must do. At the same time, de and the forefronted free form of the pronoun probably also indicate a change in topic from how Titus is to deal with false teaching to how he is to teach the believers sound doctrine.

CONT One question on this verse is whether the standard of reference, "the sound teaching/doctrine" (note the article in **tē hugiainousē didaskalia**) with which Titus' teaching is to be consistent, includes both teachings about moral conduct and the theological doctrines of the gospel or basically refers to the theological doctrines of the gospel of salvation that Paul will be discussing in 2:11-14 and 3:3-7, and which are there clearly seen to be the basis for godly living. As for the latter viewpoint, Erdman says, "Titus is to give practical instruction as to moral conduct which is consistent with the gospel and indeed is inspired by its truths." This viewpoint is consistent with the restatement of the theme of 3:3-7 as found in 3:8, "I want you to confidently teach the believers this trustworthy message [that God has mercifully saved us] in order that they will be constantly concerned with doing what is good for others." (See discussion on that section theme.) The three motivational purpose clauses of this paragraph also appear to be built on a closely related truth--godly living reveals correct theological doctrine--expressed in what is, in effect, a double negative in the purpose clause of 2:5b, live godly lives "in order that the word of God may not be discredited"; expressed in 2:8b-c as "in order that any opponent will be ashamed having nothing bad to say against us"; and in 2:10c as "in order that by means of all (they (the slaves) do) (people) will perceive that the teachings about God our(inc) Savior are very good." Notice how this contrasts with 1:16, "They (false teachers) deny God by their actions." Finally, it must be said that, although it may very well be that Paul means by **tē hugiainousē didaskalia** the theological doctrines of the gospel on which all moral conduct should be based (especially when considered on the basis of the epistle as a whole), these two ideas of moral conduct and theological doctrine are so closely connected that it is very difficult to say that one is in focus and not the other in **tē hugiainousē didaskalia**, especially because there is no compelling factor in the immediate context to help make the decision.

CONT **Lalei**, literally "speak," is often translated in this verse as "teach." "Speak" does not collocate very well in English with a teaching situation as this obviously is, though **lalei** apparently was able to do so in Greek (cf. Mark 2:2, **elalei autois ton logon** `he taught/preached the word to them').

Lalei is a present imperative. Titus is commanded to continuously teach the believers what is appropriate conduct in relation to the correct teaching of the gospel.

CONT For the meaning of **hugiainousē**, literally "sound," see notes on 1:9b. **Didaskalia**, literally "that which is taught, teaching," in contexts such as this one is often translated as "doctrine." The fact that **tē hugiainousē didaskalia** here refers to a standard of reference suggests that "doctrine" would be a proper translation. Notice that the focus here would have to be doctrine in the sense of that which is taught (or revealed) rather than the sense of that which is believed.

2:2a. **(Specifically, tell) the older men (that they should) be temperate, (that they should) behave in such a manner that all people will respect them, (that they should) be self-controlled. (presbutas nēphalious einai, semnous, sōphronas**, `old-men temperate to-be, worthy-of-respect, self-controlled')

REL The basic relationship between 2:1 and 2:2-10 is that of generic-specifics. The specific things that are to be taught the various groups within the church are all included in **ha prepei tē hugiainousē didaskalia** `what is consistent with sound doctrine'. This can be seen by the fact that **ha prepei tē hugiainousē didaskalia** and the infinitives of 2:1-5 all relate directly back to **lalei** `speak'. (In 2:6 **parakalei** `urge' replaces **lalei**, and the infinitives relate back to **parakalei** but ultimately back to **lalei**.) Ellicott remarks, "The infinitive with the accusative specifies the substance of the order which was contained in what Titus was to enunciate."

CONT Although **lalei** was rendered in 2:1 as "teach," it seems more appropriate (in English) to use "tell" here when dealing with the specific things which Titus must encourage in the believers. **Parakalei** `exhort, urge, encourage' in 2:6 is apparently meant to be quite synonymous with **lalei** in 2:1, which would indicate that **lalei**, literally "speak," has a full hortatory sense here.

CONT Regarding **presbutas** `old men', apart from his discussion of the slaves, Paul divides all the members of the Cretan church into four divisions by the use of two factors, age and sex. Since the age factor is dichotomous, and we would expect Paul to have in mind men and women of all ages, in English "older" and "younger" men and women would be more correct than "old" men and women and "young" men and women.

CONT The first characteristic to be required of the older men is that they be **nēphalios**. It is very difficult to determine, however, if this word is to be taken in its literal sense of "temperate or sober in the use of wine," or in its figurative sense of "well-balanced, self-controlled." The following data support the figurative sense of **nēphalios** here:

1. The corresponding verbal form, nēphō 'be sober, be well-balanced, be self-controlled' occurs six times in the New Testament (1 Thess. 5:6,8; 2 Tim. 4:5; 1 Pet. 1:13; 4:7; 5:8), always in its figurative sense. One of these occurrences is in the Pastorals, 2 Tim. 4:5. This shows that the verbal form at least, at the time of and in the context of the New Testament, either was used wholly figuratively or that the figurative sense was a very strong one.
2. In three of the nine occurrences of **nēphalios** and nēphō in the New Testament (**nēphalios** occurs elsewhere in the New Testament only in 1 Tim. 3:2,11), the word occurs either contiguous to, or in close proximity to, either **sōphroneō** 'be self-controlled' (1 Pet. 4:7) or **sōphrōn** 'self-controlled' (1 Tim. 3:2; Titus 2:2), a quality that is similar in meaning to the figurative sense of nēphō and **nēphalios**.

   The meaning of nēphō in the New Testament, "be well-balanced, be self-controlled," is, of course, determined by the contexts in which it occurs; these contexts show clearly that the figurative sense is intended. However, the adjective form **nēphalios** always occurs in lists where it is more difficult to determine the context. But, even in lists, there is a tendency for words of similar meaning to occur contiguously instead of in a haphazard conglomeration with no perceptible ordering. If one looks closely at the desired characteristics of the older men, it is obvious that the six qualities mentioned are divided into two parts. Those three of the first part depend on the infinitive **einai** 'to be' while the second three depend on, and are qualified by, the participle **hugiainontas** 'being sound'--"sound in faith, (sound) in love, (sound) in perseverance." **Hugiainontas** thus binds the second part together grammatically and semantically. The first part is bound together grammatically by **einai** 'to be' which is very weak semantically. It is very likely, then, that the semantic component that binds the first three qualities together is similarity in meaning.

It seems that **nēphalios** in its figurative or wider sense is indicated here unless it can be proven that its adjectival form always occurred in Greek in its literal sense, i.e., only in reference to the use of wine. Since there is no strong evidence for this (indeed it would be hard to prove that it was never used in a figurative or wider sense), the word "temperate" without qualification to the use of wine is used in the display text. By thus choosing the generic form, a word is being used that may well be very close to the meaning of **nēphalios** in the New Testament and, at the same time, it indirectly includes temperance in the use of wine.

CONT/TRNS The second characteristic that is to be required of the older men is that they be **semnos** (found elsewhere in the New Testament in 1 Tim. 3:8,11; Phil. 4:8; cognate noun **semnotēs** found in 1 Tim. 2:2; 3:4; Titus 2:7). The difficulty in understanding the precise meaning of this word is perhaps because it has no exact one-word eqivalent in English. **Semnos** designates a person who has those moral characteristics that are respected by others. He is respected because of the moral quality of his life, not because of the position he holds or any seemingly pleasing outward deportment that is not based on inner moral quality. This might be rendered as "(that they should live lives) worthy of respect" or, in more propositionalized form, "(that they should) behave in such a manner that all people will respect them." Regarding translation into other languages, no doubt in some, a one-word equivalent for **semnos** will be found, but it should focus on moral qualities rather than other factors that promote respect in the particular society.

CONT/TRNS Arndt and Gingrich give as the meaning of **sōphrōn** 'prudent, thoughtful, self-controlled'. It occurs also in 1:8 and 2:5. The cognate verb

sōphronein occurs in 2:6 and the cognate adverb **sōphronōs** in 2:12. From these uses (and especially from the fact that it is the only quality mentioned to be encouraged in the younger men), it appears to be quite a generic term for self-control. It includes self-control in one's sex life (which seems to be the meaning in 2:5), and it possibly is being used in contrast to the venting of such passions as anger and self-will in 1:7-8. It would be difficult to say how this word contrasts with **nēphalios** in that word's wider sense of "temperate, self-controlled." Whereas one might expect that **nēphalios** would retain some of its original sense of temperance in the use of wine and thus its wider meaning would take off from that point of reference, the use of the cognate **nēphō** in 2 Tim. 4:5 seems to indicate a much wider meaning. Note that NIV translates **nēphe** there as "Keep your head [in all situations]" and TEV translates as "you must keep control of yourself [in all circumstances]."

All in all, there does not seem to be a lot of difference between the meaning of **sōphrōn** and that of **nēphalios** in its wider sense. In translation into other languages, there would seem to be no problem, however, in taking **nēphalios** in the sense of self-control in such things as drinking wine, and taking **sōphrōn** as self-control in a wider sense.

2:2b. **(And tell them that they should) firmly believe in the correct teachings, (that they should) sincerely love (others), (and that they should) always be steadfast. (hugiainontas tē pistei, tē agapē, tē hupomonē.** 'being-sound in-the faith, in-the love, in-the steadfastness')

CONT In 2:2b, there is skewing between the deep structure and its surface representation. While the participle **hugiainontas** 'being sound' is the grammatical head of 2:2b, semantically the meaning represented by the nouns is more nuclear, and "sound" is the intended modifier of each of them. See the note on 1:9b for discussion of the meaning of **hugiainō** 'be sound'.

CONT Some commentators take **hugiainontas tē pistei** 'being sound in the faith' as "subjective" while others say the "objective" sense is intended. Kelly says, "he is not referring to correctness of doctrine, 'faith' being equivalent to 'the faith', but to the old men's subjective attitude; this is borne out by the subjective connotation of the two other nouns." But the application of a typical subjective-objective contrast may not be telling the whole story here. Is the basic question whether **hugiainontas** 'being sound' modifies the way they believe (subjective) or what they believe (objective)? Or can any subjective faith be sound or correct if it is not based on correct objective faith, i.e., doctrine? It is inconceivable that Paul would have as one of his main themes of the full discourse (epistle), and especially of this section (cf. 2:1), the theme of teaching sound doctrine, and would not have any special reference to this when he says that the older men should be **hugiainontas tē pistei** 'sound in the faith'. In verse one, this sound doctrine is dealt with from the teaching perspective, **lalei ha prepei tē hugiainousē didaskalia** 'speak that which is consistent with sound teaching'; while here, it is dealt with from the believing perspective. At the same time, Paul no doubt means that that correct belief should be a firm belief; a lukewarm belief in sound doctrine is not enough. Thus, the display text rendering is, "(And tell them that they should) firmly believe in the correct teachings."

CONT There seems to be no question that **hugiainontas...tē agapē** 'being sound...in love' means to sincerely love. The intended object of that love may well be other people, since the main purpose clauses of the paragraph indicate that one of the motivations for behaving in a consistent manner with sound doctrine is so that outsiders will be favorably impressed with Christians and their doctrine (cf. especially 2:5b and 2:10c). However, there is no reason why love for God could not also be intended (though not to the exclusion of love for other people), especially since **pistis** 'faith' and **hupomonē** 'steadfastness' are qualities that deal with God rather than men.

CONT "Sound in steadfastness" does not collocate in English quite as well as "sound in the faith." However, the meaning is quite clear, "being truly steadfast," "completely steadfast," or "always steadfast."

TRNS Does Paul have some special context in mind when he mentions steadfastness? Is it steadfastness in the faith in the face of so many influences that would seek to weaken or destroy their faith? Or, is it steadfastness in the faith in the face of persecution? It would seem best to keep the translation into another language rather generic, if possible, since there is nothing in the immediate context to indicate what particular situations Paul might have had in mind. However, if, in any language, the idea of steadfastness cannot be expressed without specifying a context, steadfastness in the faith in the face of those teaching opposing doctrine would most likely be the appropriate context, since this is one of the major themes of the epistle. Gealy remarks, "steadfastness in the context means primarily unwavering loyalty to the received faith."

2:3a. **(As for) the older women, similarly, (tell them that they should) behave in a holy, reverent manner;** (**presbutidas hōsautōs en katastēmati hieroprepeis**, 'old-women likewise in behavior reverent')

REL The occurrence of the initial accusative **presbutidas** 'old women' identifies them as the topic of the second group in the church to be instructed in proper behavior. **Hōsautōs** 'likewise, similarly' acts as a connecting link grammatically between the first two constituent groups, while semantically it shows that what is to be taught each group is generically similar. Here, and in 2:6, it is very awkward to propositionalize using both "specifically" and "similarly" together, so "specifically" is omitted.

CONT The behavior (**katastēmati**) of the older women is to be **hieroprepeis**, a word that can mean "befitting a holy person or thing, holy, worthy of reverence," or here perhaps may even have the specialized meaning of "like a priest(ess)" (Arndt and Gingrich). (It is a word that occurs only here in the New Testament.) Here, it is in the context of moral character, so must at least have the sense of "holy." The question is whether an additional component of "priestly dignity" or "reverence" is also intended here. Is the intended meaning similar to that of **semnos** 'worthy of respect' that is required of the older men? That is, does Paul specifically have in mind that both older men and women should have that holiness of character that permeates their whole lives and gives them a dignity that is respected by all? It seems that this very possibly was Paul's meaning. A translation, then, would need to carry both the component of "holy" and a component of "priestly dignity" or "reverence." The best rendering may be "(As for) the older women (tell them that they should) behave in a holy, reverent manner." "Reverent" here should have the sense of the outward working of holiness in all areas of life--deportment, speech, dress.

2:3b. (specifically, they should) not slander (others) (and they should) not be addicted to (drinking) much wine. (mē diabolous mē oinō pollō dedoulōmenas, 'not slanderous not to-much wine enslaved')

REL The first two phrases following **en katastēmati hieroprepeis** 'in behavior reverent' are negative specifics of this generic phrase. Women who slander others and are addicted to wine are certainly the exact opposite of what a holy, reverent woman should be. As mentioned in the discussion of 1:6d, Paul appears to use a recurring pattern in Titus of a positive generic followed by two or more negative specifics. 1:7 and 1:13c-14 are clear examples of this. 1:6d-f may also be an example, and our present case in 2:3a-b certainly seems to be one. But is the fourth requirement of the older women, **kalodidaskalous** 'teaching what is good', a third specific of **en katastēmati hieroprepeis** 'in behavior reverent', or does it have some other relationship to it? It has been analyzed here as a separate Head from 2:3a and its negative specifics since:

1. The generic-specific relationship between **en katastēmati hieroprepeis** 'in behavior reverent' and **kalodidaskalous** 'teaching what is good' is not especially obvious.
2. The positive generic with the two negative specifics form a coherent unit.
3. **Kalodidaskalous** 'teaching what is good' begins the reference to a new semantic domain which is now to be discussed, the training of the younger women. Granted **kalodidaskalous** could be considered as a tail-head link to this new topic, but it seems to act better as a second Head rather than a third specific. The older women are (a) to be holy in behavior themselves and (b) trainers of the younger women in correct behavior.

However, **kalodidaskalous** 'teaching what is good' could alternatively be considered as a third specific of 2:3a.

CONT The participle **dedoulōmenas** 'enslaved' is used in a metaphorical sense meaning "addicted." It is a dead metaphor.

2:3c. (Tell them that they should) teach (the younger women) what is good, (**kalodidaskalous**, 'teaching-what-is-good')

CONT **Kalodidaskalous** could be either an adjective "teaching what is good" or a noun "teachers of what is good." There is not much difference in meaning; formal teaching is, of course, not intended here. **Kalodidaskalos** does not occur elsewhere in the New Testament, nor in any extant Greek literature.

Huther remarks on **kalodidaskalos**, "not so much by example as by exhortation and teaching, as appears from what follows [i.e., the **hina** purpose clause]." This is the interpretation followed in the display; it is discussed more fully under 2:4a.

CONT "The younger women" is supplied as those who are to be taught rather than a more general term such as "others" or "people," because the **hina** purpose clause which depends on **kalodidaskalous** 'teaching what is good' designates the younger women as those who will be trained (**sōphronizōsin**) by the older ones.

2:4a. in order that they may train the younger women (**hina sōphronizōsin tas neas** 'in-order-that they-may-train the young-women')

REL/CONT **Sōphronizōsin** means "train," or "advise, encourage." The context (2:4-5) shows the type of training that is intended, that of right relationships within the home. We have taken the **hina** purpose clause beginning in 2:4a as relating most directly to **kalodidaskalous** 'teaching what is good' rather than relating equally to all components of verse three (which would indicate that the example of the older women as an influence on the younger ones was in focus) for the following reasons:

1. **Sōphronizōsin** 'train, advise, encourage' relates most closely to **didaskalous** 'teachers/teaching' in thought. If the main idea in 2:3-5 were that the older women were only to be an example to the younger women, then an expression indicating this should be expected here (cf. 2:7 where Titus is to be a model of good works). But both words used (**kalodidaskalous**, **sōphronizōsin**) definitely suggest teaching or training by word of mouth rather than by example only.
2. Further, the correlation between the specific qualities encouraged in the older women, "not slandering, not addicted to much wine," and those encouraged in the younger women is not very apparent. The qualities that the younger women are to learn are specifically related to the home--**philandrous** 'husband-loving', **philoteknous** 'children-loving', **oikourgous** 'working at home', **hupotassomenas tois idiois andrasin** 'submitting to their husbands'. And even **sōphronas** 'self-controlled' and **hagnas** 'pure' appear to relate especially to a proper husband-wife relationship. If teaching were only by example, we should expect a closer correlation between the qualities mentioned for the older women and those mentioned for the younger women.

Undoubtedly Paul also has in mind the example of the older women, but this is not the relationship he focuses on here. He is telling the older women to train the younger ones by word of mouth.

2:4b-5a. **to love (their) husbands (and) love (their) children, (5a) to be self-controlled (and) chaste, to be good workers at home (and) submissive to their own husbands. (philandrous einai, philoteknous, sōphronas, hagnas, oikourgous agathas, hupotassomenas tois idiois andrasin**, 'husband-lovers to-be, children-lovers, self-controlled, pure, workers-at-home good, submitting-to their-own husbands')

REL In English the infinitive construction following such words as "train" and "teach" expresses the content of the training or teaching. Here in the Greek text of 2:4-5a, there is a similar construction. There seem to be two differences semantically between this type of orienter-content construction and others. One is that the content is very closely allied with the purpose of the orienter verb--"the older women should train the younger women to love their husbands"; "the older women should train the younger women in order that they will love their husbands." Secondly, and probably related to the first, the natural prominence is not necessarily on the content construction. In the present passage, it seems best to analyze them as having equal prominence, since there is nothing here that would suggest that one is more prominent than the other.

Note that the infinitive construction in English handles the content of such orienters as "train" and "teach" much more naturally and unambiguously than a finite construction beginning with "that" does, though we normally prefer to use finite constructions in the propositionalized text.

CONT The qualities that the younger women are to learn may well be presented in a symmetrical pattern even as those for the older men (see notes on 2:2) and the older women (positives on either end with two negatives in the middle) have been.

The qualities for the younger women appear to be presented in pairs. **Philandrous** `lovers of/loving their husbands', **philoteknous** `lovers of/loving their children' are very obviously a pair, as are **sōphronas** `self-controlled' and **hagnas** `holy, chaste, pure' with their closely related meanings. And if **agathas** `good' is taken as modifying **oikourgous** `workers/working at home', there is a third pair, **oikourgous agathas** `good workers at home' and **hupotassomenas tois idiois andrasin** `submitting to their own husbands'. The outer two pairs deal specifically with relations within the home. (Note that the first and last characteristics deal specifically with relations with their husbands.)

The inner pair seems, at first, more general, but if we accept the following analysis of Arndt and Gingrich, we see that the inner pair is intricately tied up with the other family relationships. Arndt and Gingrich give the following entry for **sōphrōn** after its general entry of "prudent, thoughtful, self-controlled": "Especially of women `chaste, decent, modest.'" And for **hagnos** there is a similar entry: "Especially of women `chaste, pure.'" To have a proper family life, chastity is essential. Thus the whole unit on the younger women has to do with right relationships within the family.

Of the words found in this unit of 2:4b-5a, **philandros** `loving her husband', **philoteknos** `loving one's children', and **oikourgos** `working at home' are not found elsewhere in the New Testament.

CONT/TXT There is a variant for **oikourgous** `workers/working at home' in some texts, **oikourous**. Liddell and Scott give the meaning of **oikourous** as "the mistress of the house." The difference in meaning in this context between the two variants would be slight.

"Good workers at home" or "good mistresses of the house" would both suggest that not only should the younger women spend most of their time at home (cf. 1 Tim. 5:13), but that the time spent there should be taken up with faithfully carrying out the duties necessary for good family life.

2:5b. (The younger women should behave like this (2:4b-5a)) in order that the message about God will not be spoken against (by anyone). (hina mē ho logos tou theou blasphēmētai. `in-order-that the word of-the God not be-blasphemed')

REL This **hina** purpose clause is analyzed as relating directly back to 2:4b-5a, i.e., the qualities the younger women should learn, since it can be seen that there is a very close relationship between how well their lives are lived and the reaction of the unbelievers to their lives. There is ultimately a relationship back to 2:3c and 2:4a, but it is an indirect relationship. The only way that the teaching of the older women can be related to the purpose clause is through the behavior of the younger women. We may try to represent all these relationships by supplying at 2:5b as follows, "(The older women should train the younger women to behave like this) in order that the message about God will not be spoken against (by anyone)," but even this places too much emphasis on the teaching of the older women and not enough on the lives of the younger ones. It is the lives of the younger women that will discredit or not discredit the gospel.

At the same time, there is no obvious reason for relating the **hina** purpose clause only to the sixth requirement (submission to husbands) rather than to all six of them.

CONT/TRNS Ho logos tou theou `the word of God' here refers to that message which is both from God and about God, the gospel in general and no special facet of it. The three motivational purposes of this paragraph (5b, 8b-c, 10c) show that Paul is very concerned that the message of God not be discredited, but that the behavior of those professing to believe that message be such that the world will recognize the word of God for what it truly is. Thus, for those languages which can translate "the word of God" rather generically, that would seem to be the best way to handle it. For those languages that must translate either "the word from God" or "the word about God," the latter is the better translation unless the former in any language also carries the idea that the message is also about God.

CONT Blasphēmētai means "blaspheme, defame, discredit, malign." If the younger women who claim to be believers do not learn to practice the traits mentioned in 2:4b-5a, unbelievers will certainly discredit the gospel.

2:6. **As for the younger men, similarly, urge them to be self-controlled in all things.** (tous neōterous hōsautōs parakalei sōphronein: peri panta `the younger-men similarly urge to-be-self-controlled in-respect-to all(things)')

REL The forefronted tous neōterous `the younger men' indicates the new topic. Hōsautōs `similarly, likewise' grammatically links this new unit with the prior ones and semantically indicates similarity in subject matter. As in 2:3a, "specifically" is omitted here in the display text since it is too awkward to use both "specifically" and "similarly" together. And here, the second imperative of the paragraph, parakalei `urge', substitutes for the first, lalei `speak, teach' (2:1), and governs the rest of the paragraph grammatically.

CONT The only quality which is directly indicated as to be encouraged in the younger men is that of self-control. Notice that this is a quality that Titus is also to encourage in the older men (2:2) and the younger women (2:5). For Paul, this quality (which is also mentioned in 1:8) is one that is very essential in the present situation in Crete and the Christian life in general.

CONT Parakalei `exhort, encourage, urge' is, like lalei (2:1), a present imperative form indicating that Titus should continuously be exhorting the younger men.

REL It is not obvious whether peri panta `in all respects, concerning all things' should modify seauton parechomenos tupon kalōn ergōn `showing yourself a model of good works' or sōphronein `to be self-controlled', i.e., "in all things showing yourself a model of good works" or "to be self-controlled in all things." Modifying either one makes good sense, but we have analyzed peri panta as modifying sōphronein `to be self-controlled' for the following reasons:

1. It appears that Paul is using a generic quality here (sōphronein `to be self-controlled') instead of a number of specific qualities to indicate what is to be required of the younger men. Thus, we would expect the general statement peri panta `in all respects' to further broaden the scope of Paul's requirements for the younger men, something he does in other units by using specifics.
2. If peri panta modifies sōphronein which it immediately follows, then seauton `yourself' comes at the very beginning of the constituent about Titus. It comes in the forefronted topic position which is the place it would be expected to occur. All the other major topics of this paragraph are forefronted to the very first position in their unit: presbutas `old(er) men' (2:2), presbutidas `old(er)

women' (2:3), **tous neōterous** 'the younger men' (2:6), and **doulous** 'slaves' (2:9). Also, **presbutas** and **doulous** have no other grammatical features except forefronting to mark a new topic, as would be the case with **seauton** here. Just as we would not expect **en pasin** 'in all things' to occur before the topicalized **doulous** 'slaves' in 2:9, we should not expect **peri panta** 'in all respects' to occur before **seauton** here.

In research on **en pasin** 'in all things', **en panti** 'in everything', and **peri pantōn** 'in respect to all things', there were no examples of any of them occurring before a topic in the listings in the Arndt and Gingrich lexicon. **Peri pantōn**, however, does occur sentence initial (after the vocative) in 3 John chapter 2.

Peri 'concerning, in respect to' does itself mark topics, but, when it does so, it occurs with the genitive and almost always is followed by **de**. Here in Titus 2:7, **panta** is accusative, there is no **de**, and **panta** cannot be shown semantically to be the topic of the unit.

2:7a. **You yourself (must continually) do what is good in order that (others) will see how they should behave.** (**seauton parechomenos tupon kalōn ergōn**, 'showing yourself(sg) a-model of-good works')

REL Many see the exhortation that Paul addresses to Titus about his own life in 2:7-8 as actually part of the unit on the younger men. Titus, because he is a younger man himself, should be an example to other young men (**seauton parechomenos tupon kalōn ergōn** 'showing yourself a model/pattern of good works'). Thus, the remarks are made more to instruct the younger men than to instruct Titus himself, since Titus himself is the teacher, as can be seen by **lalei** 'you(sg) teach' (2:1) and **parakalei** 'you(sg) urge'. The fact that 2:7-8 is a participial construction depending on the main verb **parakalei** 'urge' (2:6) is given as support for this analysis. But the fact that 2:7-8 deals mainly with teaching instead of remarks that would apply more generally to the behavior of younger men brings this analysis into question. In fact, the sense one gets as he reads 2:7b-2:8 is that Paul has Titus' actions squarely in mind, that he is focusing on Titus himself and not on the younger men. Also, the forefronting of **seauton** 'yourself' indicates stress on Titus himself. Again, if the final purpose clause were, for example, "in order that the younger men will know how to act," then it would be obvious that Paul's intention here was primarily that of Titus' example to the younger men; but instead, the final purpose clause deals with outsiders' reaction to Titus' teaching.

Because of this, we have analyzed 2:7-8 as a manner constituent. While the specifics deal with the content of what Titus is to teach, this constituent deals with the manner of his teaching. The teaching (**en tē didaskalia** 'in teaching') is to be accompanied by an example of good works and is to be done with "integrity" (**aphthorian**), "seriousness" (**semnotēta**), and must be "correct teaching which no one can criticize" (**logon hugiē akatagnōston**). While the content of the teaching is indicated by infinitive constructions (**einai** 'to be' 2:2, **sōphronein** 'to be self-controlled' 2:6, **hupotassesthai** 'to submit' 2:9) depending on the imperatives **lalei** 'speak, teach' (2:1) and **parakalei** 'urge' (2:6), the manner of the teaching is indicated by a participle, **parechomenos** 'showing', relating grammatically directly to **parakalei** 'urge, exhort' in 2:6 but indirectly and semantically also to **lalei** 'speak, teach' in 2:1. Titus was to teach and urge the believers to do all these things, and the teaching was to be accompanied by a good example, was to be sincere, serious, sound, and above reproach.

CONT Parechomenos is a present middle participle, "showing (yourself)," indicating that Titus was to continually show himself as an example of good works. Tupon kalōn ergōn 'a model of good works' is a genitive construction meaning that, as Titus did good works, others could copy him so as to do good works themselves. Because of the dependency of this participial construction on the imperative parakalei 'urge' in 2:6, it, also, is hortatory, "You yourself (must continually) do what is good in order that (others) will see how they should behave."

REL Parechomenos 'showing' governs all the accusative forms of the participial clause: seauton 'yourself', tupon 'model', aphthorian 'integrity', semnotēta 'seriousness', logon 'word, speech'. The question is whether tupon kalōn ergōn 'model of good works' is a generic and the other accusatives which follow it are specifics of it, or whether tupon kalōn ergōn is to be taken as referring to something different from the three following accusatives, e.g., tupon kalōn ergōn referring to the good life that reinforces the teaching, while the following three accusatives would have more to do with the teaching itself. Since en tē didaskalia 'in teaching' occurs between tupon and the other accusatives, thus tending to divide them, and, since Paul undoubtedly has more in mind than just the model for the manner of teaching (integrity, seriousness, sound word beyond reproach) when he mentions tupon kalōn ergōn 'model of good works', it is probably better to analyze 2:7a and 2:7b-8 as conjoined constituents rather than generic-specific.

CONT See notes for 1:16 for a discussion of the meaning range of "good works."

2:7b-8a. **Teach sincerely (and) seriously, (8a) (and) teach what is correct which no one can (justly) criticize. (en tē didaskalia aphthorian, semnotēta, logon hugiē akatagnōston,** 'in the teaching integrity, seriousness, a-sound word irreproachable')

REL The prepositional phrase en tē didaskalia 'in (your) teaching' signifies that the following two nouns and the noun phrase have to do with Titus' teaching. There is a question, however, whether the first noun, aphthorian 'integrity', and the noun phrase, logon hugiē akatagnōston 'sound word beyond reproach', refer to the content of the teaching or the manner of the teaching. The second noun, semnotēta 'seriousness, dignity', undoubtedly applies to the manner of his teaching, and, as Ellicott says, "of two similarly abstract substantives, it would seem hardly natural to refer one to teaching and the other to the teacher." Although that is not conclusive evidence, the context, as a whole, also points more to the person of Titus and the manner of his teaching rather than the content of his teaching (note especially the preceding remark stating that Titus needs to show himself as a model of good works).

Though there is a division among commentators as to whether aphthorian 'integrity' applies to content or manner of teaching, most commentators see logon hugiē akatagnōston 'sound word/speech beyond reproach' as referring to the content of the teaching. Logos, however, can refer to speech (2 Cor. 8:7, and especially Col. 4:6). But the question is whether hugiēs is ever meant to apply to the manner of speaking, or always refers to the content of the teaching, since the cognate word hugiainō 'be sound' always refers to the content of the teaching elsewhere in the Pastorals. And the fact that hugiainontes logoi 'sound words' in 1 Tim. 6:3 and 2 Tim. 1:13 definitely refers to the content of the teaching argues strongly that logos hugiēs 'sound word' here in Titus also refers to the content of the teaching. Thus, we have rendered logon hugiē akatagnōston in the display text as "teach what is correct which no one can (justly) criticize." (In the final analysis, however, this is not very different in meaning from a manner-based rendering such as "Teach so accurately/correctly that no one can criticize you.")

CONT Aphthorian literally means "incorruption" but, in this context, a better translation would be "integrity, sincerity, purity of motive"; thus the rendering in the display text of "teach sincerely." Titus must be completely committed to the Christian message with no ulterior motives, and this must be clearly seen by those who oppose the faith in order that they will be ashamed of anything bad they have or would intend to say against the Christians. This is the only occurrence of **aphthoria** in the New Testament.

CONT Coupled with "sincerity" is "seriousness" (semnotēta). This, of course, does not refer only to an outward display of seriousness but signifies a deep commitment to the message which naturally shows itself in seriousness of presentation of that message. Semnotēs is also found in 1 Tim. 2:2 and 3:4. Compare the use of the cognate semnos 'serious' in Titus 2:2.

CONT As has been mentioned above, the instructions or message that Titus gives must be "sound" (hugiē). Here "sound" should be taken in a general sense. Paul is not only referring to the "sound" or "true" message of the gospel as specific truths or doctrine but also to the fact that any instruction that Titus gives which is not specified in the set doctrines of the gospel must (1) be conformable to that gospel and (2) thus also be considered by thinking men in general as sound and respectable teaching. That Paul is thinking about more than just set doctrines is shown by the fact that, in the context of 2:1-10, the instructions to be given are generally practical ones of a wide variety. That the teaching should also be sound as far as the public in general is concerned is shown by the fact that **akatagnōston** 'beyond reproach' and the purpose clause **hina ho ex enantias entrapē mēden echōn legein peri hēmōn phaulon** 'in order that the opposition will be put to shame having nothing bad to say against us' indicate the general public's view of the teaching.

CONT Akatagnōston 'beyond reproach, not open to criticism' modifies **logon hugiē** 'sound word', indicating that the message Titus gives must be so sound that no one can justly criticize it. Any teaching that is the least bit unwholesome will be immediately held up by Titus' opponents as evidence of the weakness or incorrectness of the Christian position. **Akatagnōstos** occurs only here in the New Testament.

2:8b-c. **(Do this (2:7a-8a)) in order that anyone who opposes (us(inc)) may be put to shame (8c)(because) there will be nothing bad that he can (justly) say about us(inc). (hina ho ex enantias entrapē mēden echōn legein peri hēmōn phaulon.** 'in-order-that the-one of opposite(side) may-be-put-to-shame nothing having to-say about us (that is) bad')

REL This **hina** purpose clause could relate grammatically only to **logon hugiē akatagnōston** 'sound word beyond reproach' or to all of 2:7-8a. **Akatagnōston** 'beyond reproach' has a close relationship in meaning to the **hina** clause, i.e., "be sound and beyond reproach in your teaching in order that any opponent will not be able to reproach us." However, the other qualities that Titus is to strive for in 2:7 also relate very well semantically to the purpose clause, i.e., Titus is to be an example of good works, to be sincere and serious in his teaching, in order that any opponents will not be able to reproach the Christians. So it seems better to take the **hina** clause as depending on **parechomenos** 'showing' and so semantically on all of 2:7-8a. Commentators who mention the connection of the **hina** clause tend to favor this view. This **hina** motivational purpose clause is one of three in the paragraph (the others are 2:5b and 2:10c) which appear to be placed in strategic places at the end of their units and are all dealing with the outside world's view of the church and the gospel. This strongly suggests that this hina clause (along with the others) depends on more than just the immediately preceding constituent. In other words, we would expect a wider base for the motivational purpose clause than just one specific constituent.

CONT Ho ex enantias literally means "the one of the contrary/opposite (side)," i.e., "the opponent, a member of the opposition." There is no reason to think that the singular here indicates a specific person or the devil, since there is nothing in the context to suggest this. The idea is probably any opponent. The two other motivational purpose clauses of the paragraph (2:5b, 2:10c) have in view the attitude toward Christianity of people wholly outside the church (see especially 2:5b where it would be difficult to understand people who profess Christianity as blaspheming the word of God) and this may be the main idea here, though it would certainly be difficult to rule out the false teachers who are so much on Paul's mind. Thus, it is best to take "the opponent" here in the general sense of "any opponent." This is rendered in the display text as "anyone who opposes (us(inc))." "Us(inc)" is used instead of "you(sg)" in order to be parallel with the end of the verse, "(because) there will be nothing bad that he can (justly) say about us(inc)," where "us" (hēmōn) does occur in the Greek text.

CONT Arndt and Gingrich give for the meaning of entrepō in the passive sense "be put to shame, be ashamed" and give only two references for this passive sense in the New Testament, this one and 2 Thess. 3:14. The reference in 2 Thess. 3:14 is translated in the NIV as "Do not associate with him, in order that he may feel ashamed." The 2 Thessalonians reference then definitely refers to the sense of "being ashamed" or "feeling ashamed." RSV translates 2 Thess. 3:14 as "that he may be ashamed." There a brother within the church is being talked about, but here in Titus 2:8, it is the opponent that is being referred to, who would like to have bad things to say about Titus and the Christians. Here, entrapē is translated by RSV as "may be put to shame." In the 2 Thessalonians passage, the focus is squarely on the feelings of the disobedient brother. But, in the Titus passage, there is an added component of "defeat" or "frustration" on the part of the opponent. It is difficult to say just how deep his shame goes and whether there is any real guilt involved, as there presumably is in 2 Thess. 3:14. Paul is saying that he will be defeated and the reason for this is that he doesn't have anything to stand upon in his opposition to Titus and the believers--mēden echōn legein peri hēmōn phaulon 'having nothing bad to say about us', i.e., because he has nothing bad with which to attack us.

In the display text, "put to shame" is used, since, although it is idiomatic in English, there is no other word that adequately expresses the meaning of entrapē here.

2:9-10. REL Before discussing relations within 2:9-10, it should be decided whether en pasin 'in all (things)' modifies hupotassesthai 'to be submissive' or euarestous einai 'to be well-pleasing'. En pasin may relate grammatically to either one and may also collocate semantically with either one. The other occurrences of en pasin in the Pastorals (1 Tim. 3:11; 2 Tim. 2:7; 4:5; Titus 2:10) are all apparently unambiguous in what they modify (except possibly 2 Tim. 4:5), each one occurring after the word it modifies. Notice especially Titus 2:10 where it occurs at the very end of the paragraph. Also, if en pasin were to modify euarestos einai 'to be well-pleasing', it would be very prominent on the basis of its being forefronted before the verbal nucleus, which is less plausible in a list of this sort. Therefore, we analyze **en pasin** `in all things' as relating to **hupotassesthai** `to be submissive'.

REL 2:9a is analyzed as a generic Head with 2:9b and 2:10b (along with their contrastive propositions 2:9c and 2:10a) as specifics (see display). The reasons for this analysis are:

1. Semantically **hupotassesthai en pasin** `to be submissive in all things' is quite an inclusive statement certainly covering **euarestous einai** `to be well-pleasing, to give satisfaction' and **mē antilegontas** `not talking back'. And it is not too difficult to see that **mē nosphizomenous** `not pilfering' and **pasan pistin endeiknumenous agathēn** `showing that they can be completely trusted' could also be specific characteristics of being submissive to their masters. Note Barrett's comment, "they must be careful `to respect their masters' authority in everything.' The next words illustrate the requirement in practical terms; `to comply with their demands without answering back; not to pilfer, but to show themselves strictly honest and trustworthy'"--in other words, specific instances of the generic requirement. Notice, also, that **en pasin** `in all (things)' would tend to indicate a generic statement.
2. The chiastic structure of 2:9b, 2:9c, 2:10a, and 2:10b would also favor the generic-specific relationship, since the four specifics are then in the chiasmus while the generic proposition stands outside of it. The structure of the chiasmus is:

A	positive	(2:9b)
B	negative	(2:9c)
B′	negative	(2:10a)
A′	positive	(2:10b)

2:9a. As for slaves, (specifically, urge them) to be submissive to their masters in everything. (doulous idiois despotais hupotassesthai en pasin, `slaves to-their-own masters to-submit in all(things)')

REL The forefronted accusative **doulous** `slaves' at the very beginning of the unit marks a new topic, how the slaves are to be instructed in accordance with sound teaching. In addition to belonging to one of the categories in 2:1-6, a considerable number of Cretan believers were slaves. This called for further exhortation regarding their behavior toward their masters. Grammatically, the infinitive **hupotassesthai** `to be submissive' relates back to the imperative **parakalei** `urge' in 2:6--"Urge slaves to be submissive...." 2:9-10 is the final grouping of specifics of 2:1 about a topic, here slaves.

CONT **Doulos** is a generic term for all types of slaves. Hendriksen (commentary on 1 Tim. 6:1) says that slaves in the Roman world "had become slaves: a. as prisoners of war, or b. as condemned men, or c. through debt, or d. through kidnapping...or e. as those who had been sold into slavery by their parents."

CONT As in 2:5, **idiois** `own' is not contrastive in the sense of "Urge slaves to be submissive to their own masters (rather than someone else's master)." Many English translations (NIV, RSV, 20th Century, TEV) translate as "their masters/owners" and do not include "own." Dibelius, in commenting on an almost identical phrase in 1 Tim. 6:1, says, "`Their (own)' (**idios**) is used here in a weakened sense." However, Ellicott remarks on the passage in 1 Tim. 6:1, "`their own masters,' those who stand in that distinct personal relation to them, and whom they are bound to obey." A study of **idios** in other contexts indicates that, though sometimes there is no contrast (as here), it is very difficult to determine that it otherwise loses its force. However, since in English "their own masters" can indicate a contrast between their masters and someone else's master, the phrase is rendered as "their masters" in the display text.

2:9b. **(Specifically, they should) please (them (their masters)); (euarestous einai**, 'well-pleasing to-be')

CONT/REL A more literal rendering for 2:9b would be "(Urge them (slaves)) to please (their masters)" since it follows the imperative-infinitive structure of the Greek, but the above rendering is used since it is less redundant.

CONT Everything in the context strongly suggests that the relationship Paul has in mind in 2:9b, as well as 9c and 10a-b, is between the slaves and their masters. Therefore, "them (their masters)" is supplied as the object of "pleases"; similar references to the masters in 2:9c-10b are made explicit. The slave-master relationship is set up in 2:9a, **doulous idiois despotais hupotassesthai** 'slaves own masters to-submit-to', and in Greek there is no need for additional surface structure reference to either one.

CONT **Euarestous einai** 'be well-pleasing, give satisfaction' has been rendered in the display as "(They should) please (them (their masters))." Alternate renderings would be: "(They should) do what pleases (them (their masters))" or "(They should do what (their masters) request them to do."

2:9c. **(in particular, they (slaves) should) not refuse (to obey them (their masters)). (mē antilegontas**, 'not contradicting')

CONT/TRNS From its senses of "contradict" and "oppose," **antilegō** applied to a master-slave relationship would appear to refer to the slave expressing his will (audibly) against the will of his master. This has been rendered in the display text as "refuse (to obey)," as this appears to be the most appropriate rendering in English. However, "they should not refuse to obey" is basically a double negative and, in some languages, would need to be translated as a positive statement. Therefore, the following alternate renderings for the display text are suggested: "(they (slaves) should) not contradict (them (their masters))"; "(they (slaves) should) not argue with (them (their masters))." Some languages will have a word that more exactly fits this context.

REL Since pleasing their masters is still quite generic, while refusing to obey them is more specific, 2:9c is analyzed as a negative specific of 2:9b. As has been mentioned above, there seems to be a pattern of a positive generic followed by negative specifics in Titus (1:6d-f,7,13c-14; 2:3a-b). Here, however, there is only one negative specific following the positive generic.

2:10a. **(Specifically, they (slaves) should) not pilfer (things that belong to their masters), (mē nosphizomenous**, 'not pilfering')

REL This third constituent of the chiastic structure is also expressed negatively, but its sense is expressed positively by the statement in 2:10b. Since the negative statement appears to be more specific than the positive one, "pilfering" being quite specific, but the positive statement stressing complete honesty in all situations, the relationship between 10a and 10b is analyzed as (negative)specific-generic.

When **alla** 'but' occurs in a negative-positive construction, it usually introduces the positive side and generally marks prominence on the clause that it introduces. This supports the analysis of 2:10b as the Head proposition of 2:10a-b.

CONT **Nosphizō** means "put aside for oneself, misappropriate, pilfer." White says, "The particular form of theft implied is the abstraction or retention for oneself, of a part of something entrusted to one's care."

2:10b. **instead (they (the slaves) should) always be completely honest/reliable (and thus) show (their masters that they (their masters)) can completely trust them.** (**alla pasan pistin endeiknumenous agathēn**, 'but all good fidelity showing')

CONT Since all the grammatical and semantic features of the chiasmus point to 2:10b being a positive restatement of 2:10a, the construction **pasan pistin endeiknumenous agathēn** 'showing all good faith/trust' does not refer to the trust the slaves should put in their masters, as the words could be taken in another context, but to the complete fidelity they should show to their masters, not pilfering or doing any such thing. The use of **endeiknumenous** 'showing' indicates the significance of how the slaves' masters and the unbelieving world in general perceive the faithfulness of the Christian slaves. They are to show their masters (and others) that they can be completely trusted in order that they might also show them that the teaching about our Savior God is noble (2:10c) and thus true.

CONT **Agathēn** 'good' denotes the genuineness of the fidelity. **Pasan** 'all' denotes that the slaves should at all times be faithful and reliable. The double modifiers stress the importance of carrying out this exhortation fully.

CONT 2:10b might be rendered in the display text as "(They (the slaves) should) show that (their masters) can always completely trust them." However, there is a question as to whether "show" would thus be used with its primary meaning, or whether it actually means here "do those things that show." Thus, the rendering in the display text is "instead (they (the slaves) should) always be completely honest/reliable (and thus) show (their masters that they (their masters)) can completely trust them." Although this, in effect, expresses **pasan pistin...agathēn** ('all good fidelity') twice, it nonetheless probably best expresses all the implied components of **endeiknumenous** 'show' in this context. Of course, if, in any language, a translation of the first rendering given above adequately represents the meaning, then that may be followed.

2:10c. **(They (slaves) should behave like this (2:9a-10b)) in order that by means of all (they (the slaves) do) (people) will perceive that the teachings about God our(inc) Savior are very good.** (**hina tēn didaskalian tēn tou sōtēros hēmōn theou kosmōsin en pasin**. 'in-order-that the teaching of-the Savior of-us God they-may-adorn in all')

REL Although there is a very close relationship between 10b and 10c as has been indicated by the significance of **endeiknumenous** 'showing' in the discussion above, the **hina** purpose clause appears to be related to all of the constituent on the slaves' behavior since--

1. the resultant meaning makes excellent sense;

2. this **hina** motivational purpose clause is the third one of the paragraph, each of these being placed at a strategic place, i.e., at the end of its unit, and each relating to the outside world's perception of the church, thus indicating the general motivating purpose for the individual constituent as a whole or for a substantial part of it;
3. **en pasin** 'in all (things)', i.e., "by all that they do," definitely indicates the wide scope of the means, thus showing that all Paul has said concerning slaves is the means to this purpose clause.

Endeiknumenous 'showing' may well function as a transition from the means to the purpose.

CONT The genitive construction **tēn didaskalian tēn tou sōtēros hēmōn theou** 'the teaching of our Savior God' is rendered in the display text as meaning that the teaching is about him. At the same time the teaching is also from God. See discussion under 2:5b.

"The teaching of our Savior God" means Christian doctrine, and refers not only to the practical outliving of the faith as described in 2:1-10b but especially to the great doctrines of salvation. This is shown by the forefronting of **sōtēros** 'Savior' before **theou** 'God' and the many references to the doctrine of

salvation in 2:11-14. In fact, "the teaching of our Savior God" is a tail-head link with 2:11-14.

CONT **Kosmōsin** 'they may adorn' is a dead figure well established in Greek usage, meaning that as slaves who follow the teaching about God behave in an obedient and completely trustworthy manner, their masters and others will connect the doctrine with the results and be favorably impressed as to the value and effect of the doctrine. This will result only if there is absolute consistency on the part of the slaves "in all things" (**en pasin**), that is, in all that they do.

SECTION CONSTITUENT 2:11-14 (Paragraph) (Role: grounds for 2:1-10)

THEME: God very graciously sent Jesus Christ to earth in order that God might save all people and God graciously trains us(inc) to behave in a godly manner.

DISPLAY

RELATIONAL STRUCTURE				CONTENT
HEAD$_1$				(2:11) (You should teach the believers to behave in this manner (2:1-10)) since God very graciously sent (Jesus Christ) to earth (in order that he (God)) might save all people [PERS]
HEAD$_2$	HEAD			(2:12a) (and since) God graciously trains us(inc) [PERS]
		step		(2:12b) to stop doing what God dislikes and stop lusting for the things in this world
	content	HEAD		(2:12c) (and) to be self-controlled and do what is right and do what God is pleased with (while) we(inc) live in this present age.
			contraction	(2:13a) (We(inc) should act like this (2:12b-c) since) we(inc) are waiting expectantly for that which will make (us(inc)) (very) happy (indeed) [METY],
		grounds	HEAD	(2:13b) that is, (we(inc) are expectantly waiting for) our(inc) great God and Savior, Jesus Christ, to come gloriously.
amplif.	HEAD			(2:14a) He (willingly) gave himself/his own body (to die) on our(inc) behalf, (in the same way as someone would give himself to die in order that others might be set free).
	purpose$_1$			(2:14b) (He (Jesus) did this (2:14a)) in order that he might cause us(inc) to be free from all sin, (that is, in order that he might enable us(inc) not to sin at all) [METR].
	purpose$_2$	HEAD		(2:14c) (He gave himself to die on our(inc) behalf) in order that he might make us(inc) his very own holy people,
		DESC. of "people"		(2:14d) (a people, moreover, who) are eager to do what is good.

BOUNDARIES AND COHERENCE

The initial boundary has been discussed under Boundaries and Coherence for 2:1-10.

The coherence of the paragraph is evident in the following features:

1. There are several words and phrases in the semantic domain of salvation: **charis** 'grace' (2:11), **sōtērios** 'saving' (2:11), **tēn makarian elpida** 'the blessed hope' (2:13), **sōtēros** 'Savior' (2:13), **edōken heauton huper hēmōn** 'he gave himself in behalf of us' (2:14), **lutrōsētai** 'he may redeem' (2:14), and **katharisē** 'he may cleanse' (2:14).
2. The first person plural and the third person singular predominate.
3. The subject matter centers around what God (the third person singular reference) has done or is doing for man (the first person plural reference).
4. There is only one nonsubordinated finite verb, **epephanē** 'it appeared' (2:11), to which the whole paragraph is grammatically related. The only other finite verb, **edōken** 'he gave' (2:14), is in a relative clause (though it actually governs the whole of 2:14 and may be in more of an appositional relationship with what is more directly governed by **epephanē**).

The boundary between 2:14 and 15 is evident by the return of the mood to the imperative, the change of verb aspect from punctiliar (aorist) to progressive (present), and the change of the predominant person from third to second singular.

PROMINENCE AND THEME

Gar 'for, since' at the beginning of 2:11 suggests that 2:11-14 may be grounds for the exhortations of 2:1-10. As mentioned above, 2:11 contains the only finite and thus nuclear verb of 2:11-13 (**epephanē** 'appeared'), and since 2:14 begins with a relative pronoun, the construction in that verse appears to be subordinated at least in some way to 2:11-13. Since 2:11 is introduced by **gar**, comes at the beginning of an apparent grounds paragraph immediately following the hortatory paragraph, and contains the main verb of the paragraph, it expresses the central support theme for the hortatory paragraph, i.e., (Believers should behave in a godly manner) since God has very graciously sent (his Son) Jesus Christ in order to save them. The great things which God has done for us should be a powerful incentive or motivation for us to live godly lives. That Paul places value on the importance of motivation as an impetus for holy living has been seen earlier in the section in the three motivational purposes of 2:1-10.

2:11-14 is the first of two paragraphs dealing with the great truths of the gospel as the basis and motivation for holy living. The second paragraph is 3:3-7. Both of these paragraphs deal with salvation (**sōtērios** 'saving' (2:11) introduced by a tail-head link in 2:10c, **tēn didaskalian tēn tou sōtēros hēmōn theou** 'the teaching of God our Savior'; Christ our Savior (2:13) giving himself to redeem us (2:14a); **esōsen** 'he saved' (us) as the main verb of 3:3-7 where "God our Savior" and "Christ our Savior" also occur) through grace (**hē charis** 2:11), kindness and love (**hē chrēstotēs kai hē philanthrōpia** 3:4), and his mercy (**to autou eleos** 3:5). As Barrett (p. 138) says, the author is presenting "the redemptive truth upon which the moral requirements of the paragraph are based, the 'indicative' of the Gospel which is the ground of the 'imperative' of the commandment."

In 2:12 and 14, however, there also appears to be a focus on the enablement that God graciously supplies to live holy lives. 2:12 deals with the actual process of God's training (**paideuousa**) which produces godly lives. 2:14, which is the amplification of 2:11-13, deals with Christ giving himself for us that he might deliver us from the dominion of sin and might purify us, i.e., might make us his own holy people who are thus eager to do what is good. So this grounds paragraph presents the grace of God as both the motivation and enablement for holy living. Note that Christ's second appearing is also a motivation for holy living (2:13).

Since 2:11 and 2:12a are the main Heads of the paragraph, they form the main theme. Although propositions 2:12b-c are not considered thematic since they are, in effect, a repetition of the information in 2:1-10 and not grounds, still the content of the "training" needs to be filled out to complete the sense. No part of 2:14 is added to the theme statement since it is an amplification of 2:11, though it is evident that the ideas of redemption from all lawlessness (enabled not to sin at all) and being purified to become Christ's very own people eager for good works are important as grounds for 2:1-10.

NOTES ON 2:11-14

2:11. **(You should teach the believers to behave in this manner (2:1-10)) since God very graciously sent (Jesus Christ) to earth (in order that he (God)) might save all people [PERS] (Epephanē gar hē charis tou theou sōtērios pasin anthrōpois,** 'for appeared the saving grace of God to-all people')

REL As has been discussed under Prominence and Theme, **gar** at the beginning of 2:11 is used in its common function of marking grounds for hortatory material.

REL The fact that **epephanē** 'appeared' is the only clearly nonsubordinated finite verb of the paragraph suggests that it and the clause in which it occurs are central to the semantic structure of the paragraph. And the fact that this clause deals with grace and salvation, subjects fundamental to the support for the hortatory statements of 2:1-10, also suggests its prominence. Thus, 2:11 is to be considered as the main Head, or at least one of the main Heads, of 2:11-14.

CONT **Epephanē** 'appeared' is aorist indicative passive in form. Does **epephanē** refer only to the announcement of the fact of saving grace or to the actual activity of saving grace--that is, Christ's advent and death for the purpose of our salvation? Lock remarks on **epephanē**, "The essential meaning is to appear suddenly on a scene, and it is used particularly (a) of divine interposition, especially to aid (cf. Gen. 35:7, 3 Mac. 6:9...) (b) of the dawning of light upon darkness (Nu. 6:25, Ps. 30:16, 117:27...). The context here (**sōtērios**) suggests the former shade of meaning. The grace of God came to the aid of our need, the reference being to the whole life of Christ, Incarnation and Death, cf. [verse] 14."

In its passive form, **epiphainō** 'appear' is found only here and in Titus 3:4 in the New Testament. In its active form, it is found in Acts 27:20 of the sun and stars appearing and in Luke 1:79 in a figure of the rising sun shining on those living in darkness. The cognate **epiphaneia** 'appearing, appearance' occurs in 2 Thess. 2:8; 1 Tim. 6:14; 2 Tim. 4:1,8; and Titus 2:13, all in reference to Christ's second coming; and in 2 Tim. 1:10 in reference to his first coming. There are no other occurrences in the New Testament.

The best commentary on the meaning of **epephanē** in 2:11 is the meaning of the cognate noun **epiphaneia** 'appearance, appearing' in 2:13 where it definitely refers to the second appearance (coming) of Christ on earth, and, without doubt, is being used by Paul as the second occurrence of the "appearance" motif in this paragraph. The fact that 2:11 refers to Christ's first coming as 2:13 refers to his second coming is even more clearly seen by the likeness in form of the phrases in which **epephanē** 'appeared' and **epiphaneian** 'appearing' occur:

2:11	**epephanē**	**hē**	**charis**	**tou**	**theou**	**sōtērios**
	appeared	the	grace	(art.)	of-God	saving

'the saving grace of God has appeared'

2:13	**epiphaneian**	**tēs**	**doxēs**	**tou**	**megalou**	**theou**	**kai**	**sōtēros**
	appearance	of-the	glory	of-the	great	God	and	Savior
	hēmōn	**Iēsou**	**Christou**					
	of-us	Jesus	Christ					

'the appearing of the glory of our great God and Savior Jesus Christ'

The third occurrence of the "appearance" motif is in 3:4 and refers to the first appearance of Christ:

3:4	**hē**	**chrēstotēs**	**kai**	**hē**	**philanthrōpia**	**epephanē**
	the	kindness	and	the	love-for-man	appeared
	tou	**sōtēros**	**hēmōn**	**theou**		
	of-the	Savior	of-us	God		

'the kindness and love of our Savior God appeared'

Each occurrence of the "appearance" motif (or "epiphany" formula) includes the following constants: (1) some form of the word "appear," either **epephanē** 'appeared' or **epiphaneian** 'appearance'; (2) some reference to salvation, either **sōtērios** 'saving' or **sōtēros** 'Savior'; (3) reference to God, always in the genitive (**theou**). The reference to God is always in genitive form, since the variable factor is always referred to as belonging to God. The variable factor in 2:11 is **hē charis** 'the grace', in 2:13 **tēs doxēs** 'the glory', and in 3:4 **hē chrēstotēs kai hē philanthrōpia** 'the kindness and the love'. These variable factors are not personification in the sense of standing for Christ himself, but are, however, intricately connected with his personal appearings and thus refer to those appearings.

These considerations clearly indicate that **epephanē** in 2:11 refers to the actual activity of God's saving grace and not just to the announcement of it.

CONT/REL In 2:11-12a, there is a great amount of skewing between the Greek surface structure form and the standard SSWC propositionalized form which seeks to match nouns only with animate beings/inanimate objects (T=thing), verbs only with events (E=event), and attributes only with adjectives or adverbs (A=attribute, R=relational).

Greek text form	Lit. Eng. transl.	Part of speech	Subj. of verb/verbal adj.	TEAR classif.	Event referred to	Agent of event	Propositional form
epephany	appeared	finite verb	hy charis tou theou	event	appearance of Christ on earth	Christ	sent (Christ) to earth
hy charis tou theou	the grace of God	noun phrase	--------	event/ attribute	God acting graciously	God	God very graciously sent Christ
swtyrios	saving, bringing salvation	adj.	hy charis tou theou	event	saving people	God	(in order that he (God might save
paideuousa	training	participle	hy charis tou theou	event	God training us	God	God graciously trains us

CONT **hē charis tou theou sōtērios** 'the saving grace of God' is here personified, as can be seen not only by the fact that it is said to have appeared as a divine person would appear (**epephanē**), but also by the fact that it is said to "teach/train" (**paideuousa**). It does not seem necessary to see in **hē charis tou theou** 'the grace of God' a metaphorical reference to Christ himself as if he were being called "the grace of God"; however, his coming to earth to bring salvation is certainly being referred to.

CONT/TRNS Since **epephanē** 'appeared' refers to Christ's first advent, and since God is also active in the event (**hē charis tou theou** 'the grace of God'), a causative construction is indicated, "God...caused Jesus Christ to appear on earth." This is expressed in more normal English usage in the display text as "God...sent Jesus Christ to earth."

"Grace" is a noun, yet depending on the context and other factors, it may represent manner (God (acts) graciously), attribute (God is gracious), or an event (God acts graciously, cf. SSA of 2 Thessalonians p.51). Here in 2:11, a specific event is being referred to, so it is not necessary to use the generic verb "act." In the display text, the specific event "sent" (i.e., "caused to appear") is modified by "graciously." In some languages, however, the concept of "grace" cannot be expressed by an adverb, so an adjective (God is gracious), and in some even a verb ("God loves and is concerned very much," Bahnar of Viet Nam) will need to be used in translation.

It should be remembered that "graciously" here is to be interpreted with the full meaning of **charis** 'grace' in mind as applied to this context, and not with any interpretation based on senses of grace that do not relate to God's unmerited favor.

PROM Since **hē charis tou theou** 'the grace of God' is presented by Paul as the subject of the main verb of 2:11-12a (and for that matter of all 2:11-13) and also as the variable factor in the "epiphany" formula, the grace of God is to be understood as very significant in the paragraph. This means that, when this noun phrase which expresses the manner/motive of God's action is necessarily represented in the propositionalization by something other than a noun phrase, the prominence of **hē charis tou theou** must be maintained. "Very" is used in the display text to help retain the significance of **hē charis tou theou.**

CONT **Sōtērios** 'saving, bringing salvation' is an adjective found only here in the New Testament in its nonsubstantive form. In this context it refers to Christ's first advent bringing salvation.

CONT There is a question as to whether **pasin anthrōpois** 'all people' is to be connected with the verb **epephanē** 'appeared' or the adjective **sōtērios** 'saving, bringing salvation'. Thus NIV translates, "For the grace of God that brings salvation has appeared to all men" and RSV translates, "For the grace of God has appeared for the salvation of all men." It is difficult to decide grammatically which relationship is the intended one, but the general meaning is the same either way--God's saving grace is intended for all mankind. (Note that the rendering in the display text does not support universalism any more than John 3:17, "For God sent not his Son into the world to condemn the world; but that the world through him might be saved" AV.)

CONT Many commentators take **pasin anthrōpois** to mean "all classes of people." Since in 2:1-10 Paul has been referring to various classes of people, male and female, old and young, and especially slaves, it is thought that Paul is referring here to the fact that the grace of God has brought salvation to all classes of people. A study of the thirteen other occurrences of **pantes anthrōpoi** listed by Arndt and Gingrich seems to show that its primary meaning is not "all kinds/classes of people." It is difficult, for instance, to see how, in Phil. 4:5, **to epieikes humōn gnōsthētō pasin anthrōpois** 'let your gentleness be evident to' **pasin anthrōpois** could mean primarily "let your gentleness be evident to all kinds/classes of people" rather than "let your gentleness be evident to everyone/all people." Of all those references, Titus 2:11 is more likely than any of the others to mean "all classes of people," and so the other references are not support for Titus 2:11 meaning "all classes of people." Since "all people" is at least as inclusive as "all classes of people," and since the matter of all classes of people is not focal to the theme of 2:11-14, **pasin anthrōpois** is rendered as simply "all people" in the display text.

2:12a. **(and since) God graciously trains us(inc) [PERS] (paideuousa hēmas** 'training us')

REL The relation of 2:12a, **paideuousa hēmas** 'training us', to 2:11, **epephanē hē charis tou theou sōtērios pasin anthrōpois** 'the grace of God has appeared bringing salvation to all people' or 'the saving grace of God has appeared to all people', is considered to be a conjoined relation, as expressed in the display text, for the following reasons:

1. While the grammatical structure does not indicate a coordinate relationship, the semantic structure suggests that there are two actions which God performed or performs in relation to mankind, (a) he graciously sent Jesus Christ to earth in order that he might save all people (**epephanē hē charis tou theou sōtērios pasin anthrōpois**) 2:11, and (b) he graciously trains us (**paideuousa hēmas**) 2:12a. This is parallel with the amplification unit 2:14, which states that Christ demonstrated his grace by voluntarily giving his life for us in order to deliver us from all sin, i.e., to enable us to live a sinless life (see notes there). So 2:11-14 as a grounds for 2:1-10 presents grace as both an incentive for holy living and the enablement (**paideuousa** 'training' us to live godly lives; **lutrōsētai hēmas apo pasēs anomias** 'he might redeem/free us from all lawlessness'; **katharisē heautō laon periousion** 'he might purify for himself a people that are his own') for holy living. As far as the relation of 2:11-12a

with constructions outside itself are concerned, the finite verb construction of 2:11 has a more direct connection (semantically) to 2:1-10 as grounds, while the participial construction of 2:12a has a more direct connection with the content construction of 2:12b-c. This does not mean that 2:1-10 has no semantic relationship with 2:12a, or that 2:11 has no semantic relationship with 2:12b-c, but that these are not the most immediate relationships.

2. **Paideuousa** 'training' is not a specific of **epephanē hē charis tou theou sōtērios pasin anthrōpois** 'the grace of God has appeared bringing salvation to all people' since (a) **epephanē** 'appeared' is in the aorist tense, indicating an action that occurred at one time in the past, while **paideuousa** 'training' is present tense indicating action that is continuing, and (b) the reason for the differences in tenses is that **epephanē** 'appeared' refers to the incarnation (with all its attendant events including Christ's death and resurrection), while **paideuousa** 'training' refers to the continuous activity of God "training" his people. Since the "training" does not refer to any part of the "appearing," it is not in a specific-generic relationship to it.
3. It does not seem necessary to consider "God acts graciously" as a generic and "God graciously sent Jesus Christ to earth in order that he might save all people" and "God graciously trains us" as the specifics. This would be a step farther away from the form of the Greek of 2:11 than the rendering of the display text is.
4. **Paideuousa hēmas** 'training us' might be analyzed as the purpose of **epephanē hē charis tou theou sōtērios pasin anthrōpois** 'the grace of God has appeared bringing salvation to all people/the saving grace of God has appeared to all people'. However, this would tend to overly restrict the function of **epephanē hē charis tou theou sōtērios pasin anthrōpois**. The purpose of the appearing would be for training in godliness. This is certainly only one of the purposes of the appearing, and it would be difficult to prove that it was the only purpose intended to be focused on here.

CONT The present active participle **paideuousa** 'training, teaching' is the grammatical nucleus of 2:12-13. The agent is the grace of God personified (**hē charis tou theou**) and 2:12a is propositionalized as "God graciously trains us(inc)." The present tense indicates a continuous activity.

The meaning of **paideuō** can range from "teach, instruct" to "discipline, discipline with punishment." Note Acts 7:22, **epaideuthē Mōusēs pasē sophia Aiguptiōn** 'Moses was educated in all the wisdom/culture of the Egyptians' (cf. Acts 22:3), and Luke 23:16, **paideusas oun auton apolusō** 'therefore, I will punish him and then release him' (NIV, underlining mine). As for its occurrence in the Pastoral Epistles, it is found in 1 Tim. 1:20, **hōn estin Humenaios kai Alexandros, hous paredōka tō Satana hina paideuthōsin mē blasphēmein** 'of whom are Hymenaeus and Alexander whom I have handed over to Satan to be taught not to blaspheme'. Certainly its use in 1 Tim 1:20 has some idea of discipline; it is not through mere instruction that they will learn not to blaspheme. The other reference in the Pastoral Epistles is 2 Tim. 2:25, **en prautēti paideuonta tous antidiatithemenous, mēpote dōē autois ho theos metanoian eis epignōsin alētheias** 'those who oppose him he must gently instruct, in the hope that God will grant them repentance leading them to a knowledge of the truth' (NIV, underlining mine). In this reference, the meaning could be "correct" in the sense of bringing those who think differently back to the truth.

These references suggest that **paideuousa** here in Titus 2:12a could mean "train," including training by discipline, as well as simply "teach." "Train" has been used in the display text as an attempt to use the most generic of the English words that translate paideuō, especially since it is difficult to determine which of its specific senses is intended here. We are not told here how the training/teaching is carried out. However, there is no support for understanding paideuousa here or in any of its other New Testament references as "teach" in the sense of "show," i.e., "God has acted graciously on our behalf in saving us and this teaches/shows us that we should live in a godly manner." What Christian has not recognized the training of God in his life in various ways for the purpose of enabling him to live a more godly life?

2:12b. to stop doing what God dislikes and stop lusting for the things in this world (hina arnēsamenoi tēn asebeian kai tas kosmikas epithumias 'that having-denied the ungodliness and the worldly desires')

REL The hina clause, **hina arnēsamenoi tēn asebeian kai tas kosmikas epithumias sōphronōs kai dikaiōs kai eusebōs zēsōmen en tō nun aiōni** 'that having denied ungodliness and worldly desires, in a self-controlled manner and uprightly and in a godly manner we may live in this present age', expresses the content of the "training" (paideuousa). As pointed out in the notes for 2:4b-5a, when the content is closely allied with the purpose of the verb it relates to (here paideuousa 'training'), the normal natural prominence of the content constituent is no longer predictable. Since 2:11-14 is a grounds paragraph, it is the grounds for 2:1-10 that is prominent here. The hina clause here is a reiteration of the contents of the hortatory paragraph 2:1-10 and therefore less prominent. Notice that the nonsubordinated finite verb epephanē 'appeared' in 2:11 and the finite verb edōken 'he gave' in 2:14, which is basically nonsubordinated, express grounds or means for godly living.

The participial phrase immediately following hina, i.e., **arnēsamenoi tēn asebeian kai tas kosmikas epithumias** 'having denied ungodliness and worldly desires', depends on the subjunctive verb zēsōmen 'we may live' which governs the hina clause. Since the participle arnēsamenoi 'having denied' is aorist preceding the main verb, it indicates action that is prior to the action indicated by the main verb, zēsōmen 'live', thus indicating that denying ungodliness and worldly desires is a prerequisite to living a self-controlled, upright, and godly life. This has been represented in the diagram of the relational structure as step-HEAD(GOAL). There is, of course, a negative-positive contrast here too, but note that this is not marked in the Greek.

Some commentators take the aorist tense of the participle arnēsamenoi 'having denied' to indicate reference to a specific time, e.g., at baptism, when this denial took place. Gealy says, "Perhaps the aorist tense of the Greek participle...should be taken as referring to a specific event in the Christian's life, such as baptism, when an overt renunciation of the world and the flesh was publicly made." However, the aorist participle here does not necessarily indicate a specific event. Harold Greenlee (personal communication) classifies the aorist participle here (arnēsamenoi 'having denied') as a participle of coordinate circumstance. In his book A Concise Exegetical Grammar of New Testament Greek (p. 67), he describes the participle of coordinate circumstance thus: "Normally is an aorist participle, stands before the leading verb and precedes it in time. Its action is coordinate with, prior to, and of the same mood sematically as the leading verb, although not equal in importance.... May be translated by the same tense and mood as the leading verb and connected to it by 'and.'" The aorist tense in this type of participle primarily indicates action prior to that of the leading verb and does not differentiate whether that action is a specific one-time event or not. The rendering in the display text of 2:12b-c is in line with the characteristics of the participle of coordinate circumstance as described in the quote above.

CONT **Arneomai** means "deny," i.e., the opposite of "confess by word of mouth" as in Luke 8:45, **arnoumenōn pantōn** 'when all denied' (that they had touched Jesus); or "disown" as in Jude 4, **ton monon despotēn kai kurion hēmōn Iēsoun Christon arnoumenoi** 'disowning our only Sovereign and Lord, Jesus Christ', where the situation does not refer to a verbal denial but to actions that show that one has disowned another (cf. 1 Tim. 5:8). The meaning here in Titus 2:12 seems to be closer to the sense of "disown" and has the idea of "renounce," a word often used to translate **arnēsamenoi** here. This has been rendered in the display text as "stop doing."

CONT **Asebeia** 'ungodliness' is the opposite of **eusebeia** 'godliness' (the adverbial form of which, **eusebōs** 'in a godly manner', occurs later on in this **hina** clause). In his comments on **tēn asebeian** here Lock remarks, "Impiety, all wrong thoughts about God, and the actions that follow from it, which marked the heathen (**tēn**) life, cf. Jude 15-18." Since the whole context of 2:1-14 deals with conduct, it seems like actions contrary to God's will would be in focus here, though it cannot be denied that the word may also denote, in this context, false concepts about God such as idolatry. **Tēn asebeian** has been rendered in the display text as "those things which God dislikes," but a rendering such as "those things which are evil/sinful/ungodly" would also be appropriate.

CONT The adjective **kosmikas** 'worldly' occurs only here in the New Testament with the sense of "that which is at enmity with God or morally reprehensible" (Arndt and Gingrich). But the cognate noun, **kosmos** 'world', occurs often with the same meaning as indicated here in Titus 2:12. As Lock suggests, 1 John 2:16 is a good commentary on the meaning here.

CONT **Epithumia** 'desire' is a generic word which may have a good, bad,or neutral sense according to the context. Here, of course, it has a bad sense as it does in by far the most of its occurrences in the New Testament. **Arnēsamenoi...tas kosmikas epithumias** 'renouncing worldly desires/lusts' has been propositionalized as "stop lusting for the things in this world" where "lust," of course, has a bad connotation. Note that while "stop desiring/lusting for the evil things in this world" might seem appropriate, in some cases, things that are not evil in themselves, such as money, are lusted after, and it is this action that is wrong.

2:12c. **(and) to be self-controlled and do what is right and do what God is pleased with (while) we(inc) live in this present age.** (**sōphronōs kai dikaiōs kai eusebōs zēsōmen en tō nun aiōni**, 'in-a-self-controlled-manner and uprightly and in-a-godly-manner we-may-live in the present age')

PROM **Sōphronōs kai dikaiōs kai eusebōs** ('in a self-controlled manner and uprightly and in a godly manner') are three adverbs occurring before **zēsōmen** 'we may live'. This indicates prominence on the manner of living, which would be expected in this section. Further prominence is indicated by the repetition of **kai** 'and' between the adverbs, which invites measured consideration of each sucessive adverb. In the display text, each of the adverbs is represented by a separate clause joined by "and" to express the prominence signalled in the Greek.

CONT An adjectival cognate of **sōphronōs** \`in a self-controlled manner' is discussed in 1:8. There also the adjectival cognate of **dikaiōs** \`uprightly' occurs contiguous to the cognate of **sōphronōs** (**sōphrona**, **dikaion**). This occurrence in 2:12 is the sixth occurrence in the epistle of a form built on the root **sōphron-** (though one, **sōphronizōsin** \`train, advise' in 2:4 has a somewhat different meaning). The other occurrences are in 1:8; 2:2,5,6. This would indicate the significance Paul places on this personal characteristic and probably indicates that this quality was thought of as quite generic, which is also suggested by the fact that it is the only trait mentioned to be encouraged in the younger men (2:6).

CONT **Dikaiōs** \`uprightly' signifies living in accordance with the laws of God and man. **Eusebōs** \`in a godly manner', as has been mentioned earlier in the discussion on this verse regarding its nominalized antonym **asebeia** \`ungodliness', generally signifies both a right relationship toward God and the resulting right behavior of life. In the display text, this is rendered as "do what God is pleased with"; an alternate rendering would be, "behave in a godly manner."

Some commentators see in these three adverbs a description of the believer's correct relationship to himself (**sōphronōs** \`in a self-controlled manner'), to others (**dikaiōs** \`uprightly'), and to God (**eusebōs** \`in a godly manner'). Though this is certainly within the realm of possibility, each of these words may also indicate relationships with other categories than these narrower limits, e.g., **dikaiōs** may indicate not only one's relationship to his fellowmen but also to God.

CONT In relation to **sōphronōs**, **dikaiōs**, and **eusebōs** (\`in a self-controlled manner', \`uprightly', and \`in a godly manner'), **zēsōmen** \`we should live' refers to the conduct of "life" and thus not to the primary meaning of "life" which, in most languages, is physical life. For this reason, it would not be necessary to use the term "live" in the propositional display in relation to conduct. But the prepositional phrase **en tō nun aiōni** \`in the present age' suggests that physical life is also being referred to, so the concept of "living" has been included in the display text, though not in reference to conduct.

CONT The primary meaning of **aiōn** is "age," not the spatial concept of "world," and so the display text rendering of "in this present age." This "age" is in contrast with that which is to come when Christ appears the second time. However, in some contexts, **aiōn** is closer to the spatial concept than "age" would suggest. Thus, in Heb. 1:2, **di' hou kai epoiēsen tous aiōnas** is translated "through whom he created the worlds/universe" (cf. Heb. 11:3). A translation in Titus 2:12 of "world" instead of "age" thus seems also permissible (both AV and RSV translate "world" here), especially since "this present age" and "this present world" are often equated.

2:13a. **(We(inc) should act like this (2:12b-c) since) we(inc) are waiting expectantly for that which will make (us(inc)) (very) happy (indeed) [METY]**, (**prosdechomenoi tēn makarian elpida** \`awaiting the blessed hope')

REL The present participle **prosdechomenoi** \`waiting for, expecting' occurring in a temporal context would suggest the translation "while we are waiting for." But the larger context strongly suggests that the expectation of Christ's return is a further grounds for self-controlled, upright, and godly living. In the notes for 2:11, it was shown that there are references to the two appearances of Christ (i.e., his first and second coming) in 2:11-14, and that the form of the Greek phrase stating the first appearing (2:11) has many similarities with the form of the statement of the second appearing (2:13). The contextual meanings of 2:11 and 2:13

are different enough that no such similarity would be expected unless the author definitely planned the similar form for some purpose. Within the context of 2:11-14 as grounds for godly living, the most obvious purpose for such highlighting of the two appearances is that both appearances are grounds for godly living. It is not only the gracious actions connected with the first appearance that are incentives and tools for godly living, the second appearing of Christ is also an incentive for such living. Lenski remarks, "Our expectation of Christ's second epiphany moves us to live as we do."

2:11-13 might be seen as a sandwich structure with the "appearances" on either end and the desired characteristics of believers expressed as a content construction in the middle. Another way to analyze 2:11-13 would be as a chiasmus with the "appearances" on either end and the negative and positive characteristics as the two middle constituents. However, since this chiastic structure would be basically semantically-based instead of grammatically-based and would not give any further insights into the meaning than the sandwich structure does, it is not pursued further here. In any case, it is the outer components of the structure (2:11 and 2:13) which are more thematic since they form the grounds for 2:1-10, while the inner component(s) is a generic repetition of 2:1-10 in the form of a content construction.

A propositional representation of the meaning of the overall Greek semantic structure should thus indicate that the second appearing is grounds for 2:12b-c and so the rendering in the display text is "(We(inc) should act like this (2:12b-c) since) we(inc) are waiting expectantly for that which will make (us(inc)) (very) happy (indeed)."

CONT Regarding elpida `hope', Hendriksen says, "This is metonymy for `the realization of that hope' (that is, the realization of our earnest yearning, confident expectation, and patient waiting)." Since we are "waiting for" that "hope," it is the realization of the hope that is being referred to.

Makarios may be translated as "blessed" or "happy." Since "hope" here refers to the realization of the hope, i.e., the second coming of Christ, his coming is said to bring us blessing or happiness. In the display text, this is rendered as "we(inc) are waiting expectantly for that which will make (us(inc)) (very) happy (indeed)." "Very" and "indeed" are used to modify "happy" since the context is highlighted by the use of such prominence-marking content words as doxēs `glory' and megalou `great' which tend to raise the intensity of the constituent as a whole. "Happy" unmodified does not seem to connote the intensity of happiness or blessedness that is implied in the Greek text.

CONT While elpida `hope' refers to the realization of the hope here, i.e., the second coming of Christ, it also indicates that the waiting (prosdechomenoi) is a waiting accompanied by hope. Therefore, "expectantly" is used in the display text to modify "waiting."

2:13b. that is, (we(inc) are expectantly waiting for) our(inc) great God and Savior, Jesus Christ, to come gloriously. (kai epiphaneian tēs doxēs tou megalou theou kai sōtēros hēmōn Iēsou Christou, `and/namely appearance of-the glory of-the great God and Savior of-us Jesus Christ')

REL The kai between tēn makarian elpida `the blessed hope' and epiphaneian tēs doxēs tou megalou theou...`appearing of the glory of the great God...' does not coordinate these two constituents as two different things, but it is that use of kai as described in the Arndt and Gingrich lexicon under I.3., "often explicative; i.e., a word or clause is connected by means of kai with another word or clause, for the purpose of explaining what goes before it `and so, that is, namely.'" The blessed hope is the glorious appearing of our great God and Savior Jesus Christ.

Since the statement following kai is marked as more prominent than the one preceding it by the use of such prominence-marking content words as doxēs `glory' and megalou `great' and especially the titles and person of Jesus Christ himself, the relationship between 2:13a and 2:13b is analyzed as a contraction-Head type of restatement relation.

CONT Tēs doxēs `of the glory' is the second element introduced in and by the "epiphany" formula ("appearance" motif, see under 2:11). Tēs doxēs could be interpreted as (1) the actual radiance and splendor that will accompany Christ at his second coming, (2) qualifying epiphaneian, translated in English as "the glorious appearing," (3) the personification of the glory that will accompany Christ, or (4) Christ himself.

Since Christ himself is mentioned and his personal appearing is certainly being talked about, it does not seem appropriate to interpret tēs doxēs `the glory' as personification.

As far as tēs doxēs `the glory' meaning Christ himself, this is an interpretation advocated by a small minority of commentators including Hort. In the other two occurrences of the "epiphany" formula, hē charis `the grace' (2:11) and hē chrēstotēs kai hē philanthrōpia `the kindness and the love' (3:4) are quite certainly not references to Christ himself but to the attributes that are associated with his coming, so those passages give no support for tēs doxēs meaning Christ here from that aspect. However, those attributes are most likely personified in those passages, and the fact that personification is inappropriate in 2:13 as described above might suggest that there is a possibility that tēs doxēs `the glory' means Christ. Hort (as in Lock) shows how this is grammatically possible by taking Iēsou Christou `Jesus Christ' in apposition to tēs doxēs (tou megalou theou kai sōtēros hēmōn) `the glory (of the great God and Savior of us)', that is, the glory of the great God [the Father] and Savior [the Father] of us, Jesus Christ. The reference to "the great God and Savior of us" is to God the Father, while the glory of the great God and Savior is Jesus Christ. While this is grammatically possible, it does not seem to be the most natural reading of the Greek. And, while there is some evidence for this interpretation from the standpoint of the prominence given to tēs doxēs `the glory' by the epiphany formula, there is little other evidence to support it. The passages given from the New Testament to support it--2 Cor. 4:4; Eph. 1:3 compared with Eph. 1:17; James 2:1; and Col. 2:2--are not very convincing. Nowhere else in scripture is Christ called "the glory of God." There is even less commentator and version support for it. Also, the fact that the next verse, beginning with a relative clause, deals with salvation through Christ would strongly suggest that Savior refers to Christ here in 2:13. It seems more likely that tēs doxēs `the glory' refers to the radiance, splendor, and power that will accompany Christ at his coming, but with no reference to the personification of "the glory" nor any reference to "the glory" as a title of Christ.

Though the introduction of tēs doxēs `the glory' in and by the epiphany formula would seem to mark "glory" as prominent to some extent, it would be hard to believe that "glory" is more prominent than Christ himself. Thus "glory" in the epiphany formula (and this second occurrence of the epiphany formula as a whole) may have more of a binding effect, tying the two grounds (2:11 and 2:13) together as mentioned above. As mentioned under (2) above, it would be quite natural to understand **epiphaneian tēs doxēs** 'appearance of the glory' as **tēs doxēs** 'the glory' qualifying **epiphaneian** 'appearance', a construction in Greek that translates into English as "the glorious appearing." In fact, there is very little difference in meaning whether it be taken as "the glorious appearing" of the great God and Savior, Jesus Christ, or "the appearing of the glory" of the great God and Savior, Jesus Christ. Either one refers to (1) Jesus Christ, (2) to his appearing, and (3) to the fact that that appearing is accompanied by glory associated with his person. The difference between the two is basically in the English surface structure, not in the deep structure. (Certainly "the appearance of the glory" does not refer to the glory alone, i.e., apart from Christ; it is his glorious appearing that we are waiting for.) This, then, is the basis for the rendering in the display text, "come gloriously."

CONT Down through the centuries commentators have been divided as to whether **epiphaneian tēs doxēs tou megalou theou kai sōtēros hēmōn Iēsou Christou** 'appearing of the glory of the great God and Savior of us Jesus Christ' refers to both God the Father and Christ, or only to Christ. One of the grammatical arguments for the reference to just one person (Christ) is that if Paul definitely wanted to indicate two persons (God the Father and Christ), the natural thing to have done according to Greek grammar rules would have been to use the article before **sōtēros** 'Savior', which he does not do. Though the absence of the article in a construction like this does not necessarily mean that only one person is intended, it is important to note that in the five other occurrences of **sōtēros** 'Savior' (all genitive forms) in Titus (1:3,4; 2:10; 3:4,6), the article **tou** always occurs before **sōtēros**. If this expression refers to two persons, it seems strange that in the very place where the article would be needed to definitely show that two persons are intended, the article is lacking, whereas it is found in all the other occurrences.

This argument in support of the one-person theory (Christ) is given even greater support when it is considered that **ho sōtēr hēmōn theos/Iēsous Christos** 'the Savior of us God/Jesus Christ' is a motif occurring six times in Titus and is predictable in form. The five occurrences other than 2:13 are:

tou	**sōtēros**	**hēmōn**	**theou**	'of our Savior, God' 1:3; 2:10; 3:4
of-the	Savior	of-us	God	

Christou	**Iēsou**	**tou**	**sōtēros**	**hēmōn**	'Christ Jesus our Savior' 1:4
Christ	Jesus	the	Savior	of-us	

Iēsou	**Christou**	**tou**	**sōtēros**	**hēmōn**	'Jesus Christ our Savior' 3:6
Jesus	Christ	the	Savior	of-us	

The formula for these five occurrences of the motif is:

± **Iēsou**	**Christou**/	**Christou**	**Iēsou** +	**tou** +	**sōtēros** +	**hēmōn** ±	**theou**
Jesus	Christ	Christ	Jesus	the	Savior	of-us	God

with **Iēsou Christou/Christou Iēsou** being mutually exclusive with **theou** 'God' but with one or the other always occurring.

According to this formula, we would expect the sixth occurrence of this motif in 2:13 to be **Iēsou Christou/Christou Iēsou tou sōtēros hēmōn**, but we find instead that there is no article and also that **Iēsou Christou** comes after **sōtēros hēmōn** 'Savior of us'. This latter is easily explainable, since the personal name/reference may come either before or after **tou sōtēros hēmōn** 'the Savior of us' as shown by the fact that **theou** 'God' occurs after it three times in Titus. But the best explanation for the lack of the article immediately before **sōtēros hēmōn** 'Savior of us' is that the article in that position would have indicated that ***tou sōtēros hēmōn Iēsou Christou** 'the Savior of us Jesus Christ' was distinct from **tou megalou theou** 'the great God'. The article does occur, but it occurs before **megalou theou** 'great God' and it modifies both **megalou theou** and **sōtēros hēmōn** 'Savior of us', thus indicating that only one person is being referred to. As stated above, this is a natural Greek construction for indicating one person or thing. In conclusion, the interpretation that one person is indicated here fits the grammatical patterns of the language and the formal context of Titus very well, while the two-person theory does not. There are other arguments on both sides but none of them are as conclusive as the above, therefore the display text renders **tou megalou theou kai sōtēros hēmōn Iēsou Christou** 'of the great God and Savior of us Jesus Christ' as a reference to Christ only.

Other arguments for a reference to Christ only include:

1. **Epiphaneia** 'appearing' and the whole idea of divine appearances elsewhere in the New Testament never applies to the Father but always to the Son.
2. The fact that nowhere else in the New Testament is God the Father described as "great" since this is taken for granted.
3. A parallel construction in 2 Pet. 1:11, (**tēn aiōnion basileian**) **tou kuriou hēmōn kai sōtēros Iēsou Christou** '(the eternal kingdom) of the Lord of us and Savior Jesus Christ', is generally accepted as referring only to Christ. The only basic difference is that **kuriou** 'Lord' occurs in 2 Pet. 1:11 while **theou** 'God' occurs in Titus 2:13.
4. "The frequent occurrence in pagan texts of 'God and Savior' as a formula applicable to a single personage" (Kelly).
5. It is supported by the majority of the Greek fathers.

Arguments for a reference to two persons (God the Father and Christ) include the following:

1. In this type of construction, an article before the noun after **kai** 'and' is not always necessary to denote two persons. For example, 2 Thess. 1:12 is generally held to indicate two persons: **tēn charin tou theou hēmōn kai kuriou Iēsou Christou** 'the grace of the God of us and Lord Jesus Christ'.
2. Paul nowhere else, except possibly Rom. 9:5, explicitly refers to Christ as God.
3. In the Pastoral Epistles and elsewhere, Paul often mentions God and Christ together as two persons.
4. Most of the very early versions translate as referring to two persons.

It should be noted that the doctrine of Christ's deity is evident throughout the New Testament, so the question is not whether some new doctrine is being introduced here by the one-person interpretation of this passage; it is simply a question of the most accurate interpretation of the Greek text itself in this verse.

2:14a. **He (willingly) gave himself/his own body (to die) on our(inc) behalf, (in the same way as someone would give himself to die in order that others might be set free). (hos edōken heauton huper hēmōn** 'who gave himself for us')

REL 2:14 could be considered as either a second Head or an amplification of 2:11-13. It seems better to analyze it as amplification, since the subject matter of Christ's giving himself for us in order to redeem and purify us is certainly a further expansion of the topic of "saving grace," and there appear to be parallels between the grace that trains us to live a godly life and the purifying that results in a people eager to do good works. The fact that 2:14 begins with a relative, **hos** 'who', would suggest, though not prove, that 2:14 is an amplification rather than a separate Head.

CONT The original statement about Christ's giving himself as a ransom, i.e., "price of release" (**lutron**), was made by Christ himself (Mark 10:45; Matt. 20:28), **ēlthen...dounai tēn psuchēn autou lutron anti pollōn** 'he (the Son of Man) came...to give his life a ransom for many'. This would certainly appear to form the background for the statement in Titus 2:14a-b which refers to Christ's giving himself (**edōken heauton**) in order to redeem/ransom us from all lawlessness (**hina lutrōsētai hēmas apo pasēs anomias**). Therefore, although "he gave himself on our behalf" expresses something here that might be different from what the primary meaning of those words would express, especially in extra-Biblical English, the "giving" concept needs to be retained to form the basis for the idea of the ransom price. In other words, "he willingly died on our behalf" would express the meaning of **hos edōken heauton huper hēmōn** well, except that the reference to the ransom price would be lost.

Although "he gave himself on our behalf" forms the basis for expressing the ransom price, it does not completely express it in itself. The original reader had both the familiarity of this Christian concept that had originated with Christ himself and the context of **lutrōsētai** 'he might ransom/redeem' in 2:14b to help him understand the full meaning of **edōken heauton huper hēmōn** in 2:14a. In the propositionalization of 2:14b, it seems better for various reasons to translate **lutrōsētai** as "cause to be free," so the need to clearly communicate the idea of ransom price in 2:14a. Following are two alternate ways to handle the propositionalization, depending on whether "ransom (price)" is considered acceptable to be used in the propositionalized form of the display text, since it is some type of abstract noun. Also, for translation into other languages, some would have a term for ransom (price) and others would not.

1. He (willingly) gave himself (to die) on our(inc) behalf (in the same way as someone would give himself to die in order that others might be set free).
2. He (willingly) gave himself (to die as a ransom (price)) on our(inc) behalf.

Lock says, "The gift is the gift of the whole life, but principally of the life surrendered in death." "He gave himself on our behalf" communicates the idea of Christ's death for us to those who have been taught the truths of the gospel, but in extra-Biblical English "he gave himself on our behalf" does not necessarily communicate the idea of death, and "he gave himself up for us" might have the idea of surrender but not necessarily of death. Literal renderings of "he gave himself on our behalf" would communicate the true meaning even less accurately in many other languages. For these reasons, "to die" is included in the display text.

Although it is true that "he gave himself on our behalf" also refers to the sacrifice of Christ for us, especially in light of **katharisē** 'he might purify' in

2:14c, the primary or focal reference in 2:14a-b is to redemption, and it seems better not to mix these concepts in 2:14a-b by any explicit reference to sacrifice, especially since the case frames for "giving himself as a ransom" and for "sacrifice" would not be the same.

CONT As mentioned above under REL, Paul is stressing in 2:14a the voluntariness of Christ's giving himself on our behalf. He is amplifying and reinforcing what he has said in 2:11-12a about God's saving grace, his wholly unmerited favor. Thus **edōken heauton huper hēmōn** 'he gave himself on our behalf' expresses both the concept of the ransom and the voluntariness of his giving of himself. It may be best to express this voluntariness in the display text by "willingly."

2:14b. **(He (Jesus) did this (2:14a)) in order that he might cause us(inc) to be free from all sin, (that is, in order that he might enable us(inc) not to sin at all) [METR].** (**hina lutrōsētai hēmas apo pasēs anomias** 'in-order-that he-might-ransom/redeem us from all lawlessness')

REL **Hina** signals the purpose for which Christ "gave himself."

CONT "He might cause us to be free from all sin" is the display text rendering of the figurative sense of **lutrōsētai hēmas apo pasēs anomias** 'he might ransom/redeem us from all lawlessness', while "enable us not to sin at all" is the nonfigurative meaning. Certainly, the point in focus here is the deliverance from the power of sin, since this is what the whole context is about. This **hina** purpose clause is similar in purpose and content to the content construction of 2:12b-c. It expresses in a purpose clause what 2:1-10 expresses in imperatives and other hortatory forms--godly, sinless living.

Since the figure itself does not imply anyone to whom the ransom was to be paid, the emphasis in the rendering of the figure of redemption is on the freedom of those redeemed rather than filling out the whole case frame of "ransom/redeem."

In the display text, "at all" is used to render **pasēs** 'all' (lawlessness).

2:14c. **(He gave himself to die on our(inc) behalf) in order that he might make us(inc) his very own holy people,** (**kai katharisē heautō laon periousion**, 'and purify for-himself a-people (his)own-possession')

REL **Kai** 'and' signals the addition of a second purpose of Christ's giving himself for us. In the display text, a generic representation of 2:14a must be supplied at the beginning of 2:14c in order to make the proper means-purpose connection between 2:14a and 2:14c. Since the implication of 2:14a in reference to 2:14c is one of Christ's giving himself as a sacrifice, as seen by the use of **katharisē** 'he might purify', rather than the sense of giving himself as a ransom as in 2:14a in relation to 2:14b, "He gave himself to die on our(inc) behalf" is supplied at the beginning of 2:14c, rather than the more generic "He did this (2:14a)."

CONT **Katharisē** 'he might cleanse/purify', as used here, appears to be a dead metaphor, since it was so widely used in this spiritual sense. However, there is still the comparison of that which is physically pure with that which is spiritually pure. The meaning is to have everything that has to do with sin removed from us--the actual doing of sin, the inability to stop doing it, the guilt for doing it--just as when one is physically cleansed, all dirt and filth are removed. The most accurate and concise nonfigurative way to propositionalize this seems to be "to make us holy." An alternate might be "cause us(inc) to be/become holy," but in English this causative does not seem to carry as well the sense of Christ's direct involvement that **katharisē** 'he might purify' demands.

Of course, if in any language a literal translation of "purify" adequately expresses the spiritual concept, this should be retained.

CONT **Periousion** is translated as "chosen, especial" by Arndt and Gingrich and as "of his own" by others. The ICC paraphrase (Lock) combines these two in the rendering "a people of His own choice." This Greek word occurs only here in the New Testament.

CONT There is a question as to the implication of **heautō** 'for himself' in the clause **katharisē heautō laon periousion** 'he might purify for himself a people of his own'. Lock, in his paraphrase, translates **heautō** as "for his own service"--"and purify for His own service a people of His own choice." He does not discuss **heautō** 'for himself' in the notes, however. Do **heautō** 'for himself' and **periousion** 'own possession' basically reinforce each other in getting across the idea of "his very own possession," or does **heautō** 'for himself' carry the added idea of "for his own purposes"? Although the latter is certainly implied in the overall scheme of Christ's redeeming and purifying us to be his own people, it is questionable whether it is made explicit by **heautō** 'for himself', or whether it is focal enough to the theme to be included in the propositionalization if it is only implicit. In other words, there is no hard evidence for including it in the display text. I know of no translation other than Lock's paraphrase that includes it.

CONT It does not seem necessary to render 2:14c with two separate propositions, "in order that he might make us holy and in order that he might make us his very own people." At the same time, the force of **katharisē** 'purify, make holy' must not be lost.

Those people that he has ransomed and delivered from sin he makes his very own purified, holy people.

2:14d. **(a people, moreover, who) are eager to do what is good.** (**zēlōtēn kalōn ergōn**. 'zealots of-good works')

REL Since **zēlōtēn** 'zealot, enthusiast' shows concord of case and number with **laon** 'people', even as **periousion** 'own' does, these people not only become Christ's very own people, they also become enthusiasts for good works. This suggests a relationship of Head-description between 14c and 14d. The description proposition is considered as marked prominent, since strong prominence is placed on "good works" in the epistle as a whole. As mentioned in the note on 1:16e, the motif or theme of "good works" comes at the very end of sections in Titus three times (1:16; 2:14; 3:8) and also comes at the very end of the body of the epistle (3:14). At the end of section 3:1-8, it is marked very prominent by various devices. In this present section, which contrasts overall with the one immediately preceding it (1:10-16), the eagerness of Christ's people to do good works is contrasted with the inability of the false teachers "to do any good work."

The marked prominence of this proposition (2:14d) is expressed in the display text by the use of "moreover."

CONT **Kalōn ergōn** 'good works' is to be taken quite generally. Though in some contexts it refers to acts of charity and help (1 Tim. 5:10a,b; 6:18; Titus 3:14), in Titus 1:16, where the false teachers are said to be "unprofitable for any good work" (**pros pan ergon agathon adokimoi**), the sense seems to be any good action whether in aid to others or doing what is right and godly, and this would seem to be the case here in 2:14, too. This very wide sense of "good works" would seem to fit the context of 2:1-14 well, with its emphasis on all kinds of good actions, and also contrasts well with the false teachers' absence of good actions.

DIVISION CONSTITUENT 2:15 (Propositional Cluster) (Role: manner of 1:10--3:11)

THEME: With full authority teach these things (1:10--2:14), urge the believers to do them, and correct those believers who do not follow them.

DISPLAY

RELATIONAL STRUCTURE	CONTENT
HEAD	(2:15a) Teach (the believers) these things (1:10--2:14), urge (them to do them), and correct (those who do not follow them).
MANNER	(2:15b) (Do this (2:15a)) with full authority;
restatement (neg.)	(2:15c) do not allow anyone to disregard you.

BOUNDARIES AND COHERENCE

For the initial and final boundaries, see Boundaries and Coherence for 2:1-10 and 2:11-14.

The coherence of this propositional cluster centers around the following:

1. There are four verbs, all of which are imperative.
2. The first three verbs are grammatically linked by **kai** 'and' and by parallel association with the prepositional phrase **meta pasēs epitagēs** 'with all authority'.
3. The final imperative, set off grammatically from the others by asyndeton and by being a third person imperative rather than second person like the others, is closely associated semantically with the prepositional phrase "with all authority." Both the prepositional phrase and the final imperative deal with the authority with which Titus is to teach, exhort, and correct--the first positively stated, the second negatively stated.

PROMINENCE AND THEME

The fact that **meta pasēs epitagēs** 'with all authority' and its negative restatement, **mēdeis sou periphroneitō** 'let no one disregard you', is the only new lexical information in 2:15 shows that it is focal to the theme. Thus, the manner proposition (2:15b), "(Do this (2:15a)) with full authority," has been analyzed as marked prominent, and "with full authority" should be included in the theme statement. It is not necessary, however, to include the negative restatement (2:15c) in the theme statement since it is a restatement.

Since **parakalei** 'urge' serves as a substitute verb for **lalei** 'speak, teach' in 2:6, having the same grammatical and semantic functions there as **lalei** does in 2:1, i.e., as the head hortatory verb governing the various instructions Titus is to give to the believers, and since 2:15 is at least in some sense a restatement of 2:1-14, it could be argued that only one of these imperatives needs to be included in the theme statement for 2:15. We have decided to keep them both, however, since "urge" expresses the hortatory context and the importance of what was to be urged more appropriately than "teach" does, and since "teach" is needed to cover any reference to the grounds for the exhortations, as in 2:11-14. "Correct" is included since it represents all that has been said regarding correcting those who follow false teaching, something that must be done with full authority.

NOTES ON 2:15

2:15a. **Teach (the believers) these things (1:10--2:14), urge (them to do them), and correct (those who do not follow them).** (**Tauta lalei kai parakalei kai elegche** 'these(things) speak and urge and correct/reprove')

CONT For a discussion as to what is included in **tauta** 'these things', see Boundaries and Coherence for 2:1-15. As discussed there, we analyze **tauta** as referring to all of 1:10--2:14. Each of the first three imperatives of 2:15--**lalei** 'teach', **parakalei** 'urge', and **elegche** 'correct'--occur in 1:10--2:14 as the main hortatory Heads (all as imperatives) of these two sections.

REL To which of these verbs does **tauta** 'these things' relate? Grammatically, not only **lalei** 'speak, teach' but **parakalei** 'urge, exhort' can take the accusative of the thing (cf. Luke 3:18). **Elegche** can also take the accusative of the thing, especially when it has the sense of "expose." Thus Arndt and Gingrich would translate it in 2:15 as "declare this." But, because of the context, it seems better to render it as "reprove" or "correct," i.e., "correct (the believers regarding) these things."

Semantically, there is certainly a tie between all three imperatives and **tauta** 'these things'. Titus is to teach, encourage, and convince/correct the believers regarding all these things that Paul has mentioned. This verse is dealing with generics, and this is expressed in **tauta** 'these things' and in three verbs that are used to cover the full ministry of teaching and leading the church. Therefore, the display text rendering is, "Teach (the believers) these things (1:10--2:14), urge (them to do them), and correct (those who do not follow them)."

CONT For discussion of **lalei** 'speak, teach', **parakalei** 'urge, exhort', and **elegche** 'refute, convince, correct, reprove', see notes on these words in 2:1, 2:6, and 1:13 respectively; and see notes on the latter also in 1:9.

While it does not seem necessary to change the renderings for **lalei** and **parakalei** that were used in 2:1 and 2:6 ("teach" and "urge" respectively), is it best to keep the rendering of **elegche** as "convince...that they are wrong" as in 1:13? (There the full statement is, "Convince (those Cretan believers who follow false teaching) that they are wrong.") The answer to this revolves around another question, Is **elegche** used in relation to wrong actions or wrong belief? Since it has already been used twice in the epistle with a strong leaning toward the sense of wrong belief (1:9 and 1:13), it would be difficult to discount that here. And yet, **elegche** could also apply to correcting those who are not behaving in the right way. To remain generic in an obviously generic verse, this has been rendered "Correct (those who do not follow them)" where "them" refers to both the fundamental beliefs and appropriate behavior based on these beliefs.

2:15b. **(Do this (2:15a)) with full authority;** (**meta pasēs epitagēs**: `with all command')

REL The reason for treating this Greek prepositional phrase, **meta pasēs epitagēs** `with all command/authority', as a separate proposition is that it would be difficult to adequately handle a rendering of this prepositional phrase along with the expanded propositional form of 2:15a. There are basically three components of 2:15. One is the subject matter, **tauta** `these things' which refers to all that Paul has said in 1:10--2:14. The second is what is to be done with "these things." These are the imperative verbs referring to the actions Titus must take. The third component is the manner in which Titus is to carry out these actions--"with full authority" not allowing anyone to disregard him (**mēdeis sou periphroneitō** `let no one disregard you'). It is this third component, the manner of teaching, urging, and correcting, that is the new information here, thus presumably focal to the theme of 2:15. Therefore, this manner constituent 2:15b is considered as being marked prominent.

And again, it is the significance of **meta pasēs epitagēs** `with all authority' as new information that strongly suggests that all three imperative verbs (**lalei** `teach', **parakalei** `urge', and **elegche** `correct') relate to it, instead of just the closest verb, **elegche**, relating to it. Paul wants Titus not only to correct with full authority, he also wants Titus to teach and exhort with full authority. The strengthening of the statement "with full authority" by the adding of its negativized antonym "let no one disregard you" (**mēdeis sou periphroneitō**) also suggests the significance of the manner relationship and, thus, the relation to all three imperatives.

CONT **Epitagē**, literally "command," occurs also in Titus 1:3. Paul has been entrusted with the revealed word of God "by the command of God our Savior" (**kat' epitagēn tou sōtēros hēmōn theou**). Titus should teach this message with all command/authority since it has been entrusted to Paul and now to Titus by the command of God. The following statement in 2:15c, **mēdeis sou periphroneitō** `let no one disregard you', shows that the meaning here in 15b is not only that Titus has full authority to teach these things but that he is also to show and use that full authority.

"Authority" is an abstract word that might be propositionalized as "someone has allowed someone else to tell other people what they should do." This type of thing, of course, is too complicated to use in a display text so "authority" has been used.

2:15c. **do not allow anyone to disregard you.** (**mēdeis sou periphroneitō**. `no-one should-disregard you(sg)')

CONT **Mēdeis sou periphroneitō** `no one should disregard you, let no one disregard you' contains a third person imperative (**periphroneitō**). Kelly translates **mēdeis sou periphroneitō** as "no one must underrate you" (which is a literal translation of the third person imperative) and says, "In this case, as Calvin acutely observes, the remark is intended more for the Cretan churches than for Titus himself." However, when third person imperatives are accompanied formally by a negative subject as **mēdeis** `no one' (or with **tis** `anyone' plus the negative **mē**, see 2 Thess. 2:3), semantically they function as second person commands to the addressee. Here, of course, that is Titus. He should teach, exhort, and correct with full authority, not allowing anyone to disregard him or what he says. No one should be allowed to disregard him as a person since he represents authority and, thus, they must not disregard what he says. At the same time, there is no doubt that this instruction is meant by Paul as a warning to the Cretan believers, too. So, formally (i.e., as far as the actual Greek grammatical form is concerned), **mēdeis** 'no one' is the subject of the imperative, semantically, Titus would normally be understood as the agent of the command ("you must not allow anyone to disregard you"), but, as far as intentionality is concerned, it would seem that both Titus and the Cretan believers are to be the agents of this command. The propositional form in the display text is that of the regular semantic function of this grammatical construction.

Notice a similar passage in 1 Timothy 4:11-12: **Paraggelle tauta kai didaske. mēdeis sou tēs neotētos kataphroneitō, alla tupos ginou tōn pistōn en logō...** 'Command and teach these things. Let no one despise your youth (or, 'no one should despise your youth'), but be an example for believers in speech...' **Kataphroneitō** 'no one should despise, let no one despise' is a third person imperative, while **paraggelle** 'command', **didaske** 'teach', and **ginou** 'be' are all second person imperatives. It would seem quite unnatural for the agent of these imperatives to change from Timothy to others and then back to Timothy again in a hortatory constituent clearly addressed to Timothy. Undoubtedly **kataphroneitō** means "do not let anyone despise" in which Timothy is the agent, instead of "no one should despise." The same would appear to be true for Titus 2:15 as far as semantic function is concerned.

REL Since 2:15c has as its nucleus an imperative, **periphroneitō** 'disregard', it is most natural to consider it to have a conjoined relationship with the three other imperatives, **lalei** 'teach', **parakalei** 'urge', and **elegche** 'correct', though these three are more closely related to each other than to **periphroneitō**. Since we have considered **meta pasēs epitagēs** 'with all authority' to modify all three of the preceding imperatives, 2:15c is a negative restatement of 2:15a-b especially in reference to "with all authority."

DIVISION CONSTITUENT 3:1-8c (Section) (Role: Head B′ of 1:10--3:11)

THEME: Remind the believers to act appropriately toward authorities, to act kindly toward everyone, and to do what is good for all people, since God acted kindly toward us(inc) and mercifully saved us(inc), even though formerly we(inc) were behaving sinfully.

DISPLAY

RELATIONAL STRUCTURE	CONTENT
HEAD	(3:1-2) Remind the believers to act appropriately toward authorities and kindly toward everyone,
GROUNDS	(3:3-7) since God acted kindly toward us(inc) and mercifully saved us(inc), even though formerly we(inc) were behaving sinfully.
RESTATEMENT	(3:8a-c) I want you to confidently teach this trustworthy message (3:3-7) to the believers in order that they will be constantly concerned with doing what is good for others.

BOUNDARIES AND COHERENCE

See earlier for boundary between 2:15 and 3:1.

In 3:1-7, there are three grammatical sentences in the Greek. The first one, 3:1-2, is connected to the second, 3:3, by **gar** `for, since′, which is at the beginning of verse 3. The second, in turn, is connected with the third, 3:4-7, by **de** `nevertheless′ at the beginning of verse 4, and by the relationship between **pote** `formerly′ (3:3) and **hote** `when′ (3:4a), the relation between these two units being concession-contraexpectation.

Coherence is shown in 3:1-7 by such words as **amachous** `peaceable′, **epieikeis** `kind′, and **prautēta** `consideration′ which are the believers′ obligation (3:1-2), since God has shown **chrēstotēs** `kindness′, **philanthrōpia** `love for man′, and **eleos** `mercy′ to us even though we were formerly sinful (3:3-7).

At the end of the third sentence, there is asyndeton (end of verse 7). Verse 8 begins with **pistos ho logos** `trustworthy is the saying/word′. This is a prominence-marking evaluative device found five times in the Pastorals and can be used either anaphorically or cataphorically. Before considering whether it refers backward or forward here, however, we must examine what follows it. 3:8b, **kai peri toutōn boulomai se diabebaiousthai** `and concerning these things I want you to speak confidently′, is an exhortation to Titus, while 3:8c gives the purpose of that exhortation. If **toutōn** `these things′ is taken to mean the preceding truths of the gospel as found in 3:3-7 (although verse 3 expresses our former state, it provides necessary background and so is closely connected with 4-7), then 3:8b-c acts as a restatement of 3:1-7 as shown in the following chart indicating which communication relations express the topics under consideration:

	3:1-7	3:8b-c
Good works	exhortation (3:1-2)	purpose (3:8c)
Sound doctrine	grounds (3:3-7)	exhortation/means (3:8b) (necessarily includes orienter)

In 3:8a-c, Paul attacks the topic of 3:1-7 from a different direction. The motivational grounds of 3:3-7 now become the focus of exhortation, while the exhortations of 3:1-2 become the purpose. Note that, as motivational grounds, it is implied that the great truths of 3:3-7 were to be taught or stressed upon the believers as incentives for doing good works; they were certainly not incentives for Titus alone.

If **toutōn** 'these things' is taken to refer to what precedes it, 3:3-7, then **pistos ho logos** 'trustworthy is the saying' would most naturally refer to that also rather than something else. 3:8a-c thus acts as a powerful restatement, reinforcing both the grounds (sound doctrine) and the exhortations (doing good works) of 3:1-7, in other words, doubling the stress on doing good works. Whereas, if **pistos ho logos** and **toutōn** are taken as referring forward, only the doing of good works in itself is stressed.

It is true that most, if not all, of the other occurrences of **pistos ho logos** in the Pastorals refer to what follows. But there is no grammatical reason why the phrase in itself cannot refer to what precedes.

By far the majority of commentators and versions take **pistos ho logos** here to refer to what precedes.

Thus, at least 3:8b-c appears to be a restatement of 3:1-7. But it still must be determined whether 3:8a, **pistos ho logos**, even though it appears to relate back, is more closely related to 3:3-7 or to 3:8b-c; and also, whether 3:8d is more closely related to 3:8b-c or 3:9.

We have taken 3:8a, **pistos ho logos** 'trustworthy is the saying', as belonging to the constituent of which 3:8b-c is a part for the following reasons:

1. There is no connective marker in the Greek text between 3:7 and 3:8a, while there is one between 3:8a and 3:8b-c.
2. If that connective marker, **kai**, is taken as not only expressing basic coordination but also a logical relationship (grounds-exhortation) as in such passages as Matt. 23:32 and 2 Pet. 1:19a (in English most similar to "and so," see Arndt and Gingrich,I.2.f), then 3:8a-c forms a coherent logical unit of grounds-exhortation-purpose, "These things which I have said are trustworthy, therefore, I want you to confidently teach them to those who have believed in God in order that they will be constantly concerned with doing what is good for others."
3. If **kai** began a new unit, then it would be more natural for it to express connection on a higher level, but the lower-level connection between **pistos ho logos** and 3:8b appears to be the most meaningful one. Some translations, such as RSV, NEB, TEV, which take 3:8a with the preceding unit, do not translate **kai**.

This may be because a connector on the higher level would not be significant here semantically.

Basically **pistos ho logos** is a connective statement itself. Together with **kai** it relates the truths of 3:3-7 with the restatement exhortation of 3:8b-c.

Before deciding where 3:8d, **tauta estin kala kai ōphelima tois anthrōpois** 'these things are good and profitable for people', belongs, the antecedent of **tauta** 'these things' must be determined. It could refer to (1) the great doctrines of 3:3-7, (2) the good works (**kalōn ergōn**) of 3:8c, or (3) possibly to both (1) and (2). Although **kalōn ergōn** is the closer antecedent, we have analyzed **tauta** to refer to the great doctrines of 3:3-7 for the following reasons:

1. **Tauta** is contrasted with the false doctrines in 3:9 rather than evil deeds. The most probable and focal contrast would be between the sound doctrine of 3:3-7 and the false doctrine of 3:9. (Note that, though 3:9 also focuses on arguments, the contents of these arguments are false doctrine.)
2. If **tauta** were to refer to **kalōn ergōn** 'good works', then it would be difficult to understand why Paul would repeat himself and call the works **kala** 'good' again in his very next statement. It seems as though he would have at least used a synonym to avoid being overredundant.

A majority of commentators take **tauta** to relate to 3:3-7 (or 4-7).

Taking **tauta** 'these things' to refer to the truths of 3:3-7, the following considerations would suggest that 3:8d belongs to the constituent that follows it:

1. There is no connective marker (other than **tauta**) between 3:8c and 3:8d. (Thus the proposed constituent 3:8a-c would be bounded by asyndeton on both sides.)
2. There is no doubt about the semantic relationship between 3:8d and 3:9. There is a definite intended contrast between the profitableness (**ōphelima** 'profitable') of **tauta** 'these things' and the unprofitableness (**anōpheleis** 'unprofitable') of the foolish disputes about genealogies and the law. If **tauta** is taken to refer to the great truths of 3:3-7, then the primary semantic relationship here is between 3:3-7 and 3:9. The basic function of 3:8d would be to relate 3:3-7 with 3:9, setting up the contrast. Therefore, since the basic anaphoric relationship of 3:8d is not to 3:8a-c but to 3:3-7, it seems better to analyze 3:8d as part of constituent 3:9ff. rather than constituent 3:8a-c.
3. There is no doubt that 3:8d is summary-type information as is 3:8a-c. However, the coherence that this suggests is more general than the specific coherence involved in the contrast between 3:8d and 3:9. If there were a connector marking 3:8d as grounds for 3:8b-c, then it would definitely belong to the preceding constituent. If taken with 3:8a-c as it is, it seems to stand alone, and to be rather anticlimactical, as a final summary statement that doesn't tie in well anywhere, except with 3:9.

Finally, it must be said that some boundaries are not as distinct as we would like them to be. Where there is definite semantic relationship, sometimes the two constituents blend into each other at the borders, and it is difficult to make an exact cut.

In our analysis, the two evaluative/prominence-marking statements, 3:8a and 3:8d, both of which refer to 3:3-7, act as connectors. 3:8a relates 3:3-7 to the restatement exhortation of 3:8b-c, while 3:8d relates 3:3-7 to the contrast in 3:9ff.

PROMINENCE AND THEME

The theme statement includes the theme of the naturally prominent exhortation unit 3:1-2 plus the theme of the grounds for 3:1-2 which is considered as marked prominent for the following reasons:

1. The grounds has many prominence-marking signals--notice the high-impact words used in verse 3, almost every content word is intensive to some degree to emphasize the depth of our sin. Notice the piling up of synonyms to emphasize God's love in verses 4 and 5--kindness, love, mercy. And to show that our salvation is all from God, notice the forefronting of "not of works of righteousness" and "because of his mercy" before the main verb and the piling up of other phrases that prove the same point--regeneration and renewal of the Holy Spirit, being justified by God's grace. Kelly mentions "the rhythm and heightened tone of the passage" and sees this as evidence (along with many other commentators) that this was probably some inserted hymn or liturgical piece. It seems better to me to take these as prominence-marking devices instead of analyzing this unit as an insertion without adequate proof that it is such.
2. Verse 8 also shows the importance of verses 3-7. **Pistos ho logos** `trustworthy is the saying/word' is a prominence-marking device. (Note that only one other of Paul's five uses of **pistos ho logos** in the Pastorals definitely refers to what might be called a liturgical quotation (2 Tim. 2:11), the others refer to what Paul himself is saying.) As mentioned under Boundaries and Coherence, **pistos ho logos** is best considered to point backward to 3:3-7.
3. In the restatement (3:8a-c), the topic of the grounds unit 3:3-7 becomes the focus of the exhortation (see Boundaries and Coherence for 3:1-8c).

Paul is saying that these truths about God and his salvation are the basic truths upon which all our Christian actions and behavior are based--"I want you to affirm these things in order that those who have trusted in God will be concerned with doing good deeds" (3:8). Note also the preview of the theme of the epistle in 1:1, **epignōsin alētheias tēs kat' eusebeian**, which could well be translated as NIV, "the knowledge of the truth that leads to godliness."

As a restatement of 3:1-7, 3:8a-c might be thought to add nothing significant enough to the theme to be included in the theme statement. However, 3:8a-c is a powerful reinforcement of what has been said in 3:1-7, this time attacking the topic with the focus on confidently affirming the great truths of the gospel to motivate the believers to good works. Coming at the end of the sections on teaching sound doctrine, and being marked highly prominent itself, it is certainly one of the main peaks of the epistle. The fact that maintaining "good works" is found in the purpose construction at this strategic point and also at other strategic points in the epistle, as mentioned earlier under the notes for 1:16e, argues for the inclusion of a reference to "good works" in the theme statement. This has been included as "do what is good for all people."

SECTION CONSTITUENT 3:1-2 (Paragraph) (Role: Head of 3:1-8c)

THEME: Remind the believers to act appropriately toward authorities and kindly toward everyone.

DISPLAY

RELATIONAL STRUCTURE	CONTENT
ORIENTER	(3:1a) Remind them (the believers)
HEAD	(3:1b-2) that (they should) submit to (and) obey those who rule (them and) have authority (over them). Anything that is good, (they should) be ready to do. (2) (They should) never say bad things about anyone, (they should) not quarrel (with people), (they should) be kind (to people), (and they should) always act considerately toward all people.

BOUNDARIES AND COHERENCE

For intial boundary of this paragraph, see above under final boundary for the previous section. This paragraph coheres by being a single list with a single orienter which is the only nonsubordinated finite verb in the paragraph. The final boundary is marked by the change in subject matter, mood, aspect, and person that takes place at 3:3. These contrasts may be charted as follows:

	3:1-2	3:3-7
Subject matter	godly living	God's saving grace--the basis for godly living
Mood	imperative	indicative
Aspect	progressive (present)	punctiliar (aorist)
Person	second singular third plural	third singular first plural

A similar pattern was observed between 2:1-10 and 2:11-14. The same semantic relationship, exhortation-grounds, holds between the two paragraphs here and between those in chapter two.

PROMINENCE AND THEME

Since the basic construction of this constituent is an imperative that acts as orienter, plus a list of specific instructions that form the content, the theme statement should include the orienter plus a generic representation of the specific instructions for godly living. Although there is nothing on the grammatical level that differentiates one set of the specific instructions from another set, on the semantic level the first two instructions (or possibly three, see notes) refer to the believers' relationship to those in authority, while the rest refer to the believers' relationship to people in general (**pantas anthrōpous** 'all people, everyone'). Also, the semantic domain of the verbs of the first relationship, "submit" and "obey," might be taken as somewhat different from that of the verbs, adjectives, and nouns of the second set, which deal more with kindness and consideration for others.

However, the grounds support unit for 3:1-2 (3:3-7) deals with the kindness of God as an incentive for our being kind to others, and the restatement of 3:1-7 (3:8a-c) summarizes the exhortations of 3:1-2 as doing good works (kalōn ergōn proistasthai), so that, as far as the higher-level theme is concerned, "be kind toward everyone" would appear to be more thematic than "submit to and obey rulers and authorities."

For the theme of 3:1-2, then, there are these choices:

1. Exclude any specific reference to submission to authorities, and use only a very generic reference that fits in well with the overall theme, e.g., "Remind the believers to act appropriately and kindly to everyone," where "appropriately" is meant to cover the relationship to those in authority.
2. Use a generic verb like "appropriately" as in 1 above to represent "submit to" and "obey" but also include a reference to those in authority, e.g., "Remind the believers to act appropriately toward those in authority and kindly toward everyone."
3. Keep a specific reference to the relationship with those in authority, e.g., "Remind the believers to submit to those in authority and to act kindly toward everyone."

We have used the second choice in the theme statement in an attempt to remain relevant to the theme of the section while, at the same time, including some reference to submission to those in authority, which seems to have a certain amount of prominence shown by its occurring first in the list of instructions. The third choice does not fit the overall theme as well. There is nothing in the text itself that separates the relationship with authorities from the relationship with all people, and so we would expect the grounds unit of 3:3-7 to apply to all the instructions.

NOTES ON 3:1-2

3:1a. **Remind them (the believers)** (**Hupomimnēske autous** 'remind them')

CONT By using the present imperative **hupomimnēske** 'remind', Paul commands Titus to remind the believers to do what is shown in the content (3:1b-2). The present tense shows that he was to do so continually and repeatedly, and suggests that he was already doing this and was to continue. **Autous** 'them' refers to all the classes of believers mentioned in 2:2-10.

3:1b-2. **that (they should) submit to (and) obey those who rule (them and) have authority (over them). Anything that is good, (they should) be ready to do. (2) (They should) never say bad things about anyone, (they should) not quarrel (with people), (they should) be kind (to people), (and they should) always act considerately toward all people.** (**archais exousiais hupotassesthai, peitharchein, pros pan ergon agathon hetoimous einai, mēdena blasphēmein, amachous einai, epieikeis, pasan endeiknumenous prautēta pros pantas anthrōpous.** 'to-rulers, to-authorities to-submit, to-be-obedient, for every good work ready to-be, to-speak-evil-of no-one, uncontentious to-be, kind, showing-forth all meekness to all people')

CONT The references to **archais** `rulers' and **exousiais** `authorities' in 3:1 are not to the church leaders referred to earlier in the letter (1:5c-9). In the New Testament, **archē** and **exousia** (when referring to human beings) are not used for leaders in the Christian church but for civil authorities and possibly for Jewish religious authorities. Also, some commentators see 3:1-2 as referring to the pagan world generally, that is, what the attitude of the Christian should be toward the pagan world. Notice "all people" at the end of 3:2, and the fact that Paul says that "we" also formerly lived like these people (3.3).

CONT **Archē** `rule, ruler' and **exousia** `authority' occur together ten times in the New Testament and are always in this order. They are joined by **kai** "and" in every other instance. Here there is asyndeton. Accordingly, the second "and" is enclosed within parentheses. The nouns are anarthrous, which suggests that rulers and authorities in general are referred to, rather than the specific incumbents.

CONT In the environment of the imperative **hupomimnēske** `remind', the infinitives **hupotassesthai** `to submit to', **peitharchein** `to be obedient', **einai** `to be', and **blasphēmein** `to speak-evil-of', and the participle **endeiknumenous** `showing' carry on the specific commands of which they are to be reminded. "They should" is supplied in the text to indicate this obligation.

CONT There is also asyndeton between the infinitive constructions **hupotassesthai** and **peitharchein**. **Peitharchein** `to be obedient' is closely linked semantically with **hupotassesthai** `to submit to'. In the display text, "obey" has been linked with "submit to" as having those who rule and have authority as the object of both verbs. Some commentators believe that **peitharchein** `to be obedient' is best taken absolutely, that is, to be generally obedient. But it would seem that here the believers are specifically enjoined to obey those in authority. The reasons for this conclusion are the close semantic link between obedience and submission, and the fact that all the relations in 3:1-2 have to do with the believers' attitude toward other people and not toward God, so obedience to God would not be in focus here.

CONT In 3:1b-2, the content propositions, which function as individual specific commands, can be seen to begin with the believers' relationship to rulers and authorities (**archais exousiais**) and end with the believers' relationship to all people (**pantas anthrōpous**). **Mēdena** `no one', in the construction **mēdena blasphēmein** `to say bad things about no one', indicates that the switch has already changed to a general application by this point and that the relationship is no longer just to rulers and authorities. But where exactly does that switch occur?

As mentioned above, it seems best to take **peitharchein** `to obey' with **hupotassesthai** `to submit to' as both showing a relationship toward rulers and authorities. This, then, might be the first couplet of the six infinitive constructions in 3:1b-2. **Peitharchein** and **hupotassesthai** are close in meaning and are especially relevant to the relationship to those in authority. Actually, the first couplet itself could be taken as symmetrically constructed with two nouns linked by asyndeton immediately followed by two verbs linked by asyndeton.

We, then, notice that constructions five and six, **amachous einai, epieikeis** `uncontentious to be, kind (to be)', are alike in that they both contain adjectives, they both depend on the one **einai** `to be', the construction for each is very brief, and the meaning of the two is very similar. The construction following, **pasan endeiknumenous prautēta pros pantas anthrōpous** `showing all consideration for all people', Is participial and shows semantic dependence on constructions five and six. The question is, then, Is there anything that ties together constructions three and four (**pros pan ergon agathon hetoimous einai, mēdena blasphēmein** 'for every good work to be ready, to say bad things about no one'), or, as many commentators suggest, does construction three relate more closely to constructions one and two, and construction four relate more closely to constructions five, six, and seven? There may be an intended connection between constructions three and four in the contrast between **pan ergon agathon** 'every good work' and **mēdena** 'no one'. If we take **erga agatha** 'good works' in its common (though not necessarily primary) sense of good done to help others, then construction three does relate very well to all of verse two. In fact, the basic semantic structure of 3:1-2 could very well be, "Submit to authorities and do good to everyone." Based on these considerations and the fact that there is no grammatical evidence for relating **pros pan ergon agathon hetoimous einai** 'for every good work to be ready' to **archais exousiais hupotassesthai peitharchein** 'to submit and be obedient to rulers and authorities', it seems better to keep the application of this construction general rather than specific to the rulers and authorities, e.g., always being ready to do whatever good thing the authorities might request. On the other hand, there certainly is the possibility of an intended semantic link between obedience and readiness to do good, so that the alternate solution of taking readiness to do good works as part of the believers' obedience to authorities has considerable merit.

CONT For a discussion of the general meaning of "good works," see 1:16e. Since we have considered the reference to those who are the beneficiaries of the "good works" as general, it seems best to take "good works" here in a rather generic sense, though with the sense of doing good for others and helping them rather than the sense of good behavior, since there is no contextual evidence that the latter would be in focus here.

CONT Regarding the word **prautēs** which we have rendered as "act considerately," Callow (1983a:185) says, in his discussion of the word as it occurs in Col. 3:12, that it "seems to have two components. One is a consideration for others, an ability to see things from the other's point of view. The other is a willingness to waive legitimate rights (Martin), 'to suffer injury rather than to inflict it' (Hendriksen). There does not seem to be any English word that covers both of these senses...." In Col. 3:12, Callow uses words giving both senses in the display text ("be meek/considerate") "because there is no contextual reason to choose one rather than the other." Here in Titus, the fact that there is a definite relationship between **prautēs**, which we, as believers, are to show to others, and **chrēstotēs** 'goodness, kindness, generosity', **philanthrōpia** 'love for mankind' (3:4), and **eleos** 'mercy' (3:5), which God has shown to us, would suggest that "considerate" is the more appropriate sense here.

PROM Very strong prominence is put on **pasan** 'all' as modifying **prautēta** 'consideration'. The adjective occurs first in the participial phrase and is separated by the participle from the noun which it modifies. Believers should invariably exhibit a considerate attitude toward all others.

SECTION CONSTITUENT 3:3-7 (Paragraph) (Role: Grounds for 3:1-2)

THEME: God acted kindly toward us(inc) and mercifully saved us(inc), even though formerly we(inc) were behaving sinfully.

DISPLAY

RELATIONAL STRUCTURE				CONTENT
	concession			(3:3) Formerly we ourselves(inc) were also foolish even as (they (all people who do not believe in Christ) are now). (We(inc)) did not obey (anyone). (We(inc)) were being deceived (by others). (We(inc)) could not stop ourselves from lusting after all sorts of (evil) pleasures. (We(inc)) were continually doing what is evil. (We(inc)) were envying (others). (We(inc)) were causing people to hate us(inc) (and we(inc)) were hating one another.
		CIRCUM.		(3:4) (Even though we(inc) were behaving sinfully like this (3:3),) nevertheless (the time came) when God our(inc) Savior acted kindly and lovingly (to us(inc)) [PERS],
HEAD	HEAD	HEAD		(3:5a) (and then) he saved us(inc).
		contrast		(3:5b) (He saved us(inc)) not because we ourselves(inc) did what is right,
	REASON	HEAD		(3:5c) but because he himself is merciful (to us(inc)).
	means			(3:5d-e) (He saved us(inc)) by means of (his) washing (us(inc)) (and making us(inc) holy) (5e) (at which time) the Holy Spirit regenerated (us(inc)), (that is,) the Holy Spirit caused (us(inc)) to begin a new (spiritual) life.
amplif.	HEAD			(3:6) By means of Jesus Christ our(inc) Savior, God (graciously) gave the Holy Spirit to us(inc) (in order that the Holy Spirit might act) mightily (on our(inc) behalf).
	purpose	HEAD		(3:7a) (God did this (3:6)) in order that we(inc) might become (his) heirs* (and, as a result,) confidently expect to live* forever.
		reason	HEAD	(3:7b) (We(inc) became God's heirs* because) he declared (us(inc)) righteous,
			reason	(3:7c) (because) he is gracious.

BOUNDARIES AND COHERENCE

The intial boundary was discussed under 3:1-2, the final boundary under 3:1-8c.

The two major constituents of this paragraph (3:3 and 3:4-7) are related by de 'but, nevertheless' (3:4) and the temporal progression from pote 'formerly' (3:3) to hote 'when' (3:4) which represents a subsequent event. These connectives, plus the content of the two clusters manifest the relationship of concession-contraexpectation. The last major constituent (3:7) is linked to 3:6 by hina, signalling the purpose relationship.

The referential unity of the paragraph revolves around the Head proposition, esōsen hēmas 'he (God) saved us' (3:5), and deals with the basis, means, and purpose of our salvation. 3:3 gives the background showing that it was of true mercy that we sinners were saved and that our salvation is not of anything that we have done.

It should be noted that the order of units in the display does not strictly follow the order in the Greek in some cases. The reason unit 3:5b-c occurs before esōsen hēmas 'he saved us' in the Greek text. In the display text, the reason unit was put after "he saved us" in order to facilitate the signalling of relations in the English gloss. Also 3:7a-c has been reordered. See notes on those propositions for the reasons.

PROMINENCE AND THEME

The theme statement includes the Head proposition of the paragraph, "he (God) saved us." **Esōsen** 'he saved' is the only nonsubordinated finite verb in 3:4-7, the contraexpectation part of the paragraph.

The basis or reason for his saving us--his kindness, love, and mercy (3:4-5)--is thematic, since it is the point of comparison in the grounds which relates to believers' being kind to others (3:1-2). Also **chrēstotēs** 'kindness' and **philanthrōpia** 'love' are marked prominent by their occurrence with **epephanē** 'appeared' in the motif that also occurs in chapter two. See the notes on 2:11. The focal point of this type of motif is marked prominent by the use of this rhetorical device. The focal point in the formula of the motif is that point which is variable --here **chrēstotēs** 'kindness' and **philanthrōpia** 'love'. Notice that in the verse under consideration, 3:4, **chrēstotēs** and **philanthrōpia** "kindness" and "love" are further highlighted by forefronting, whereas **charis** 'grace' and **doxēs** 'glory' in the other occurrences of the motif are not forefronted. Because of these various reasons, "God acted kindly toward us(inc)" is included in the theme.

Further reasons for considering **to autou eleos** 'his (God's) mercy' (3:5c) as being marked prominent are (1) the forefronting of **kata to autou eleos** 'according to his mercy' before the verb **esōsen** 'he saved', and (2) the highlighting given it as the positive in a negative-positive contrast, all coming before the main verb.

Since 3:6-7 is a parallel semantic construction with 3:4-5, adding new information but still dealing with the same general categories of basis and means for our salvation as found in 3:4-5 (see notes on 3:6-7), 3:6-7 is considered an amplification unit and is not separately represented in the theme statement.

Since 3:4-5 and 3:6-7 are composed of multiple references to the basis and means of our salvation, and both the basis and fact of our salvaion are included in the theme statement, the next question is whether the means should also be represented. There are at least four references to the means--"washing," "regeneration," "renewal," and the outpouring of the Holy Spirit upon us. This number of references to the means would tend to mark it prominent, combined with the fact that one of these, the outpouring of the Holy Spirit, is represented by a finite verb **execheen** 'he poured out' in a construction that could be interpreted to be non-subordinate. It appears, however, that these references to the means of our salvation, which are all performed by God (either directly or through his Holy Spirit), are meant to show that we can claim nothing on our own, our salvation is brought about only through God's gracious actions on our behalf. This, then, reinforces the fact that we have no excuse for not being kind to others since God has been so kind to us. Since this has basically been included in the theme statement already, no direct reference to the means of our salvation is included in the theme statement.

Finally, the theme statement includes the concession unit in order to round out the concession-contraexpectation structure of the paragraph and thus represent the full force of the theme. The concession portion of the paragraph has been summarized in the words "even though formerly we were behaving sinfully."

NOTES ON 3:3-7

3:3. **Formerly we ourselves(inc) were also foolish even as (they (all people who do not believe in Christ) are now). (We(inc)) did not obey (anyone). (We(inc)) were being deceived (by others). (We(inc)) could not stop ourselves from lusting after all sorts of (evil) pleasures. (We(inc)) were continually doing what is evil. (We(inc)) were envying (others). (We(inc)) were causing people to hate us(inc) (and we(inc)) were hating one another.** (**Ēmen gar pote kai hēmeis anoētoi, apeitheis, planōmenoi, douleuontes epithumiais kai hēdonais poikilais, en kakia kai phthonō diagontes, stugētoi, misountes allēlous.** 'For we-were formerly also/even we-ourselves senseless, disobedient, being-deceived, enslaved to-lusts and pleasures various, in evil and envy living, hateful, hating one-another')

REL The question here is whether gar indicates a grounds role for what is to follow, i.e., a grounds role supporting the exhortation in 3:1-2, or whether gar indicates some other relationship. What is the semantic relationship between 3:1-2 and 3:3ff.? Here are some of the proposed relationships:

1. Lenski: "The argument is strong: Shall we, after having been delivered from such a state [3:3], again fall back into it?" But there seems to be no support for this in the text. It does not relate to the imperatives of 3:1-2, otherwise there would be an imperative something like, "Do not return to your former ways." The exhortations of 3:1-2 and 3:8 are more of a positive type--do good to others.
2. White: "The connexion is: you need not supppose that it is hopeless to imagine that these wild Cretan folk can be reclaimed. We ourselves are a living proof of the power of God's grace." Again, this does not support the imperatives of 3:1-2. This may be a further logical step that can be deduced from what Paul is saying, but it is not what he is saying in these verses.
3. Huther: "As we were in the state in which they are now, but were rescued by the kindness of God, it becomes us to show kindness and gentleness towards those whom we were at one time like." This seems to be a sound interpretation because it keeps the exhortations of 3:1-2 in focus ("it becomes us to show kindness and gentleness")--it ties in the kindness asked of us in 3:1-2 with the kindness shown by God as stated in verses 4ff.--and it keeps all of 3:3-7 in perspective, since it is obvious that verse 3 is subordinate to verses 4ff., so that tying verses 1-2 with 3 only, does not give the correct interpretation. The display is in agreement with interpretation number 3.
4. Lock would agree with Huther (3 above) but also states another grounds: "we ourselves were no better, and therefore are bound to be tolerant and forgiving." (This grounds is actually stated first by Lock since it is based on 3:3.) Yes, but this is really a part of, or subordinate to, the other more comprehensive grounds. I believe our display would cover both of these ideas, but it seeks to convey the more comprehensive grounds.

3:3-7 as a whole, then, is considered as grounds for 3:1-2 in our analysis. However, there seems to be no adequate way to represent this connection in the English display text. Since verse 3 and verses 4-5 are not conjoined Heads but are in a concession-contraexpectation relationship, the most direct thematic connection is between verses 1-2 and 4-5. But to express such a connection in the display text of verse 3, one has to bring into verse 3 elements of verses 4-5, and the general structure of the paragraph becomes somewhat changed. Therefore, the connection between 3:1-2 and 3:3-7 is not expressed explicitly in the display text of verse 3, but the connection can be seen in the display diagram and through the semantic ties between the hortatory unit and the grounds unit.

CONT Hēmeis 'we' includes Paul, Titus, and the Cretan Christians. Paul is included since hēmeis always includes the speaker/author; the Cretan Christians are included since the exhortations of 3:1-2 are meant for them (autous 3:1), and 3:3 deals with grounds for those exhortations based on the experience of those who are to be exhorted, "You be kind to all people since God was kind to you even though you formerly were equally sinful." Titus is included since there is no reason why Paul should be included and Titus excluded. "We(inc)" remains the only explicit participant on the human side all through 3:3-7. Though the focus is on Paul, Titus, and the Cretan Christians, it is not necessary to exclude a general reference to all believers.

CONT The kai in 3a probably means "also, likewise, as well as, even." It expresses comparison. The reading in the display text is "even as (they (all people who do not believe in Christ) are now)." The reason for supplying more than the "also" or "even" of the text is to indicate more clearly those with whom the comparison is being made. "All people" (pantas anthrōpous) occurs in the immediately preceding construction at the end of 3:2. Because of the close proximity of pantas anthrōpous and the fact that no one else besides the "we" is mentioned in the immediate context, "all people" is most obviously to be compared with "we." Of course, the implied reference in 3:3 is to all people who have not yet believed since the logic of the grounds-exhortation appears to be, "We should do good to them, after all we were once like they are now but God showed his love for us." In fact, when Paul uses pantas 'all' in 3:2, he probably does so with the suggestion of "all people no matter how sinful they may be." Kelly remarks, "The insistence on 'all men'...is deliberate. This gentle courtesy which is so essential a trait of the Christian character must be exhibited to the world in general, including those who are most hostile or whom one likes least, and not just to one's fellow-Christians or personal friends. The Cretans, Paul now suggests, have a powerful motive for behaving in a considerate, conciliatory manner to their pagan neighbours, inasmuch as 'we ourselves (with characteristic humility he brackets himself with them...) were at one time,' i.e. before our conversion, fully as bad as they are now."

CONT Each item in the list is regarded as a chronic condition, occurring repeatedly or continuously. This aspect derives from the fact that ēmen 'we were' is in the imperfect tense. Anoētoi 'foolish' here could refer to a condition of lack of spiritual understanding as in Rom. 1:14, or to thoughts or actions based on incorrect spiritual understanding as in Luke 24:25; Gal. 3:1,3; 1 Tim. 6:9. (These are the only other occurrences of anoētos in the New Testament.) Since Paul is focusing in 3:3 on our sinfulness before trusting Christ rather than the fact of our lack of knowledge of God per se, what is meant here is a condition in which people's thoughts and actions are based on a lack of spiritual understanding, they think and act foolishly because they do not know God.

CONT Apeitheis 'disobedient' could refer here either to disobedience to God or disobedience in general. Since 3:3 is a generic statement of the sinful traits of unbelievers and since several of the specific traits deal with the relations of people with one another (planōmenoi 'deceived', phthonō 'envy', stugētoi 'hateful', misountes allēlous 'hating one another'), it seems best to understand apeitheis 'disobedient' as generic too, and so the rendering in the display text is "(We(inc)) did not obey (anyone)." "Anyone" here is intended to include God.

CONT In the phrase douleuontes epithumiais kai hēdonais poikilais 'being enslaved to various lusts and pleasures', the participle douleuontes 'being enslaved' is used figuratively, the persons controlled by their desires and pleasures are spoken of as being slaves to them. However, since **doulеuō** is used in many other places in the New Testament and other Greek literature with a similar figurative sense, it functions as a dead metaphor. **Poikilais** 'various' is taken as modifying both **epithumiais** 'lusts' and **hēdonais** 'pleasures'. Both **epithumia** and **hēdonē**, more often than not, have a bad sense in the New Testament. With the context of enslavement and sin in general, certainly evil pleasures are most in focus. It is true, of course, that an unhealthy preoccupation with legitimate pleasures can also be sinful. In the display text, "lust" is used in verbal form.

CONT **Diagontes** 'living' has the sense of "passing the time" in evil and envy. **Stugētoi** 'hateful' means acting in such a way as to induce hatred from others.

3:4. **(Even though we(inc) were behaving sinfully like this (3:3),) nevertheless (the time came) when God our(inc) Savior acted kindly and lovingly (to us(inc)) [PERS], (hote de hē chrēstotēs kai hē philanthrōpia epephanē tou sōtēros hēmōn theou**, 'but when the kindness and the love-for-mankind of-the Savior of-us God appeared')

REL/PROM See Prominence and Theme for 3:3-7 for the reasons this circumstance proposition is considered as marked prominent. The circumstance or time factor is not as much in focus thematically as the statement about "God acting kindly and lovingly to us." But an indication has to be made of the change of time from what "we formerly (**pote**) were" to the time "when (**hote**) God acted kindly and lovingly to us and saved us." "The time came" is added to indicate that the time of the action here is not as prominent as the action itself; hopefully this addition helps to de-emphasize the time factor. An alternate solution might be to render 3:4-5a as "But, then God our Savior acted kindly and lovingly (to us(inc)) (and) he saved us(inc)."

CONT As mentioned earlier, we understand **epephanē** here in the same way as in 2:11 as having reference to Christ's appearing on earth the first time. Note that in the noun form, **epiphaneia** 'appearing, appearance' always refers to Christ's appearing on earth in the New Testament, whether his first or second coming, and there is no obvious reference in the New Testament where the verb in passive form (as here) means "reveal" in any other sense than "appear." That it means the appearance of Christ here is further indicated by its close comparison with the noun form **epiphaneia** in the motif in 2:13 (see discussion under notes for 2:11 and 2:13 where personification in the "appearance" motif is also discussed). Instead of making each of the meaning components of **epephanē** explicit here as in 2:11 where we rendered it as "(God) sent (Jesus Christ) to earth," in this context it seems more appropriate to use a more generic form, "(God) acted (kindly and lovingly)," in order to keep the focus on God's action.

CONT A third problem may be determining the time relationship between Christ's appearing and God's saving. A cursory reading would tend to indicate that they came one right after the other. But we know that, even for Paul, this did not happen, unless we follow Calvin, "not of that ordinary manifestation of Christ which took place when he came as a man into the world, but of the manifestation which is made by the gospel, when he exhibits and reveals himself, in a peculiar manner...both to Paul and others, when they were enlightened in the knowledge of the gospel." To follow this, however, would be to take **epiphainō** in a way not used elsewhere in the New Testament. Rather, it would seem better to follow Lenski, "'When' that [grace] made its epiphany, God 'saved us'; yet that does not mean that these acts occurred together in point of time....Paul received baptism at a later time, and the Cretans received it still later." Here Paul is speaking without reference to exact time relationships. It must be remembered, too, that for Paul, and for at least some of those he is including in the "we," Christ came after they had lived part of their lives in sin. Our time orientation today as to Christ's coming is far different from the time orientation of Paul's day.

3:5a-c. **(and then) he saved us(inc). (5b) (He saved us(inc)) not because we ourselves(inc) did what is right, (5c) but because he himself is merciful (to us(inc)).** (**ouk ex ergōn tōn en dikaiosunē ha epoiēsamen hēmeis alla kata to autou eleos esōsen hēmas** 'not of works in righteousness which we-did we-ourselves but according-to his mercy he-saved us')

REL By adding "the time came" to 3:4, 3:4 is no longer a subordinate construction and so (in English anyway) 3:5a needs to have a connector. Since "and" would be ambiguous, meaning either "and then" or "and when," it cannot be used in the display text. "At that time" could be taken to mean that the "saving" came right at the time of the "appearing," while "and then" would not be so precise (see discussion of time relationships in 3:4). Therefore, "and then" is used.

REL The relationship of 3:5c to 3:5a (note that these are the references to the propositions in the display text and they are in different order from the Greek text) is considered a reason-result relationship, since **kata** often introduces a reason for Head statements, and 3:5a "he saved us" refers to the referential aspect of the event and not to "the illocutionary act of stating, commanding, or questioning by the author" (Beekman, Callow, and Kopesec 1981:107). Therefore, the relationship is not considered to be grounds-Head.

PROM In the Greek text, the reason unit (3:5b-c) is forefronted, thus putting marked prominence on the reason unit and especially on the positive side (3:5c) of the negative-positive contrast. On the negative side (3:5b), **hēmeis** 'we' is marked for contrast (with **autou** 'his') by the occurrence of the overt nominative pronoun. **Alla** 'but' introduces the positive side and gives prominence to **kata to autou eleos** 'according to his mercy'. In the noun phrase **to autou eleos** 'his mercy', **autou** is marked as contrastive (with **hēmeis** 'we') by occurring between the article and its noun. The contrast between **hēmeis** 'we' and **autou** 'his' is reflected by the use of "ourselves" and "himself" in the display text. The contrast in the pronouns further stresses the fact that our salvation is not of anything that we have done but it is all because of his mercy.

3:5d-e. **(He saved us(inc)) by means of (his) washing (us(inc)) (and making us(inc) holy) (5e) (at which time) the Holy Spirit regenerated (us(inc)), (that is,) the Holy Spirit caused (us(inc)) to begin a new (spiritual) life.** (**dia loutrou paliggenesias kai anakainōseōs pneumatos hagiou**, 'through a-washing of-regeneration and renewal of-Spirit Holy')

REL **Dia** 'through' with the genitive signals a means relation.

CONT This prepositional phrase is one of the most difficult in Titus to analyze since there are so many grammatical and semantic possibilities as to its exact structure and meaning. The context must be relied upon to aid in the understanding of this phrase.

One clue from the context may be that **loutrou** 'washing' (generally of the whole body) is possibly being used to contrast the "washing of regeneration (and renewal of the Holy Spirit)" with the ceremonial ablutions of the Jews. (For **loutron's** ceremonial usage, see Arndt and Gingrich and cf. **louō** 'wash'.) Lock says, "There is probably a conscious reference to 1:15 and 2:14. We needed cleansing, but with more than just Jewish ceremonial ablutions, with a washing that would entirely renew our nature."

This may explain why **loutrou** is in a grammatical head position in relation to **paliggenesias** (**kai anakainōseōs**) 'regeneration (and renewal)'. Paul is saying that the washing associated with rebirth (and renewal) is the washing through which we are saved--not any other type of washing. That this washing is needed is shown by our condition in 3:3.

Many commentators see **loutron** as referring to baptism. In Eph. 5:26, where the only other occurrence of **loutron** in the New Testament is found, **loutron** is used with water, **tō loutrō tou hudatos** 'the washing of/in water', in the context "having cleansed her [the church] by the washing of water with the word" (RSV). In Heb. 10:22, the cognate verb **louō** 'wash' is also used with water, **lelousmenoi to sōma hudati katharō** 'having our bodies washed with pure water', in the context, "with our hearts sprinkled clean from an evil conscience and our bodies washed with pure water" (RSV). There would seem to be some reference to baptism in both of these verses, especially since **loutron** and **louō** are used in connection with water in both places.

However, there are a few reasons why physical baptism might not be in focus here in Titus 3:5:

1. The basic meaning of the word **loutron** is, of course, not baptism but "bath, washing." As an example of its use in other types of purification rites, in a Gospel Fragment from the Oxyrhynchus Papyri, the cognate verb **louō** 'wash' is used to refer to "the act of purification necessary before entering the temple" (Arndt and Gingrich).
2. If Paul is contrasting **loutron** here with the ablutions of the Jews, it is not baptism itself that is in focus so much as the idea of cleansing and purification.
3. It is the inward cleansing that is the means of salvation, not the outward cleansing; otherwise physical baptism alone is of no greater value than Jewish ablutions.
4. If Paul meant to focus on baptism, he could have done so more clearly by using **baptizō** 'baptize'.

For these reasons, and especially because Paul does not use **baptizō**, the word "baptize" is not used in the display text.

As will be discussed later, either God, who is the agent of "saved us" (3:5a), or the Holy Spirit, may be the agent of the washing.

Loutron 'washing' is a metaphor based on the comparison of washing away dirt and filth and making one clean, with the removal of sin and making one holy. Here it is better to keep the figurative reference since a reference to baptism certainly seems possible (though not necessarily focal). The display text rendering seeks to represent the figurative sense "washed us" and the actual event "made us holy." "And" is used instead of "that is" since there could very well be two actions intended by Paul here--the washing of physical baptism which is itself the figure and the actual event of making us holy.

REL It is difficult to determine the relation between the proposition which renders **loutrou** 'washing' and the one which renders **paliggenesias** 'regeneration'. On the Greek surface structure level, **paliggenesias** appears to be identificational, defining the kind of washing. It is quite apparent that Paul is saying that we have been saved by means of the washing which is either inseparably accompanied by regeneration or is itself regeneration. The genitive construction **loutrou paligg.** has the possiblity of expressing either of these ideas.

It seems better, however, to analyze regeneration as something that accompanies the washing rather than being wholly equivalent to the washing, since nowhere in Scripture is it indicated that spiritual washing/cleansing and regeneration are the same thing, and certainly physical baptism and regeneration are not the same thing. (We are not maintaining that spiritual washing and regeneration are definitely not the same thing, but we are saying that we know of no scriptural basis to support making a representation here that they are the same.)

For those who maintain that **loutron** and **paligg.** refer to two different, closely connected events/actions, or at least two different aspects of one general event, some maintain that the relationship here is means-result, i.e., the washing produces regeneration. For those who interpret **loutron** as basically physical baptism, this may be an appropriate relation. But for those who interpret the washing as basically a spiritual cleansing which may be symbolized by the physical washing of baptism, it is more difficult to prove that the spiritual washing produces regeneration. In fact, it does not seem necessary to mention any causal relation between the two, especially since this is not a point that Paul is trying to make here. The basic point Paul is making is that we have been saved by a washing that inherently includes regeneration, with the implication that regeneration is a means of our salvation. We are not told that the washing produces regeneration.

Based on all these considerations, we have represented the relationship between the washing and the regeneration in the display text as one of concomitant events, supplying "at which time" at the beginning of 3:5e.

REL Another question is whether **anakainōseōs** 'renewal' modifies **loutrou** and thus is either coordinate or equivalent to **paligg.** 'regeneration', or whether **anakainōseōs pneumatos hagiou** 'renewal of/by the Holy Spirit' relates to **dia** and is another means effecting our salvation coordinate with **loutrou paligg.** (or possibly even equivalent to it).

It may, at first, appear that taking **paliggenesias** 'regeneration' and **anakainōseōs** 'renewal' as coordinate modifiers of **loutrou** produces an awkward construction--"the washing of regeneration-and-renewal through the Holy Spirit"--whereas, a much more symmetrical and therefore more likely construction is that of **loutrou paligg.** 'washing of regeneration' as one means, and **anak. pneumatos hagiou** 'renewal of the Holy Spirit' as a separate means--"the washing of regeneration and the renewal of the Holy Spirit." However, there are some good reasons for favoring the former construction, as described below. (Many commentators favor the former construction; in fact, Kelly sees the former as preserving the balance of the sentence better.)

In this context, **paligg.** 'regeneration' and **anak.** 'renewal, making new' are very close in meaning. Though in other contexts in the New Testament (2 Cor. 4:16; Col. 3:10; possibly Rom. 12:2) **anakainōsis/anakainoō** refer to a continual process, that sense is not seemingly appropriate here since **esōsen** 'he saved', the main verb, is aorist denoting an action that has already taken place, and thus we would expect that the means to that action/event were also one-time actions that have already taken place. This is certainly true about regeneration, and it must be true here, also, about renewal or making new. The **anak.** is described here as to its beginning point and not as a continual process as elsewhere. What is in focus is our being made new when we experienced the washing/cleansing at the very beginning of our Christian life.

Looking at **anak.** in this way, a very close, if not identical, meaning is indicated here for both **paligg.** and **anak.** If this is true, it would be hard to see why Paul would use both words in two separate phrases, in one of which the regeneration is in the modifying position, in the other its equivalent, renewal, in the head position. It would make more sense for them to be in a parallel relationship where they reinforce one another, which is the case when both regeneration and renewal are taken as modifying washing. As has been mentioned before, one of the things characteristic about this climactic passage is the number of synonyms, or near synonyms, which help to emphasize the points being made.

When we do take both **paligg.** 'regeneration' and **anak.** 'renewal' as modifying **loutron** 'washing', then it is more natural to take **pneumatos hagiou** 'Holy Spirit' as the agent for both regeneration and renewal. As to whether the Holy Spirit should also be considered as the agent for the washing, it seems like the agency of the washing is not in focus, so that either God or the Holy Spirit might be used in those languages that need to supply an agent; otherwise, it does not need to be stated.

In the display text, then, regeneration and renewal are considered as equivalent. Note, however, that in translation into another language the equivalency relation need only be spelled out if, for some reason, that is necessary; or, if there is only one way to translate the two equivalent propositions, they may be translated as one. Otherwise, it is best to translate them as coordinate propositions, trying to stress the importance and also the different facets of the beginning of the new life, even as Paul did.

3:6-7. In the Greek text, 3:4-7 is just one sentence. However, at the beginning of verse 6, there is a relative pronoun, **hou**, referring to the Holy Spirit, which begins a relative construction. The relative construction in Greek can sometimes indicate the beginning of what, in many languages including English, would be most naturally treated as a new sentence. Therefore, 3:6 could be a more typical relative clause describing the Holy Spirit, with 3:7 returning to a **hina** construction dependent upon **esōsen** 'he saved'. Or, 3:6-7 could be a construction independent of the main verb of 3:4-5, **esōsen**, and having as its main verb **execheen** 'he poured out', with the **hina** clause of 3:7 dependent on **execheen**. The translation of these two options would be: (1) "He (God) saved us...in order that we might become heirs..."; (2) "He (God) poured out the Holy Spirit upon us abundantly...in order that we might become heirs..."

The following considerations would favor taking 3:6-7 as a construction independent of **esōsen** 'he saved', with **execheen** 'he poured out' as its main verb:

1. Otherwise the construction built on **esōsen** is very long and involved.
2. The independent construction of 2:14, which also begins with a relative (**hos** 'who') and occurs in a similar grounds paragraph, shows that an independent "relative" construction in 3:6-7 is a natural construction in this context.

3. The gift of the Spirit is elsewhere associated with the idea of becoming heirs of God (Rom. 8:15-17; Gal. 4:6-7).
4. Nowhere else in the New Testament does a hina clause depend on sōzō 'save' or sōtēria 'salvation'. In the New Testament, salvation is not presented as a means to effect a purpose, but it is always an end or purpose to be achieved.
5. Paul may very well be using two parallel constructions, 3:4-5 and 3:6-7, to present the highly important information of this paragraph. Notice the similarities there would be in these constructions:

	3:4-5	3:6-7
Savior	our Savior God	Jesus Christ our Savior
Basis for our salvation and hope of eternal life	God's kindness, love, and mercy	God's grace, justification
Means to the same	washing, regeneration, renewal	Holy Spirit poured out upon us
Result	salvation	heirs of eternal life
Involvement of the Godhead:		
God	acted kindly and lovingly (in sending Christ), is merciful, saved us	poured out the Holy Spirit, is gracious and justified us
Jesus Christ	Christ's coming referred to in epephanē 'appeared'	the one through whom we receive the Holy Spirit
Holy Spirit	regenerated and renewed us	his outpouring means we become heirs of eternal life

In 3:4-5, the main verb esōsen 'he saved' expresses the result of both the reason/basis (3:5b-c) and means (3:5d-e) for that salvation. In 3:6-7, the clause klēronomoi genēthōmen kat' elpida zōēs aiōniou 'we might become heirs in hope of 'eternal life' is the purpose of the means (3:6) and the result of the reason/basis (3:7b of display text) for becoming heirs. Therefore, the result of 3:4-5 and the purpose/result of 3:6-7 are similar in meaning and function. They are the final product or result of God's grace and actions on our behalf.

As for those who take the other view, i.e., that the hina clause relates directly back to esōsen 'he saved', Ellicott states that position as follows, "Though some prominence is given to execheen, both by the adverb plousiōs, and by the defining words dia Iēsou Christou, yet the whole context seems to mark esōsen as the verb on which the final clause depends. We were once in a hopeless and lost state, but were rescued from it by the philanthrōpia of God, who not merely saved us from the douleia [slavery] of sin, but associated with it the gracious intent that we should become klēronomoi [heirs] of eternal life." As far as commentary support n general is concerned, it would seem that a majority of commentators support aking the hina purpose clause as dependent on **execheen** 'he poured out'.

On the basis of the considerations above, we believe that Paul begins a new parallel construction at 3:6; the hina clause (3:7) is dependent on **execheen** 'he poured out' rather than on **esōsen** 'he saved'.

3:6. **By means of Jesus Christ our(inc) Savior, God (graciously) gave the Holy Spirit to us(inc) (in order that the Holy Spirit might act) mightily (on our(inc) behalf).** (hou execheen eph' hēmas plousiōs dia Iēsou Christou tou sōtēros hēmōn, 'whom he-poured-out upon us abundantly through Jesus Christ the Savior of-us')

CONT There is a question here as to what is meant by **dia Iēsou Christou.** Does it mean that the outpouring of the Holy Spirit by God is (1) through Jesus Christ as himself an intermediary, i.e., God outpours the Holy Spirit by means of Jesus outpouring the Holy Spirit, or (2) through the merits of Jesus Christ, i.e., through what Jesus Christ has done for us in dying on our behalf? In favor of the first interpretation is the fact that (1) if Paul intended to focus on Christ's death on our behalf, it seems likely that he would not have left it implicit; and (2) the concept of Christ as an intermediary in pouring out the Spirit on believers is found at the very beginning of the church, "Exalted to the right hand of God, he has received from the Father the promised Holy Spirit and has poured out what you now see and hear" (Acts 2:33, NIV).

In favor of understanding a reference to Christ's death for us is that this would be appropriate to the context here, in which there are many references to the unmerited basis of our salvation. In fact, in 3:4-7 all other constituents either refer to the basis or the means of our salvation and hope of eternal life. Also, the qualifying words **tou sōtēros hēmōn** 'our Savior' would tend to suggest Christ's sacrifice in saving us, though in the three other occurrences of the name of Christ in Titus, only the one in 1:1 does not have the modifier "our Savior," and God is referred to as "our Savior" several times, too.

It seems best, then, to take this **dia** construction as relating to the mediate agency of Christ in pouring out the Holy Spirit, with a more remote reference to Christ's death on our behalf. If the purpose of this construction is not to indicate a further aspect of the gracious basis for our salvation and hope of eternal life, it may be to indicate that all the members of the Godhead are involved in our salvation and hope of eternal life.

There is a good amount of commentary support, however, for understanding this **dia** construction as referring to Christ's death on our behalf.

There is a further problem as to how to propositionalize this **dia** construction if it is understood as mediate agency in pouring out the Holy Spirit. To express this fully semantically, on the basis of Acts 2:33, the propositionalization would be, "God gave the Holy Spirit to Jesus Christ our(inc) Savior in order that he (Jesus) might pour out the Holy Spirit abundantly upon us(inc)." There is a question, however, as to whether this full semantic form is necessary in the propositionalization, especially when it tends to skew the natural prominence of the Greek text. Callow, in his notes on Col. 1:16g-i (1983a:75-76) where a similar example of mediate agency occurs, gives the full semantic equivalent in the notes, but prefers to propositionalize in the display text as "by means of him" only, "because it is preferred to keep the topic of 'everything' as in the Greek." Here, also, it seems better to use the shortened form, "by means of Jesus Christ our(inc) Savior," in order to better preserve the natural prominence.

If the interpretation is followed that understands this dia construction to refer to Christ's death on our behalf, the following proposition would seem appropriate, "By means of Jesus Christ our(inc) Savior (dying on our(inc) behalf)."

CONT In the Greek surface structure, **plousiōs** `richly, abundantly' modifies **hou execheen** `whom he poured out' with the inference that the Holy Spirit was "poured out abundantly upon us." This is certainly some type of figure where the Holy Spirit is compared to a liquid being poured out. **Plousiōs** `abundantly' is part of the figure; it modifies **execheen** `poured out' in its figurative sense. This figure is parallel to being filled with the Holy Spirit, but here it is looked at from the perspective of God's action of giving, whereas, filled looks at it from the perspective of man's receiving, i.e., God outpours so man is filled. That the figure is not a completely dead one is shown by the fact that both words ("outpoured" and "abundantly") equally function figuratively, and there is a relationship to being filled with the Spirit. At the same time, the figure of outpouring has a wide use, being used to refer to various things that God gives to man: **charis** `grace' (Ps. 44:3; [45:2]); **hormēma** `wrath' (Hos. 5:10); **eleos** `mercy' (Jesus Sirach 18:11); **agapē** `love' (Rom. 5:5, though perhaps there is a connection with the outpouring of the Holy Spirit there).

In determining the meaning of the figure, there is a problem in knowing how to apply **plousiōs** `richly, abundantly' to the Holy Spirit. From a comparison of its other uses in the New Testament, there is no concrete evidence that it refers to anything other than an abundant measure of whatever it modifies semantically (Col. 3:16, "the message about Christ," i.e., "know thoroughly the message about Christ"; 1 Tim. 6:17, "everything"; 2 Pet. 1:11, "entrance, welcome" which seemingly must be understood in the sense of the value of the welcome as in NIV, "a rich welcome"). It always refers to measurable things. Are we then to think of the Spirit of God as in some way measurable, or should we not rather understand **plousiōs** as referring to the works or manifestation of the Holy Spirit in our lives, here specifically at the time of our regeneration? Following this second option, **hou execheen eph' hēmas plousiōs** `whom he poured out upon us abundantly' would refer to (1) the giving of the Holy Spirit, and (2) the fact that this giving is one which resulted in the Holy Spirit "abundantly" working on our behalf, i.e., he acted mightily on our behalf.

Two further questions deal with the time being referred to here. The first is whether the outpouring of the Holy Spirit mentioned here refers to Pentecost or to the individual outpouring of the Holy Spirit at the time of regeneration. There seems to be no special reason to focus on Pentecost. The aorist tense of **execheen** `poured out' could very well refer to the giving of the Holy Spirit to "us" (**hēmas**), i.e., specifically Paul, Titus, and the Cretan believers, at the time of each one's individual regeneration. **Esōsen** `he saved' (3:5), also aorist, refers basically to each person's individual moment of salvation.

Secondly, does **plousiōs** `abundantly' basically refer to the Spirit's working at the time of regeneration, or to his working in the Christian life in general, both at regeneration and ever afterward? The aorist tense of **execheen** `poured out' indicates that the focus may be on the outpouring of the Holy Spirit at regeneration and the mighty way he acted on "our" behalf at that time. All the other events in the context--salvation, washing, regeneration, justification, probably renewal, and certainly becoming heirs which is the purpose of this means clause--are events that happen at the very beginning of the Christian life. Therefore, the focus of hou execheen eph′ hēmas plousiōs ′whom he poured out upon us abundantly′ seems also very likely to be on the beginning point of our Christian life.

Paul, likely, not only used plousiōs here to describe the Spirit′s action but also to indicate another instance of God′s graciousness on our behalf. It may be on this basis that NIV translates plousiōs as "generously," where generously may indicate both the graciousness of the giver and the abundance of the gift. (A comparison of plousiōs here with its other uses in the New Testament gives no evidence that plousiōs refers only to the graciousness of the giver.) To retain this component of the total meaning of the paragraph, "graciously" has been supplied in the display text.

In trying to combine the above components into a proper propositionalization, there are problems. To definitely indicate that the Holy Spirit had already acted mightily on "our" behalf, a result proposition would be needed after the means, "God (graciously) gave the Holy Spirit to us(inc), (and as a result, the Holy Spirit acted) mightily (on our(inc) behalf)." The problem with this is an ambiguity, which, though not likely to be misunderstood, still should not occur in proper propositionalization. The means-result propositions above could be misunderstood to mean that the Holy Spirit acted mightily on our behalf only because of God′s gracious action toward him. This problem could be overcome by using a purpose proposition instead of result, "God (graciously) gave the Holy Spirit to us(inc) (in order that the Holy Spirit might act) mightily (on our(inc) behalf)." Although this does not indicate when the mighty working takes place, it is a more natural rendering of the relationships under discussion (cf. the hina purpose clause in 3:7 and the notes on it; though it refers to something that had already been accomplished, becoming heirs of eternal life, still it is expressed in a purpose clause in the Greek text).

3:7. In the Greek text, there is a participial construction, dikaiōthentes tē ekeinou chariti ′having been justified by his grace′, occurring right after hina ′in order that′ at the beginning of verse 7. This participial construction is dependent grammatically on the subjunctive verb genēthōmen ′we might become′ of the hina clause, but could be interpreted as a purpose of the means construction of 3:6; or, it could be interpreted as a separate reason/means for the construction which has the subjunctive verb genēthōmen ′we might become′ as its nucleus. The difference between these two options can be seen by the following translations:

RSV, "so that we might be justified by his grace and become heirs in hope of eternal life."
NIV, "so that, having been justified by his grace, we might become heirs having the hope of eternal life."

That either of these analyses is possible can be seen from the following examples:

1. Titus 2:12, where the participial construction arnēsamenoi tēn asebeian kai tas kosmikas epithumias ′having renounced ungodliness and worldly lusts′ (an almost identical construction to that here) appears to be part of the content of paideuousa ′training′ along with the content represented in the subjunctive construction. This analysis of 2:12 is similar to that expressed by the RSV translation of 3:7 above.

2. 2 Cor. 13:10, *tauta apōn graphō, hina parōn mē apotomōs chrēsōmai* 'I write these things being absent, in order that, being present, I may not have to act harshly', where the participle *parōn* 'being present' is not part of the purpose clause proper, i.e., it cannot be translated, *"I write you these things being absent, in order that I may be present with you and not act harshly."

Although *parōn* is a present participle instead of aorist (the participles in Titus 2:12 and 3:7 are both aorist), this example shows that participial constructions occurring after *hina* are not necessarily a purpose of the main verb. It would seem that the construction, *hina* plus aorist participle plus subjunctive verb, primarily denotes that the action of the aorist participle is prior in time to that of the subjunctive verb, and does not necessarily denote that the action represented in the aorist participle is also a purpose of the main verb on which the *hina* clause depends.

While RSV and TEV take 3:7 as double purpose, a majority of commentators, though they may not comment on it, appear (by the way they translate) to take the participial construction as other than purpose. Of course, for those who take *esōsen hēmas* 'he saved us' as the means for the *hina* construction in 3:7, "he saved us in order that we might be justified" would be unacceptable.

This participial construction would appear to be an amplification and reinforcement of the reasons (i.e., basis, 3:5a-b of the Greek text) for our salvation and accompanying privileges. This can be shown by the parallelism between Greek text 3:5a, 3:5b, and 3:7a:

3:5a *ouk ex ergōn tōn en dikaiosunē ha*
'not of works those in righteousness which

epoiēsamen hēmeis
we-have-done we-ourselves'

3:5b *alla kata to autou eleos*
'but according-to his-own mercy

(*esōsen hēmas*....)
he-saved us'

3:7a *dikaiōthentes tē ekeinou chariti*
'having-been-declared-righteous (by) his-own grace'

There is a contrast between those "righteous" actions that we have done which are an unacceptable basis for salvation, and his declaring us righteous which is an acceptable basis. And strong prominence is marked on the agent in each case, whether it be "us" or God. The same type of construction is used in both 3:5b and 3:7a to mark the agent as prominent, the pronoun occurring between the article and the noun, *to autou eleos* 'his own mercy', *tē ekeinou chariti* 'his own grace'.

Based upon these considerations, the participial construction appears very likely to be a reason/basis for our becoming heirs, rather than a purpose of *execheen* 'he poured out'. Also, we do not elsewhere find the Holy Spirit's actions as prominent in justification.

Although dikaiōthentes could be interpreted as means for our becoming heirs of eternal life, in this context it seems better to understand it as the reason/basis for our becoming heirs, as that contrasts well with 3:5a.

The construction klēronomoi genēthōmen kat' elpida zōēs aiōniou 'we might become heirs in hope of eternal life', according to the above interpretation, is both a purpose of 3:6 and a result of Greek text 3:7a, dikaiōthentes tē ekeinou chariti 'having been justified by his grace'. In Greek, both the means and the reason constructions are able to precede the purpose/result in such a situation as this. However, in the English propositionalization, it seems impossible to keep both the means and reason before the purpose/result, so the reason is placed after the purpose/result proposition.

3:7a. (God did this (3:6)) in order that we(inc) might become (his) heirs* (and, as a result,) confidently expect to live* forever. (**hina...klēronomoi genēthōmen kat' elpida zōēs aiōniou.** 'in-order-that...heirs we-might-become in-accordance-with hope of-life eternal')

TRNS For languages in which generic verbal forms are not as appropriate as specific ones in summarizing longer constructions, a more specific representation of 3:6 than "God did this (3:6)" would be "God gave the Holy Spirit to us(inc)."

REL Some take the **hina** clause to indicate the result of 3:6 instead of purpose. The arguments are not syntactic but theological, i.e., that God's purpose in saving people and/or outpouring his Holy Spirit was actually (and necessarily) accomplished. Although there is no doubt from the context that those referred to as "we" actually became heirs when God poured his Holy Spirit upon them, the most common use of **hina** in the type of grammatical construction represented here is to express purpose, and so this would be what is in focus in Paul's mind rather than result. It is looked at from the perspective of **execheen** 'he poured out', not as things are now. God's purpose in the outpouring was that we might become heirs in hope of eternal life.

CONT Another question that must be answered is whether **klēronomoi** here is a live or dead metaphor, i.e., is it live, meaning "heirs (of God)" and so possessors of eternal life, or is it dead, meaning "heirs" of eternal life with no special reference to being sons/heirs of God? If it is dead, the figure need not be retained in the propositionalization; if live, it should be. The following considerations suggest that a live metaphor is being used here:

1. In Rom. 8:14-17 where, as here, the Spirit's activity and our being heirs of God is closely tied together, it is stated, "it is the Spirit himself bearing witness with our spirit that we are children of God, and if children, then heirs, heirs of God and fellow heirs with Christ." (8:16-17a, RSV). See also Gal. 4:6-7 where the ideas are similar. These Scripture passages show that the idea of being an heir of God is consistent with Scripture, is tied in with the Holy Spirit's activity in other places than Titus 3:7, and is a live figure since it occurs with other figures in the same or contrastive domains: "children," "sons," "slave," "fellow heirs," "adoption."
2. In Titus 3:4-7 itself, **paliggenesias** 'rebirth, regeneration' may have an intended figurative relationship with becoming heirs of eternal life. We are reborn as children, and so heirs, of God.
3. The use of **klēronomoi genēthōmen** 'we might become heirs' rather than the cognate verb **klēronomeō** 'inherit' also suggests that **klēronomoi** is a live metaphor,

though even the verbal form sometimes seems to be a live figure. Of the other eight occurrences of kl**ē**ronomos `heir' in the New Testament, six are definitely live figures, and even the other two have other members of the inheritance domai in the immediate context. Also, the fact that **klēronomoi** is forefronted, suggesting its being marked prominent, tends to indicate that it is a live metaphor, since it emphasizes our position rather than the event. Therefore, **klēronomoi** is propositionalized as a live metaphor. It is marked with an asterisk, though, since it refers to spiritual heirs, and there are important differences between the ranges of meaning of spiritual heirs and earthly heirs.

CONT Before deciding how this live metaphor will be propositionalized, we mus deal with the following questions: (1) Is **zōēs aiōniou** `life eternal' an immediate constituent of **klēronomoi** `heirs' with the meaning "heirs of eternal life (in hope)," or (2) is **kat' elpida** an immediate constituent of **klēronomoi** with the meaning "heirs in reference to the hope (of eternal life)"? The following translations show the difference between these two analyses:

1. NEB, "we might in hope become heirs to eternal life."
2. NIV, "we might become heirs having the hope of eternal life." AG, "we might become heirs in accordance with the hope of eternal life."

Either choice is possible, however there would seem to be little difference in the actual meaning and propositionalization of them. Of the three components of this construction (heirs, hope, eternal life) it is clear that eternal life is that which will be received and that heirs will be the recipients of that eternal life. The only question is how "hope" modifies that relationship. "Hope" shows that the realization of eternal life is in the future, but its purpose here is not, of course, to lessen the component of assurance found in the word "heirs." On the contrary, "hope" is meant to heighten that idea of assurance.

CONT The full comparison between the live figure and the reality would be something like this:

> God poured out the Holy Spirit upon us in order that we might begin a special relationship with him, similar to that of a person becoming the child of his father. As the child, as heir, may confidently expect to inherit the possessions his father has promised to him, so we may confidently expect to receive eternal life which God has promised to those who have been regenerated (or, to those who have this special relationship with him).

This is propositionalized in the display text in a much shortened form.

CONT "Live" is marked with an asterisk, since it does not refer to physical life on this earth, which may be the primary meaning of "live" in English, but to eternal life as described in the Scriptures.

3:7b-c. **(We(inc) became God's heirs* because) he declared (us(inc)) righteous, (7c) (because) he is gracious. (dikaiōthentes tē ekeinou chariti** `having-been-justified by-that-one's grace')

REL See the discussion under the notes for 3:7 as to why 3:7b is analyzed as a reason constituent. Means would be an alternate possibility.

CONT **Ekeinou** `of that one, his' is taken by a majority of commentators to refer to God the Father. Some explain that the use of **ekeinos** here is for the purpose of referring to the more remote subject which is God, rather than Jesus Christ who has just been mentioned. However, a study of the use of **ekeinos** in the New Testament does not substantiate that it always refers to the more remote antecedent. Note such places as Mark 16:11 and John 5:37, where forms of **ekeinos** refer to the one(s) mentioned immediately before. Note especially John 8:42-44 where there is a contrast between God, Jesus' Father, and the devil, the father of those being spoken to by Jesus. **Ekeinos** in the middle of 8:44 refers to **tou patros humōn** `your father' (the devil), which is the nearest antecedent, rather than to God, the more remote antecedent. On the other hand, Mark 16:13b is a case where **ekeinos** refers to the more remote antecedent.

It seems best to understand **ekeinou** in Titus 3:7 as similar in function to any other pronoun as far as relationships to antecedents are concerned, and so to take it to refer to the subject of the sentence, God (subject of the main verb **execheen** `he poured out'), unless there are semantic reasons to take it to refer to **Iēsou Christou tou sōtēros hēmōn** `Jesus Christ our Savior', the most immediate potential antecedent. In general, the context appears to substantiate that **ekeinou** does indeed refer to God as shown by the following:

1. Grace is much more often used in connection with God the Father than with Christ in the New Testament. In Titus the grace of God is mentioned in 2:11.
2. In this grounds paragraph, the other attributes that are the basis for our salvation are all referred to God-- **chrēstotēs** `kindness', **philanthrōpia** `love', **eleos** `mercy'.
3. Justification is more often referred to God as agent ("principal cause").
4. The parallelism between those constructions of 3:5-7 which present the basis for our salvation, i.e., 3:5a, 3:5b, and 3:7a (Greek text order) reinforce the inferences of reasons 1-3 immediately above. See the notes on this parallelism under 3:7. The parallels between 3:5b and 3:7a suggest that God is agent, not only in 3:5b, but also in 3:7a.

CONT Ellicott comments on the use of **dikaiōthentes** here as follows: "**Dikaiōthentes** `justified', in the usual and more strict theological sense; not, however, as implying only a mere outward non-imputation of sin, but as involving a `mutationem status,' and acceptance into new privileges and an enjoyment of the benefits thereof." Arndt and Gingrich's comment is somewhat similar, "`be acquitted, be pronounced and treated as righteous' and thereby become **dikaios**...."

As mentioned above, the aorist tense of **dikaiōthentes** indicates that being declared righteous is a prerequisite to becoming heirs of eternal life.

SECTION CONSTITUENT 3:8a-c (Propositional Cluster) (Role: Restatement of 3:1-7)

THEME: I want you to confidently teach this trustworthy message (3:3-7) to the believers in order that they will be constantly concerned with doing what is good for others.

DISPLAY

RELATIONAL STRUCTURE	CONTENT
grounds	(3:8a) (These) things which (I) have said (3:3-7) are trustworthy,
HEAD	(3:8b) therefore, I want you to confidently teach these things (3:3-7) to those who have believed in God
PURPOSE	(3:8c) in order that they will be (constantly) concerned with doing what is good (for others).

BOUNDARIES AND COHERENCE

For initial and final boundaries, see above under 3:1-8c.

This propositional cluster may be analyzed as one sentence in the Greek text (see UBS text): a stative clause, joined by kai to a clause with a finite verb plus infinitive, followed by a hina clause. For more on coherence, see the discussion under 3:1-8c.

PROMINENCE AND THEME

Since the Head (3:8b) plus the purpose (3:8c) together summarize the exhortation and prominent grounds units of 3:1-7, they are both included in the theme of 3:8a-c. "Trustworthy," as a representation of 3:8a, is also added to modify "message" as a succinct way to include this significant, though perhaps less thematic, statement.

NOTES ON 3:8a-c

3:8a. **(These) things which (I) have said (3:3-7) are trustworthy,** (Pistos ho logos, 'trustworthy the word')

CONT/TRNS Pistos ho logos is taken here as referring to the great doctrinal truths of 3:3-7. (For more on this, see Boundaries and Coherence for 3:1-8c.) Pistos means "trustworthy, reliable, sure." For languages where there is no one-word equivalent for pistos, a statement such as "We(inc) can trust/believe completely in these things" may be appropriate. Otherwise, one may have to translate this as "true," which would be a close synonym in this context. (Cf. Rev. 21:5 houtoi hoi logoi pistoi kai alēthinoi eisin 'these words are trustworthy and true'.)

3:8b. **(therefore,) I want you to confidently teach these things (3:3-7) to those who have believed in God** (kai peri toutōn boulomai se diabebaiousthai, 'and concerning these-things I-wish you(sg) to-affirm')

REL As discussed earlier in Boundaries and Coherence for 3:1-8c, 3:8a is taken as grounds for 3:8b. Kai is taken as expressing this logical relationship.

CONT Diabebaiousthai (found elsewhere in the New Testament only in 1 Tim. 1:7) is variously translated as "affirm, stress, speak confidently." Since forms related to diabebaiousthai have the meanings of "firm, permanent, reliable" (bebaios), "make firm, establish, confirm" (bebaioō), and since the meaning of pistos (3:8a) 'trustworthy, reliable, sure' is close to this, there could well have been an intentional choice of these words with related meaning: "These are reliable words and so I want you to affirm their truth to the believers" or "These are reliable words and so I want you to speak confidently about them."

The following considerations would suggest that diabebaiousthai may have the sense of "speak confidently" here:

1. That would seem to be the meaning in 1 Tim. 1:7, which is also in the Pastoral Epistles, and which is the only other occurrence in the New Testament.
2. The peri prepositional phrase appears to indicate that the focus is on the manner of the speaking, rather than on the content of the statement, i.e., "speak

confidently about these things," rather than "stress these things" (cf. the use of the accusative with **bebaioō** in Mark 16:20, **ton logon bebaiountos** 'confirming the word').

3. Furthermore, there is no overt representation of the hearers in this clause, which might be explained by the fact that the focus here is on the speaker rather than on the hearers. But the confident speaking has a purpose, it will result in the believers being intent on doing good works.

Instead of using "speak" in the display text, however, the more specific word "teach" is used, since the context here is that of a teaching situation.

CONT Note that, in the display text, "those who have believed in God" is shifted from 3:8c where it occurs in the Greek text to 3:8b, since it is needed there in the display translation to complete the case-frame for "teach."

3:8c. **in order that they will be (constantly) concerned with doing what is good (for others). (hina phrontizōsin kalōn ergōn proistasthai hoi pepisteukotes theō.** 'in-order-that they-be-concerned good works to-maintain, those(who) have-believed in-God')

CONT **Phrontizōsin** 'be concerned about, be intent on' gives the idea that good deeds should be a constant concern of the believer.

CONT Although some commentators prefer to translate **proistasthai** according to its technical meaning in secular Greek literature "practice a profession," and thus render the Greek phrase **kalōn ergōn proistasthai** here as (e.g., NEB) "engage in honourable occupations," the fact that **kalōn ergōn** occurs in numerous other places in Titus, and the Pastorals in general, as a theme or motif meaning "good works" or "good deeds" argues strongly that this is the meaning of **kalōn ergōn** here also. **Proistasthai** may mean "be concerned with, practice." Some see **proistasthai** as possibly a metaphorical use of the technical meaning, "busy themselves with good works" (Kelly), "'make a business of all that is excellent', to be active in all good works" (Lock). It is evident that Paul is using two content-intensive verbs here (**phrontizōsin** and **proistasthai**) to stress the importance of believers always being concerned with devoting themselves to good deeds. For the display text, we have used one verb plus the adverb "constantly" to maintain this emphasis. An alternate solution would be, "in order that they will be eager to devote (themselves) to doing what is good (for others)."

CONT See earlier discussion on "good works" in notes on 1:16e; 2:14d; 3:1b-2. As mentioned in Boundaries and Coherence for 3:1-8c, "good works" in 3:8c appears to be a generic that intentionally includes the exhortations of 3:1-2. There the emphasis is on being kind and doing good for others, and the grounds unit which supports 3:1-2 deals with God's gracious and kind actions on our behalf. Therefore, doing good for others by whatever means would seem to be the primary meaning here.

DIVISION CONSTITUENT 3:8d-11 (Paragraph) (Role: Head A' of 1:10--3:11)

THEME: Have nothing to do with foolish disputes about genealogies and about the Jewish law; and do not allow divisive people who have turned away from the true teachings to influence the believers.

DISPLAY

RELATIONAL STRUCTURE					CONTENT
HEAD$_1$	contrast				(3:8d) These (teachings (3:3-7)) are beneficial and profitable for (all) people,
	HEAD				(3:9a) but (when people) foolishly* dispute about senseless (myths about) genealogies and foolishly* argue and quarrel about the (Jewish) law, have nothing to do with that,
	grounds				(3:9b) since (arguing about such things (3:9a)) is not profitable (for anyone but) is worthless.
HEAD$_2$	head$_1$				(3:10a) Any person who teaches things which are different from the true teachings and causes others to turn away from the true teachings, you must warn him (in order that he will stop doing those things).
	head$_2$				(3:10b) (If he does not stop, warn him) one more time.
	HEAD$_3$	HEAD			(3:10c) (If he still does not stop, then) no (longer) allow (him to influence the believers),
		grounds	HEAD$_1$		(3:11a) (since) you know that such a person (3:10a-c) has (deliberately) turned away from (the true teachings)
			HEAD$_2$	HEAD	(3:11b) and (since you know that) he is sinning,
				grounds	(3:11c) (since) he knows that he is doing what is wrong (yet he deliberately keeps on doing it).

BOUNDARIES AND COHERENCE

The initial boundary has been discussed under 3:1-8c, the final boundary under 1:5--3:11.

Although there is asyndeton between 3:9 and 3:10-11, 3:8d-11 is regarded as one unified paragraph for the following reasons:

1. In both 3:9 and 3:10-11, there are words in the semantic domain of divisiveness and controversy: **zētēseis** `controversies' (3:9), **ereis** `arguments' (3:9), **machas** `quarrels' (3:9), **hairetikon** `factious, divisive' (3:10).
2. Less obvious, but fairly verifiable from the total context, are words in the semantic domain of false doctrine: **genealogias** `genealogies' (3:9), **ereis kai machas nomikas** `arguments and quarrels about the law' (3:9), and **hairetikon** (3:10) which, in New Testament times, still had the primary meaning of "factious," but had a component or connotation of "heretical," as shown by the fact that not too much later its primary meaning became "heretical."
3. 3:8d-11, as a whole, deals with those people who oppose the gospel, just as 1:10-16 does. There is no doubt that these false teachers and their followers of 1:10-16 are much on the mind of Paul, and thus it is inconceivable that he is now talking about someone else. The people who are destroying whole houses in 1:11 by teaching what they ought not are the same people (or of the same kind) who are teaching false doctrine in 3:9 and could divide the church in 3:10-11. Those who propound Jewish myths (1:14) would certainly seem to be the same as those who propagate the importance of genealogies (3:9). (In 1 Tim. 1:4 "certain men" are referred to as devoting themselves to "myths and endless genealogies," showing the close connection between the two, or at least the fact that the same people were in the habit of propounding both. In fact, **muthois kai genealogiais** can mean "myths about genealogies.")

PROMINENCE AND THEME

Thus, Paul has returned to talking about the false teachers, against whom he commanded such urgent action in 1:10-16. However, 3:8d-11 is not a completely independent topic from what immediately precedes it. As the great doctrines about God's gracious salvation are used by Paul to give a powerful incentive to living a life devoted to good deeds (3:8a-c), so Paul also uses the contrast between the great and profitable doctrines of salvation and the foolish and profitless teaching and controversies of the false teachers as a warning to Titus (and the elders and Christians in general) to have nothing to do with such teaching (3:9-11).

Notice the following contrast-marking surface structure signals used by Paul:

1. De, a contrast-marking conjunction at the beginning of 3:9.
2. Pistos ho logos 'a trustworthy statement' (3:8a), referring to the great truths of salvation in 3:3-7, and mōras zētēseis 'meaningless/foolish speculations/controversies' of the false teachers (3:9a).
3. The great truths of salvation are described as kala kai ōphelima tois anthrōpois 'good and profitable for people' (3:8d), but the foolish speculations and controversies of the false teachers are described as anōpheleis kai mataioi 'unprofitable and worthless' (3:9b).
4. There is a contrast between proistasthai (from proistēmi) 'be devoted to' (3:8c) and periistaso (from periistēmi) 'avoid, have nothing to do with' (3:9a). The believers must be completely "devoted to" good deeds, but Titus (and the believers) are to "have nothing to do with" foolish controversies.

Periistaso must be understood in the sense of "have nothing to do with whatsoever," rather than "avoid" in the sense of "don't stop them but just stay clear of them," since in 1:11, Titus is told that the false teachers "must be silenced" and in 1:13, their followers are to be rigorously corrected.

The foolish speculations and arguments are forefronted in the Greek text in order to emphasize their contrast with the great, profitable truths of 3:3-7 and also to indicate a switch of topic.

As an exhortation, 3:9a has natural prominence. Since zētēseis 'controversies', ereis 'quarrels', machas 'quarrels' are similar in meaning, they are represented by one word in the theme statement--"disputes." Though this noun expresses an event, it seems best to use it in the theme statement to avoid a lengthy statement, especially because it expresses the sense of the Greek better than the verbal form with the accompanying necessarily supplied agent. This shortened form of 3:9a is the theme statement for the first part of 3:8d-11 (i.e., 3:9); it does not seem necessary to include any part of the grounds proposition, 3:9b.

3:10-11 is rather difficult to translate since several of the Greek terms are so generic. It is a second exhortation and the imperative verb is paraitou. This verb is variously translated as "have nothing (more) to do with, shun, avoid, reject." These words, however, tend to be too generic and do not really tell us how Titus was to treat the divisive man. To understand paraitou better, it is helpful to compare its use here with its use in 1 Tim. 5:11 where it is used in the sense of "refuse" or "decline" permission for younger widows to be put on the list of the widows of the "widows' order." These younger widows were not to be "avoided" or "shunned," but they were to be refused a certain position or category in the local congregation. Likewise here in Titus, "avoid," in the sense of staying clear of, is not appropriate. If a divisive person is only avoided, will he not continue in his divisive ways? We may think of it, then, as "have nothing to do with" in the sense of no longer allowing such people to have any influence in the congregations; or possibly, the case may be more parallel with the widows' case in 1 Tim. 5:11: no longer allow such people to be on any list of elders or teachers, in other words, dismiss them from any position, formal or informal, within the church. (Note that **paraiteomai (paraitou)** in secular literature did mean "dismiss, drive out.") This second interpretation, however, cannot be well supported, since we do not have enough knowledge about the total situation referred to nor the exact meaning of **paraiteomai**. An acceptable translation then might be "no longer allow him to influence (the believers)."

In the display text, 3:10a is an unpacking of the meaning of the Greek word **hairetikon**, a word that can best be understood by stating its meaning in propositionalized form. In the theme statement, this is reduced to "divisive people." Since it is not the "divisive" person, per se, that is being talked about, but the one who persists in his divisiveness and is thus shown to be **exestraptai** 'perverted', a rendering of **exestraptai** as "have turned away from the true teachings" is included in the theme. The expansion used to propositionalize "with one and two warnings" is left out, since it is long and is not the focal point of the exhortation. "Do not allow divisive people who have turned away from the true teachings to influence the believers" is thus the theme statement for verses 10-11, the second Head and second exhortation of this paragraph.

NOTES ON 3:8d-11

3:8d. **These (teachings (3:3-7)) are beneficial and profitable for (all) people, (tauta estin kala kai ōphelima tois anthrōpois**: 'these are good and profitable for-people')

REL As explained earlier in the Boundaries and Coherence section for 3:1-8c, **tauta** 'these (things)' has only two possible antecedents in the immediate context, the great truths about salvation in 3:3-7 or "good deeds" (kalōn ergōn) in 8c (unless it is taken to refer to both). It is hard to see why Paul would say that good (kalōn) deeds are good (kala 8d); certainly, that would be overredundant. But it makes excellent sense for "these things" to refer to the great truths of salvation which are compared with the unprofitable controversies/speculations of the false teachers.

CONT Matters that need to be considered here are the exact meaning of **kala** 'good' in this context, and whether **kala** is to be taken with **tois anthrōpois** 'for people' or whether only **ōphelima** 'profitable' relates to **tois anthrōpois**. Most commentators take **kala** by itself. In fact, some add "in themselves" in their translations, e.g., Lock, "These truths are excellent in themselves and full of profit to others." Their reasons for taking **kala** alone must be lexical rather than grammatical or collocational. That the collocation **kala...tois anthrōpois** is not an inappropriate one can be seen from a similar construction in 1 Cor. 7:1, **kalon anthrōpō gunaikos mē haptesthai** 'It is good for a man not to touch a woman'.

The great truths of God's gracious salvation are beneficial for mankind as 3:3-7 has so clearly pointed out. Arndt and Gingrich give as the general meaning of **kalos** under entry 2, "good, useful." Since **kala** is used along with **ōphelima** 'beneficial, profitable' and in contrast to **anōpheleis** 'profitless' and **mataioi** 'useless', there is a strong possiblity that it means "good" in the sense of "beneficial" here. Note, too, that **kalon** in such constructions as **kalon anthrōpō** in 1 Cor. 7:1 can mean "good" in the sense of "beneficial" (note Mark 9:42; Matt. 17:4; 26:24). Thus, **kala** may very well be intended to relate to **tois anthrōpois**--"these teachings are beneficial and profitable for (all) people."

Actually, it is a matter of focus. These teachings, being inherently good, are also good and beneficial for mankind. But it would seem that Paul meant to focus on their being good in the sense of being beneficial to man.

CONT/TRNS **Tois anthrōpois** here refers to mankind in general. NIV translates this as "everyone." Either "everyone" or "(all) people" could be used in the display text. In some languages, a first person plural inclusive pronoun might be more appropriate.

3:9a. **but (when people) foolishly* dispute about senseless (myths about) genealogies and foolishly* argue and quarrel about the (Jewish) law, have nothing to do with that,** (**mōras de zētēseis kai genealogias kai ereis kai machas nomikas periistaso**, `foolish questionings and genealogies and quarrels and disputes about-the-law avoid')

REL **De** indicates a definite contrast between what has come before, i.e., the statement that the doctrine of God's salvation (3:3-7) is good and profitable for all people, and the unprofitableness of arguments about genealogies and the Jewish law. Thus, 3:8d has a contrast-Head relationship with 3:9a.

REL/CONT This is one point in the text where it is difficult to retain the focus of the original and, at the same time, propositionalize without using nouns that express events, especially because the agents of these events have to be introduced and the focus is then no longer entirely on the original topic, but is shared with the people involved in the topic under discussion. Of the options available, it seems that a circumstance-Head construction, "but (when people) foolishly dispute about senseless (myths about) genealogies..., have nothing to do with that," is better than a descriptive/identificational construction, "but have nothing to do with (people who) foolishly dispute about senseless (myths about) genealogies," since the latter puts more focus on having nothing to do with the people themselves than the former does. It is not the people, but their practices, that are in focus here.

CONT **Zētēsis** has the meanings "investigation, speculation, controversial question, controversy, discussion." Though here "speculation" would make excellent sense, contrasting the foolish "speculations" of the false teachers with the "trustworthy" truths about God's salvation (3:3-7), **zētēsis** cannot be definitely shown to mean "speculation" anywhere else in the New Testament. (However, in 1 Tim. 1:4, **ekzētēsis**, in its only occurrence in the New Testament, is translated by many as "speculation.") Of its six other occurrences in the New Testament (John 3:25; Acts 15:2,7; 25:20; 1 Tim. 6:4; 2 Tim. 2:23), only in Acts 25:20 is there the probability that **zētēsis** means "investigation." In all the other passages, it probably has some sense of "controversy." (Even in Acts 25:20 **aporoumenos de egō tēn peri toutōn zētēsin**, **zētēsis** could be understood as meaning "discussion" or "controversy." Cf. NEB, "Finding myself out of my depth in such discussions...." However, it is understood in that portion by most translators as "investigation.")

Also, two of the other three subjects with which Titus is to have nothing to do here in Titus 3:9 are **ereis** `strife, arguments' and **machas** `quarrels'. Paul seems to be focusing on the arguments and controversies of false teaching here. If zētēsis does have a sense of "speculation" in this passage, it probably means speculation in which contrasting theories are being proposed--controversial speculation. Notice that in 1 Tim. 1:4 ekzētēseis, most often translated as "speculations," are said to be promoted by myths and genealogies. Since "genealogies" in that passage would mean "theory about genealogies" and not "genealogies" per se, it is the contrasting conjecture about genealogies that is being indicated by ekzētēseis.

This "controversy" or "controversial speculation" may not denote outright quarreling as shown by the fact that zētēseis in 2 Tim. 2:23 are said to produce machas `quarrels, strife'; and zētēseis and logomachiai `disputes about words' in 1 Tim. 6:4 are said to result in (among other things) eris `quarreling'. However, in a construction such as 3:9a where synonyms or near-synonyms are used side by side, it is difficult to differentiate their meanings, the piling up of synonyms being used for emphasis.

CONT It is difficult to know exactly what genealogias `genealogies' refer to here. Many commentators have interpreted the word as referring to groups of aeons in Gnostic teaching. However, the word is never found in any literature as referring to the Gnostic system of aeons. Many other commentators are of the opinion that it refers to something based on genealogies from the Old Testament. Paul mentions genealogies in 1 Tim. 1:4 in connection with myths, muthois kai genealogiais, which could mean that genealogies are the subject matter of the myths. It would seem best to interpret the mention of genealogies here in Titus as referring to myths built on family trees. Kelly, in commenting on 1 Tim. 1:4 says, "Irenaeus gives an interesting example of how the family-trees of Genesis could be worked up into myths...." Since it is not the bare genealogies themselves, but the stories or myths about them, that are in focus here, "(myths about) genealogies" is used in the display text.

TRNS Since Paul also refers to myths in Titus (1:14) in connection with the false teachers (and so may be referring to the same thing as genealogies here) and there calls them "Jewish myths," if, in a given receptor language, genealogies or ancestors must be qualified as to whom or what group they belong, the best choice would be the Jews. SSA OF TITUS 3:9a-15

CONT The three kai's joining the four nouns of 3:9a could indicate that four separate matters are being referred to. It is significant, however, that of the four nouns, three of them belong to the semantic domain of controversy-argument--zētēseis `controversy', ereis `quarrels', machas `fighting, quarrels'. It is also significant that these three are generic (when taken by themselves) while the fourth, genealogias, denotes something specific. This leaves genealogias as an odd-ball right in the middle of the other three. However, if genealogias is taken as the subject matter of zētēseis `controversies', which is a possible analysis for this type of construction, then there is a parallel with ereis kai machas nomikas where the law is the subject matter of the arguments and quarrels. Supporting such an analysis is 1 Tim. 1:4 where Paul says that "genealogies" promote ekzētēseis `controversial speculations'. This analysis understands 3:9a as referring to controversies and disputes that center around two issues--genealogies and the (Jewish) law.

And there are further reasons for such an analysis. Mōras `foolish' occurs in the prominence-marking/contrast position at the very beginning of this Greek construction. Along with 3:9b, it contrasts the value of what follows it with the value of tauta 'these things', which are kala kai ōphelima tois anthrōpois 'good and profitable for mankind'. The sequence of kai's in 3:9a strongly suggests that mōras applies to all four nouns in that part of the verse. In fact, that may be the reason for this type of construction. Notice, too, that Paul cannot refer to the law by a noun in this sequence (as he does to genealogies), since he does not want to say that the law itself is foolish; it is the arguments and quarrels about the law that are foolish. But his use of the formal coordinate construction zētēseis kai genealogias is probably to definitely indicate that not only the controversy, but also the genealogies (i.e., the myths about genealogies) in themselves, are foolish. This would make excellent sense here, since we would expect that the good and profitable doctrines of the gospel would be contrasted not only with foolish disputes, though certainly there is a strong focus on that too, but also with foolish false doctrine.

In the display text, then, "foolishly" is used to modify "dispute" and also "argue" and "quarrel," while "senseless" is used to modify "myths about genealogies." Note that "foolishly" here does not mean "in a silly manner" but refers to the senselessness of the arguments.

As far as version and commentary support is concerned, though the versions tend to translate zētēseis kai genealogias 'controversies and genealogies' as separate matters, a number of commentators take genealogias as the subject matter of the zētēseis.

CONT Most commonly when the law is referred to in the New Testament, the Mosaic (or Jewish) law is meant, and here in Titus, there would be no reason to expect another meaning. Note that the false teachers are basically of a Jewish orientation--malista hoi ek tēs peritomēs 'especially those of the circumcision', Titus 1:10. They promoted Jewish myths, 1:14. Since "Jewish" is a more comprehensive and easier understood term than Mosaic/of Moses, "Jewish" is used to describe the law. In many languages, law must be qualified, indicating what law is being talked about.

CONT See the discussion under Prominence and Theme for 3:8d-11 on the meaning of periistaso, which we have translated as "have nothing to do with." 2 Tim. 2:23-24, at first glance, seems similar to this passage: "Don't have anything to do with (paraitou) foolish (mōras as here in Titus 3:9) and stupid arguments (zētēseis as here), knowing that they produce quarrels (machas, also used in Titus 3:9). And the Lord's servant must not quarrel (machesthai)...." But the focus in Titus cannot be on keeping out of arguments only, although that is included; it must mean "have nothing to do with" in the sense of "don't allow these things to happen wherever you have influence and authority." Only this has meaning in the light of the need to silence the false teachers and rigorously correct their followers (1:11,13).

3:9b. **since (arguing about such things (3:9a)) is not profitable (for anyone but) is worthless.** (**eisin gar anōpheleis kai mataioi**. 'for they-are unprofitable and worthless')

CONT Since there is a contrast between the great teachings about salvation which are beneficial and profitable for all people and the contents of 3:9a which are here described as unprofitable and worthless, it would seem most likely that the unprofitable side of the contrast would refer not just to arguing itself but also to the things that are argued about. What is being propounded about genealogies and what the false teachers are trying to make the law say are also unprofitable, as well as the arguing itself.

3:10a-c. **Any person who teaches things which are different from the true teachings and causes others to turn away from the true teachings, you must warn him (in order that he will stop doing those things). (10b) (If he does not stop, warn him) one more time. (10c) (If he still does not stop, then) no (longer) allow (him to influence the believers),** (**hairetikon anthrōpon meta mian kai deuteran nouthesian paraitou**, 'a-divisive person after a-first and a-second warning have-nothing-to-do-with')

CONT The word **hairetikos** did not, at the time of Paul's writing, have as its primary meaning "heretical" (as it did in later writers) as shown by the fact that Paul uses the noun form (**hairesis**) in 1 Cor. 11:19 to mean "factions, divisions." Yet in the context of the epistle as a whole, and especially of the preceding verse, and because of the fact that in verse 11 a **hairetikos anthrōpos** who persists in his ways is said to be **exestraptai** 'perverted', it would appear that teaching false doctrine is the main reason behind the divisions being caused. (Cf. especially 1:9-14.) Note, too, that in Acts 24:14 **hairesis**, used with its denotative meaning "sect," has connotations of heresy, "I admit that I worship the God of our fathers, as a follower of the Way, which they call a sect [**hairesis**]" (NIV). The display text unpacks the two related ideas found in the word **hairetikos** as used in this context.

CONT Regarding the verbal form of **nouthesia**, **noutheteō** 'admonish, warn, instruct', Callow (1982:106), in commenting on 2 Thess. 3:15, says, "The verb **noutheteō** 'warn' carries the components of (a) a warm relationship between the parties concerned (such as parents and children, friends, brothers) and (b) that the one who is the object of the verb is in error of some sort, doctrinal or behavioral, or in danger of falling into error. Hence, 'warn' is a suitable translation in English. However, the old English 'admonish' represents the components of the Greek verb more accurately." The relationship here in Titus 3:10 is that within the fellowship of believers, which is the relationship most often found in the several places where the noun and verb occur in the New Testament. Since, in some contexts, the noun and verb have more of the sense of "instruction, instruct" (Eph. 6:4; Col. 3:16), a warning which includes instruction (e.g., why what they are doing is wrong and how they should change, plus the warning itself) would appear to be what Paul is referring to, rather than a warning with no special attempt at correction through instruction.

CONT "In order that he will stop doing those things" is added after "warn him" to make explicit the purpose of the warning. The conditional clauses, shown in parentheses in the display, supply the implied logical steps in the process of disciplining the offender.

CONT/TRNS See under Prominence and Theme for the discussion on **paraitou** which is rendered in the display text as "no (longer) allow (him to influence the believers)." In languages where there is no direct translation for "influence," either "no longer allow him to speak to the believers" or "no longer allow him to teach the believers" may be appropriate. The possibility that Paul meant that the "divisive" man was to be "dismissed" from the fellowship of believers has some merit, since **paraiteomai** (**paraitou**) was used in secular literature to mean "dismiss." However, if this were meant here, probably a stronger word such as **ekballō** 'expel' would have been used. Most commentators are against the view that **paraitou** here means "excommunicate" or "dismiss" from the fellowship of believers, though some do support it.

3:11a. **(since) you know that such a person (3:10a-c) has (deliberately) turned away from (the true teachings)** (**eidōs hoti exestraptai ho toioutos** 'knowing that has-been-perverted such-a-one')

CONT The question might be asked whether **exestraptai** 'has been perverted' means "no longer wants to do what is right" or "no longer believes what is right," i.e., "no longer follows the truth." In Deut. 32:20-21, its only other use in Biblical literature in the passive, the context definitely indicates perverseness of belief: "they are a perverse generation, children who are unfaithful. They made me jealous by what is no god and angered me with their worthless idols" (NIV). Also, there are other indications in the context of the epistle and the immediate context that would argue for the meaning perverseness in belief here: (1) The same or similar people are said in 1:14 to have turned from (**apostrephō**) the truth, and in 1:15 are described as "unbelieving." (2) 3:9 certainly indicates perverseness of belief with the emphasis on genealogies and wrong ideas about the Jewish law. (3) **Hairetikon** (3:10) 'factious, heretical' at least seems to have a connotation of heretical belief, especially when taken in the context of 3:9.

By the time a divisive person has been warned twice and still continues in his heretical ways, it is obvious that he has deliberately turned away from the true teaching. As a perfect passive form, **exestraptai** describes a state that the person concerned has now entered. Arndt and Gingrich translate as "such a man is perverted" (underlining mine). The best rendering for this in our propositionalized form would probably be "such a person has (deliberately) turned away from (the true teachings)."

3:11b-c. **and (since you know that) he is sinning, (11c) (since) he knows that he is doing what is wrong (yet he deliberately keeps on doing it).** (**kai hamartanei, ōn autokatakritos.** 'and he-sins being self-condemned')

REL/CONT 3:11 states the grounds for rejecting the man described in 3:10. First, he has turned from the truth (**exestraptai**). Second, he is sinning (**hamartanei**). But where does "being self-condemned" (**ōn autokatakritos**) come in? It cannot refer to self-confession, since Paul is stating the very opposite--he is stating the reasons why this man is to be rejected. Thus it must mean either number 1 or number 2 below:

1. Such a man, at least by the time he has been warned twice and still persists in disobeying a command of a servant of God, knows that he is guilty. He sins since even though he knows that he is doing wrong, he deliberately keeps on doing it.
2. Whether the man realizes that he is sinning or not is not the question, but he condemns himself before others by his action in not obeying the warnings of a servant of God, and thus also condemns himself in relation to his other "factious" practices. The fact that he does not obey the warnings shows to all that his other practices are also wrong, thus he is condemning himself.

Number 1 seems to be the better choice because it is simpler logically. Note that in Matt. 27:4 there is a similar construction:

hēmarton paradous haima athōon
'I have sinned (by) betraying innocent blood'

Arndt and Gingrich describe the participle in Matt. 27:4 (**paradous** 'having betrayed') as a supplementary participle indicating that in which the sin consists.

This, then, is support for **ōn autokatakritos** 'being self-condemned' here in Titus 3:11 also indicating that in which the divisive man's sin consists, deliberately disobeying a command of a servant of God.

PART CONSTITUENT 3:12-14 (Paragraph) (Role: $head_2$ of the Body)

THEME: Make every effort to come to me at Nicopolis. Help Zenas and Apollos on their journey. All the believers should likewise learn to devote themselves to doing good deeds for people who especially need help.

DISPLAY

RELATIONAL STRUCTURE		CONTENT
	circum.	(3:12a) When I send either Artemas or Tychicus to you, (as soon as he arrives,)
$HEAD_1$	HEAD	(3:12b) make every effort to come to me at (the city of) Nicopolis,
	grounds (explanatory)	(3:12c) since it is there that I have decided to (go and) stay during the winter.
$HEAD_2$	HEAD	(3:13a) As for Zenas the lawyer and Apollos, (when they are ready to leave Crete,) help (them) as much as you can
	purpose	(3:13b) in order that they may not lack anything they need as they travel.
$HEAD_3$	HEAD	(3:14a) Moreover, our(inc) (fellow believers) also should learn to devote (themselves) to (doing) good deeds (for people) who especially need help
	purpose	(3:14b) in order that they (our(inc) fellow believers) will not live useless lives.

BOUNDARIES AND COHERENCE

The main part of the epistle is ended, and we now come to some final instructions with a more personal and time-specific orientation and not directly related to the situation in the Cretan church. See discussion earlier under Boundaries and Coherence for 1:5--3:11.

Although the first two verses represent separate sentences in the Greek text with no conjunction between them, they are united by the fact that they both have this personal, time-specific orientation, in contrast to the rest of the body which has material that is more general, is not so time-specific, and deals directly with the situation in the Cretan church. In 3:12-13, there are instructions about a future rendezvous between Paul and Titus and a request for Titus to help two travelers on their way. Though these two verses talk about two unrelated events, they both deal with the movement of personnel. Basically, they are tied together by those things they have in common in contrast with the rest of the letter, and by their appropriateness to the closing part of a letter.

Verse 14, however, is very closely related to the material and main theme of the body of the epistle. It contains the phrase **kalōn ergōn proistasthai** 'be devoted to good deeds', an injunction upon all Cretan believers, which also occurs in 3:8 and is thematic for the epistle as a whole. But verse 14 also has a formal connection with verse 13--**de kai** 'and also'. Verse 13 deals with the meeting of the needs of two specific people, Zenas and Apollos, while verse 14 deals with meeting the needs of people in general who need help. Verse 13, with its specific need to be met, seems to bring to Paul's mind one further point that could be added in regard to good deeds--the Christians must learn to devote themselves to good deeds in order to meet the needs of people who really need help. Thus, there is unity between verses 12 and 13, and also between verses 13 and 14.

Verse 14 is set off from verse 15, since 15 is the closing of the epistle. Verse 15 is marked by the characteristics of the closing of Paul's epistles--final greetings and a benediction.

PROMINENCE AND THEME

Although there is a certain unity between verses 12 and 13 and also between verses 13 and 14 in that we may treat them as a loosely-bound unit, they each are distinctive. 12 and 13 are distinct from each other in that they give instructions for two unrelated events. 13 and 14 are distinct from each other in that 14 returns to the theme of the epistle as a whole. It seems best, then, to treat each verse, and thus, each exhortation, as a separate Head, each having equal prominence.

NOTES ON 3:12-14

3:12a. **When I send either Artemas or Tychicus to you, (as soon as he arrives,) (Hotan pempsō Arteman pros se ē Tuchikon,** 'When I-send Artemas to you(sg) or Tychicus')

CONT "As soon as he arrives" makes explicit the implied chronological step between Paul sending one of the brothers, and Titus making every effort to go to Nicopolis. Tychicus is a fellow worker of Paul and is mentioned in Acts 20:4; Eph. 6:21-22; Col. 4:7ff.; and 2 Tim. 4:12. Artemas is mentioned only here in the New Testament.

3:12b-c. **make every effort to come to me at (the city of) Nicopolis, (12c) since it is there that I have decided to (go and) stay during the winter. (spoudason elthein pros me eis Nikopolin, ekei gar kekrika paracheimasai.** 'make-every-effort to-come to me at Nicopolis, for there I-have-decided to-winter')

CONT The use of **spoudason** 'make every effort' makes the command urgent. There is no reason, from the word used or the context, to limit **spoudason** to speed only. **Spoudazō** may indicate speed when used with a verb of motion, as here, but since its primary meaning is "make every effort, do one's best," it is better to consider that as the meaning here also and not limit it to speed only.

REL There seems to be no reason to understand the **gar** construction as motivational grounds for Titus to make every effort to come to Nicopolis, as if something about the situation in Nicopolis called for a more urgent effort on Titus' part than if Paul were going to winter somewhere else. The **gar** construction, rather, is explanatory grounds. It answers the implicit question, Why do you want me to come to you at Nicopolis (rather than some other place)? The answer, Because it is at Nicopolis that I have decided to spend the winter.

CONT **Ekei** 'there', referring to Nicopolis, implies that Paul was not at Nicopolis when he wrote to Titus, otherwise he would have said "here." "Go" is supplied to make explicit the implied step Paul must take to stay in Nicopolis during the winter.

3:13a-b. **As for Zenas the lawyer and Apollos, (when they are ready to leave Crete,) help (them) as much as you can (13b) in order that they may not lack**

anything they need as they travel. (**Zēnan ton nomikon kai Apollōn spoudaiōs propempson, hina mēden autois leipē.** `Zenas the lawyer and Apollos wholeheartedly send-on-their-way in-order-that nothing to-them may-be-lacking')

CONT/TRNS The forefronted names of Zenas and Apollos announce them as the new topic. Zenas is only referred to here in the New Testament. Apollos is mentioned both in Acts and 1 Corinthians. Nomikon `lawyer' is used here for identifying purposes and Zenas' profession is not in focus in this context, so it is best to keep the description of "lawyer" as short as possible. In some languages where this profession is completely unknown, a propositionalized form such as "the man who is expert in the law," "the man who understands the law well" may have to be used. But a further problem may be that the type of law must also be indicated. There is no conclusive evidence as to whether Zenas' expertise was in Roman or Jewish law. At first glance, one might think that his Greek name may indiate that he was an expert in Roman law, but then, both Paul's and Apollos' names are also Greek but they were Jews. There is the fact that nomikos, in its other occurrences in the New Testament, always refers to the Jewish law (occurs several times in the gospels meaning "expert in the Jewish law"), and in its only occurrence in the New Testament outside the gospels, only four verses earlier in Titus (3:9), it definitely refers to the Jewish law, there meaning (quarrels) "pertaining to the law." But then, of course, the reason for its not being used elsewhere in the New Testament to mean Roman law/lawyer may be because there was no occasion to do so.

There are other arguments on both sides but none of them are conclusive.

PROM Spoudaiōs `earnestly, wholeheartedly' occurs before the verb, thus indicating the prominence given to the manner in which they should be sent on their way. This is rendered in the display text as "as much as you can."

CONT "As they travel," in the purpose unit, is a translation of a component of meaning of propempson `help on one's journey'. In the Greek, propempson comes in the Head unit but, in the English propositionalized rendering, it is more natural to have it in the purpose unit. "When they are ready to leave Crete" is implied in propempson and the context.

3:14a. **Moreover, our(inc) (fellow believers) also should learn to devote (themselves) to (doing) good deeds (for people) who especially need help** (**manthanetōsan de kai hoi hēmeteroi kalōn ergōn proistasthai eis tas anagkaias chreias**, `and also our(people) must-learn good deeds to-devote-themselves-to for the necessary needs')

REL/CONT De kai `moreover...also', at the beginning of this verse, indicates that not only should Titus help Zenas and Apollos in their needs but that the Cretan Christians (hoi hēmeteroi `our(inc) (people)') should also learn to help people who have real needs.

CONT Manthanetōsan `they must learn' is present tense indicating a continuous, on-going process. The form is third person plural imperative. Manthanō may mean "learn" from experience/practice or instruction. However, as Arndt and Gingrich indicate, manthanetōsan `learn' here would mean to learn from experience or practice more than from instruction. It is something that they apparently had not yet learned to do very well and so needed to learn to do.

CONT For a discussion of **kalōn ergōn proistasthai** 'devote (themselves) to good deeds', see notes for 3:8c. The meaning of **kala erga** here is more precisely defined by **eis tas anagkaias chreias** 'for necessary needs'.

CONT While the occasion which prompted the writing of this verse deals specifically with meeting the needs of those who are traveling, there is no reason to limit the application of 3:14 itself to people who travel, or hospitality in general. Since "doing good works" is a major theme in the epistle and is quite generic in most of its contexts, it is better to see a generic application here, both in helping believers like Zenas and Apollos and unbelievers also (as 3:1-7 so clearly points out) in all kinds of situations. Helping Zenas and Apollos is one case where the believers can learn to put into practice those things that Paul has been urging in the body of the epistle, but the believers must learn to constantly devote themselves to doing good for believers and unbelievers alike, in all types of situations. The only qualification is that the needs be **anagkaios** 'necessary', which Arndt and Gingrich translate in this context as "pressing." Paul is not asking the believers to help those who can help themselves, but those who genuinely need help from others.

3:14b. **in order that they (our(inc) fellow believers) will not live useless lives.** (**hina mē ōsin akarpoi.** 'in-order-that they-may-be not unfruitful')

CONT/REL **Ōsin akarpoi** 'they may be unfruitful' is a dead figure in New Testament Greek for "living uselessly." There is a question as to whether **hina mē ōsin akarpoi** 'in order that they may not be unfruitful' is only a negative restatement of **kalōn ergōn proistasthai eis tas anagkaias chreias** 'devote themselves to good deeds to (meet) urgent needs', or whether its main purpose is to indicate the lack of real value of a life which is not concerned with doing good for others; or, at least, connotes the lack of value, along with the denotation that the believers are doing no good deeds. The first of these options would be built upon an analysis that, in effect, takes the **hina** clause not as purpose but as negative restatement--"our people should learn to devote themselves to doing good deeds to meet urgent needs, that is, they should not keep from doing good deeds." It would seem better to take the **hina** clause as indicating purpose, "our people should learn to devote themselves to doing good deeds to meet urgent needs, in order that they (our people) will not live useless lives." While the means construction of 3:14a refers to actions, the purpose construction of 3:14b refers to a state or condition, one which is recognized by both God and man. Ellicott remarks, "**akarpoi** 'unfruitful', not solely and specially with reference to the wants of their teachers, but also with reference to their own moral state, i.e., without showing practical proofs of their faith by acts of love."

EPISTLE CONSTITUENT 3:15 (Propositional Cluster) (Role: closing of the Epistle)

THEME: Everyone who is with me greets you and the other true believers there. I pray that our(inc) Lord Jesus Christ will continue to act graciously toward all of you.

DISPLAY

RELATIONAL STRUCTURE		CONTENT
$HEAD_1$	$HEAD_1$	(3:15a) (In closing,) everyone who is with me greets you.
	$HEAD_2$	(3:15b) Greet (for us(exc)) those (there) who love us(exc) and believe (the same teachings about God as we(inc) do).
$HEAD_2$		(3:15c) (I pray that our(inc) Lord Jesus Christ will continue to) act graciously toward all of you.

BOUNDARIES AND COHERENCE

This verse is characteristic of the closing of a Pauline epistle. It is composed of three Greek sentences (as punctuated in the UBS Greek text). The typical vocabulary of greeting and benediction are present.

PROMINENCE AND THEME

Of the three Greek sentences in the closing, the first two deal with greetings, number one dealing with all those who are with Paul greeting Titus, number two asking Titus to greet the believers in Crete. These two sentences are coordinate and, since they both deal with greetings, are grouped together under main $Head_1$ as $Heads_{1}\&_{2}$. "Those (there) who love us(exc) and believe (the same teachings about God as we(inc) do)" has been shortened in the theme statement to "true believers there." The last sentence is the benediction and forms separate main $Head_2$. The theme statement represents this structure by combining sentences one and two into one sentence, and stating the benediction as a separate sentence.

NOTES ON 3:15

3:15a. **(In closing,) everyone who is with me greets you.** (**Aspazontai se hoi met' emou pantes**. 'They-greet you(sg) all those with me')

REL Sending greetings indicates that we have reached the closing of the epistle. This is made explicit in the display by adding "In closing."

CONT It is difficult to know whether **hoi met' emou pantes** 'all those with me' refers to fellow workers, e.g., Paul's traveling companions, or whether he was referring more generally to the believers in the local congregation where he happened to be. In Phil. 4:21-22 Paul mentions two groups who are sending greetings -- (1) **hoi sun emoi adelphoi** 'the brothers who are with me' and (2) **pantes hoi hagioi** 'all the saints'. It may be that, when Paul talks about "those with him," he is referring to those closely involved with him in the work as compared to the believers of a congregation in general. However, since it is not possible to know for certain to whom Paul is referring here in Titus, a more literal rendering, "Everyone who is with me," is used in the display text.

CONT/TRNS Notice that the word "greeting" is used here in a specialized sense which, in other languages, may or may not be the same word used to describe a greeting when people meet each other.

3:15b. **Greet (for us(exc)) those (there) who love us(exc) and believe (the same teachings about God as we(inc) do).** (**Aspasai tous philountas hēmas en pistei**. 'Greet those loving us in faith')

CONT The first question here is whether **hēmas** 'us' ("those loving us") is inclusive or exclusive. Paul's friends, of course, would be Titus' friends, too, but Paul is zeroing in on the fact that those people are his friends. Therefore, as far as the primary reference in this context is concerned, **hēmas** appears to be exclusive. (But as far as any reference to the basic relationship between those involved is concerned, **hēmas** would be inclusive, i.e., presumably those who loved Paul also loved Titus.)

CONT **En pistei** may mean "in the faith" or "in faithfulness, faithfully." It could mean "faithfully, loyally" here since there is no article, whereas in other places in Titus where "in the faith" is meant, there is an article (1:13; 2:2). However, the phrase **en pistei** does not occur elsewhere in the New Testament meaning "in faithfulness, faithfully," though **pistin** is used in Titus 2:10 to mean "faithfulness." In Titus, **pistis** occurs twice without the article meaning "faith" (1:1,4).

Thus the evidence is inconclusive. But, since correct belief is so important to the theme of Titus, it may be more probable that Paul also has this in mind here in the final part of the epistle. It would be thus quite similar to Paul's designation of Titus in the opening of the epistle (1:4), **gnēsiō teknō kata koinēn pistin** '(my) true son in (our) common faith'. This is the interpretation adopted for the display text here in 3:15, rendered as "believe (the same teachings about God as we(inc) do)," rather than "love us faithfully."

3:15c. **(I pray that our(inc) Lord Jesus Christ will continue to) act graciously toward all of you.** (**hē charis meta pantōn humōn.** 'the grace (be) with all of-you')

CONT In each of the final benedictions in the epistles of the New Testament where a member of the Trinity is specified in connection with grace (nine times), it is always the Lord Jesus Christ who is specified. Therefore, it is his name that is supplied as the agent of "act graciously" here in the display text for Titus 3:15c, where no explicit reference to an agent is given in the Greek text.

This last sentence in the Greek text has no verb. See the discussion under 1:4c on a similar construction.

REFERENCES

GENERAL REFERENCES

Aland, Kurt; Black, Matthew; Martini, Carlo M.; Metzger, Bruce M.; and Wikgren, Allen, eds. 1975. The Greek New Testament. 3rd ed., Stuttgart et al.: United Bible Societies.

Alford, Henry. 1865. The Greek Testament. Vol. III. London: Rivingtons.

Arndt, William F. and Gingrich, F. Wilbur. 1957. A Greek-English Lexicon of the New Testament and Other Early Christian Literature. Chicago: The University of Chicago Press.

Austing, John. 1976. "A Semantic Analysis of Titus." MS. Dallas: Summer Institute of Linguistics.

Barnes, Albert. 1861. Barnes' Notes on the New Testament. Glasgow: Blackie and Son.

Barrett, C.K. 1963. The Pastoral Epistles. The New Clarendon Bible. Oxford: The Clarendon Press.

Beekman, John and Callow, John. 1974. Translating the Word of God. Grand Rapids: Zondervan Publishing House.

Beekman, John; Callow, John; and Kopesec, Michael F. 1981. "The Semantic Structure of Written Communication." Prepublication draft, 5th ed. Dallas: Summer Institute of Linguistics.

Beekman, John and Smith, Robert E. 1981. A Literary-Semantic Analysis of Second Timothy. Dallas: Summer Institute of Linguistics.

Bendor-Samuel, Pam. 1973. "Titus: Tentative Propositional Analysis. MS. Dallas: Summer Institute of Linguistics.

_______. 1976. "Titus: Analysis of the Larger Semantic Units." Notes on Translation, No. 61. Dallas: Summer Institute of Linguistics.

Blass, F. and Debrunner, A. 1961. A Greek Grammar of the New Testament. A translation and revision of the ninth-tenth German edition by Robert W. Funk. Chicago: University of Chicago Press.

Blight, Richard. 1977. "A Literary-Semantic Analysis of Paul's First Discourse to Timothy." Prepublication draft. Dallas: Summer Institute of Linguistics.

_______. 1979. "An Auxiliary Translation of Titus." Preliminary edition. Dallas: Summer Institute of Linguistics.

Bullinger, E.W. 1898. Figures of Speech Used in the Bible. London: Eyre and Spottiswoode.

Callow, John. 1982. A Semantic Structure Analysis of Second Thessalonians. Dallas: Summer Institute of Linguistics.

_______. 1983a. A Semantic Structure Analysis of Colossians. Dallas: Summer Institute of Linguistics.

_______. 1983b. "Word Order in New Testament Greek, Part I." Selected Technical Articles Related to Translation, No. 7. Dallas: Summer Institute of Linguistics.

Calvin, John. 1558. Commentaries on the Epistles to Timothy, Titus, and Philemon. Translated by William Pringle from the original Latin. Reprinted from 1910, Grand Rapids: Wm. B. Eerdmans Publishing Company, n.d.

Dibelius, Martin and Conzelmann, Hans. 1955. The Pastoral Epistles. Translated by Philip Buttolph and Adela Yarbro, ed. by Helmut Koester. Hermeneia--A Critical and Historical Commentary on the Bible. Philadelphia: Fortress Press, 1972.

Ellicott, Charles J. 1882. A Critical and Grammatical Commentary on the Pastoral Epistles. Andover: Warren F. Draper.

Erdman, Charles R. 1923. The Pastoral Epistles of Paul. Reprinted, Philadelphia: The Westminster Press, 1966.

Friberg, Barbara and Timothy. 1981. Analytical Greek New Testament. Grand Rapids: Baker Book House.

Friberg, Timothy. 1982. "New Testament Greek Word Order in Light of Discourse Considerations." Ph.D. diss., University of Minnesota.

Funk & Wagnalls Standard College Dictionary in The Reader's Digest Great Encyclopedic Dictionary. 1966. Pleasantville, New York: The Reader's Digest Association.

Gealy, Fred D. 1955. "The Epistle to Titus." The Interpreter's Bible, Vol. II. New York: Abingdon Press.

Grayston, Kenneth. 1955. "The Pastoral Epistles." Twentieth Century Bible Commentary. New York: Harper & Brothers.

Greenlee, J. Harold. 1979. A Concise Exegetical Grammar of New Testament Greek. 4th rev. ed. Grand Rapids: Wm. B. Eerdmans Publishing Company.

Guthrie, Donald. 1957. The Pastoral Epistles. The Tyndale New Testament Commentaries. London: The Tyndale Press.

Hanson, Anthony Tyrrell. 1966. The Pastoral Letters. The Cambridge Bible Commentary. Cambridge: University Press.

Heath, Daniel P. 1976. "A Discussion of the Structure and Themes of the Epistle of Titus." MS. Dallas: Summer Institute of Linguistics.

Hendriksen, William. 1965. Exposition of the Pastoral Epistles. New Testament Commentary. Grand Rapids: Baker Book House.

Huther, John, ed. 1885. "Timothy and Titus." Meyer's Commentary on the New Testament. New York: Funk and Wagnalls.

Kelly, J.N.D. 1963. A Commentary on the Pastoral Epistles. Black's New Testament Commentaries. London: Adam and Charles Black.

Kittel, Gerhard, ed. 1970. The Theological Dictionary of the New Testament. Vols. I-X. Translated by Geoffrey W. Bromiley. Grand Rapids: Wm. B. Eerdmans Publishing Company.

Kopesec, Michael F., ed. 1980a. "A Literary-Semantic Analysis of Titus." Preliminary edition. Dallas: Summer Institute of Linguistics.

______, ed. 1980b. An Auxiliary Translation of Titus. Preliminary editon. Dallas: Summer Institute of Linguistics.

Lenski, R.C.H. 1937. The Interpretation of St. Paul's Epistles to Colossians, Thessalonians, Timothy, Titus, Philemon. Columbus, Ohio: Wartburg Press.

Liddell and Scott. 1972. A Lexicon, Abridged from Liddell and Scott's Greek-English Lexicon. Oxford: Clarendon Press.

Lock, Walter. 1924. The Pastoral Epistles. The International Critical Commentary. Edinburgh: T. and T. Clark.

Nicholson, Roy S. 1965. "I and II Timothy and Titus." The Wesleyan Bible Commentary. Grand Rapids: Wm. B. Eerdmans Publishing Company.

Robertson, A.T. 1931. The Epistles of Paul. Word Pictures in the New Testament, Vol. IV. Nashville: Broadman Press.

Scott, E.F. 1936. The Pastoral Epistles. The Moffatt New Testament Commentary. Reprinted, New York: Harper and Brothers, 1964.

Stibbs, A.M. 1954. "Titus." The New Bible Commentary. Grand Rapids: Wm. B. Eerdmans Publishing Company.

Thompson, Frank Charles, ed. 1983. The Thompson Chain-Reference Bible. New International Version. Indianapolis: B.B. Kirkbride Bible Co., Inc. Grand Rapids: The Zondervan Corporation.

Wallis, Wilbur B. 1962. "I and II Timothy, Titus." The Wycliffe Bible Commentary. Chicago: Moody Press.

White, Newport J.D. 1910. "The Epistle to Titus." The Expositor's Greek Testament, Vol. V. Reprinted, Grand Rapids: Wm. B. Eerdmans Publishing Company, 1961.

Williams, Paul M. 1978. "A Literary-Semantic Analysis of Paul's Epistle to Titus." MS. Dallas: Summer Institute of Linguistics.

VERSIONS

Beck, William F. 1963. The New Testament in the Language of Today. Saint Louis: Concordia Publishing House.

Bruce, F.F. 1965. The Letters of Paul. Grand Rapids: Wm. B. Eerdmans Publishing Company.

Dios Llega al Hombre: Version Popular. 1966. Sociedades Biblicas en America Latina.

Good News Bible: The Bible in Today's English Version. 1976. New York: American Bible Society.

Good News for Modern Man: The New Testament in Today's English Version. 1966. New York: American Bible Society.

Goodspeed, Edgar J. 1923. The New Testament: An American Translation. Chicago: University of Chicago Press.

The Holy Bible. Authorized (or King James) Version. 1611.

The Holy Bible: New International Version. 1978. New York: New York International Bible Society.

The Holy Bible: Revised Standard Version. 1953. New York: Thomas Nelson & Sons.

The Jerusalem Bible. 1966. Garden City, New York: Doubleday and Company, Incorporated.

Knox, Ronald A. 1944. The New Testament. New York: Sheed and Ward.

Marshall, Alfred. 1976. The New International Version Interlinear Greek-English New Testament. Grand Rapids: Zondervan Publishing House.

Moffatt, James. 1935. A New Translation of the Bible. Revised edition. New York: Harper and Brothers.

New American Standard Bible: New Testament. 1963. Chicago: Moody Press.

The New English Bible New Testament. 1961. Oxford and Cambridge.

Norlie, Olaf M. 1961. The New Testament: A New Translation in Modern English for Today's Reader. Grand Rapids: Zondervan Publishing House.

Phillips, J.B. 1958. The New Testament in Modern English. New York: MacMillan Company.

Taylor, Kenneth N. 1962. Living Letters. Wheaton, Illinois: Tyndale House.

The Twentieth Century New Testament. Rev. ed., 1904. New York: Fleming H. Revell.

Verkuyl, Gerrit. 1945. Berkeley Version of the New Testament. Berkeley, California: James J. Gillick and Company.

Weymouth, Richard Francis. 1902. The New Testament in Modern Speech. 5th ed., revised by J.A. Robertson. Boston: Pilgrim Press, 1943.

Williams, Charles Kingsley. 1952. The New Testament: A New Testament in Plain English. London: S.P.C.K. and Longmans, Green and Company.